H

Read

hverdy Digest !!

the
very
idea

ch very best

Dave

June 2019

David Wethey

the
very
idea

unlocking
the power of
idea economics

And introducing Jon Leach, 'The Idea Economist'

Urbane
BUSINESS

urbanepublications.com

First published in Great Britain in 2018 by Urbane Publications Ltd
Suite 3, Brown Europe House, 33/34 Gleaming Wood Drive, Chatham, Kent ME5 8RZ
Copyright © David Wethey, 2018
Cartoon illustrations © Tim Cordell

A CIP catalogue record for this book is available from the British Library.

ISBN 978-1-911583-37-0
MOBI 978-1-911583-39-4
EPUB 978-1-911583-38-7

Design and Typeset by Julie Martin
Cover by Julie Martin

Printed and bound by 4edge UK

urbanepublications.com

The Very Idea is dedicated to my parents Norman and Freda who encouraged their only child to be inquisitive. And to all my family, friends, and colleagues who have gamely put up with the consequences.

CONTENTS

PREFACE

The English language does irony brilliantly. But we must thank ancient Greek for giving us a series of figures of speech to help us deliver it stylishly. Litotes sounds so much more interesting than understatement. Euphemism and hyperbole are elegant expressions for mincing words and going over the top. But I've always thought that the phrase 'The Very Idea' was in a class of its own for conveying the opposite of what it appears to mean.

When I was a small boy my parents often left me in the care of three splendid – and quite elderly – maiden aunts at their vast, unheated, 13 bedroomed house in North Oxford. The library would have supplied the reading requirement for a good-sized town, and there was room for an audience of well over 100 people in the drawing room when it was used for amateur dramatics or lantern shows.

The aunts were kind, industrious, and dedicated to good works. They had had an interesting upbringing. Their mother was one of Alice's friends, taken out regularly in Lewis Carroll's boat. One of their uncles was Queen Victoria's surgeon, and another the Master of Magdalen College for 43 years. They had grown up in Torquay with their other two sisters and had been taught by a governess. A lonely little girl from down the road was invited to share lessons with them: Agatha Christie. They used old-fashioned pronunciation ('lahndry' for washing clothes, a 'yart' for sailing, and one stayed in 'an otel'). They of course never swore or used profane language. If anyone said anything controversial or mildly shocking, like 'there'll be a female prime minister one day', their retort would inevitably be: 'the VERY idea!'. I suppose in today's money, the expression was somewhere between 'surely not' and 'no way'. I loved hearing one of them say, 'the very ideah'. Marvellously Lady Bracknell.

So when I was searching for a title for this book on the crucial role of ideas in every aspect of our lives, I looked no further. I have two main messages. The first is that ideas are vital to progress, change and growth, and to solving problems and meeting challenges. If they are that valuable, we should create a new value system that recognises ideas are actually worth more than mere money. I call it Idea Economics. It is also a philosophy and a belief system. Idea Economics is fuelled by valuable ideas. They are its currency.

Secondly, I have observed during a long lifetime that most people (especially in business) are pretty modest about their ability to come up with original ideas. They cheerfully leave 'creativity' to the experts.

I can't tell you how much I disagree with this. I believe we all have it in us to be at the very least a creative contributor. We can all learn to be creative, and in particular to be a prolific source of ideas. When John Seifert, the new boss of the advertising agency Ogilvy, announced the agency's relaunch and new identity in June 2018, he called for 'Pervasive Creativity' in the following words:

> 'We are all created equally creative; it just comes out in different ways. David Ogilvy said that 'a good idea can come from anywhere'. Well, you are that anywhere. Creativity isn't about a department or a business card. It's about respect for good ideas and the people who have them. You. Me. Our client. Anyone. Anywhere.'

In these pages I am going to introduce you to one of the most potent and inventive forces in nature – the Idea Brain. You will find numerous suggestions and tips on how to discover, switch on, and use your own Idea Brain to generate and develop the valuable ideas that drive Idea Economics.

So with your permission, I would like to repurpose 'The Very Idea' not to indicate shock or surprise, but to represent the epitome of a terrific, winning, valuable idea, by adding an exclamation mark in the appropriate place (ie The Very! Idea).

If you will allow me to fast forward to the acceptance of Idea Economics as a more dynamic metric than bottom line or cash deposits, and to a world where creativity is the ultimate game changer, I would want to encourage new language as well as new ways of doing things. Since Idea Economics is a value system, clearly one idea is going to be far more valuable than any others. My friend Jon Leach, whom you will meet later on in these pages, calls it the one in a hundred idea – even the one in a thousand idea. As we are engaged in the treasure hunt, we are bound to wonder exactly what this exceptionally high worth idea is going to look like and how we are going to recognise it when we have found it. More about the mathematics of this later.

Meanwhile I think The Very! idea is a good way to describe it.

INTRODUCTION

Sadly, many businesses suffer from a culture where transactional competence (efficiently doing the same job day after day) is valued above inquisitiveness and the desire to be smart in the way we think and work.

My experience of the world of work tells me that ambitious people tend to be one of two things: acquisitive or inquisitive. The acquirers are very often largely transactional – doing roughly the same thing most of the time, while the inquirers are usually transformational. In other words, they want to change things. I mainly write for inquirers and transformers, while hoping that acquirers and transactors can be won over.

I have spent a complete working life in the world of commercial creativity. (We called it advertising until the word became unfashionable). Ideas have been the lifeblood of that life and, going forward, will play a crucial part in the very challenging new industrial revolution which awaits us. Short term financial measurement will not be enough. Businesses will need a radical new value system based on the long-term value and power of ideas. I call it Idea Economics.

In the same way that Behavioural Economics demonstrated that people's behaviour frequently deviates from economic orthodoxy, logic and self-interest, so Idea Economics is a more accurate and useful predictor of success and failure by using ideas, and not money, as the currency.

Just as Brand Valuation told us that the value and potential of companies depends just as much on what their brands are worth as on fixed assets and balance sheet, so Idea Economics gives businesses the tools to measure the value and impact of ideas from concept right through to implementation.

For the last thirty years my work has involved managing advertising pitches – one of the most highly-charged examples of Idea Economics in action.

All of us – not just 'creatives' and 'experts' – have the ability to come up with ideas. Some ideas are the product of our lively imagination. Most successful ideas come from the connections we make between new thoughts and stimuli and what we already have stored. It is the Idea Brain that we use to make these connections. Knowing it's there, and that it's a facility we can and must use, is the first step.

I extensively researched idea generation techniques across innovation and commercial creativity and interviewed highly successful idea people. *The Very Idea* is peppered with tips that I hope you will find useful. They are just a selection. There are no right and wrong ways. Some will work better for you than others. We can also work out for ourselves new and improved methods of firing up our Idea Brain and getting the most out of it. As Oscar Wilde said, 'you can't use up creativity. The more you use, the more you have'.

I am happy to share practical advice on how each of us can learn to use our Idea Brain both to generate original ideas and to become a creative contributor. Some of the cleverest operators, commentators, teachers and advisers on the planet have written about ideas. Reading their books, papers and presentations on the subject has been a great learning experience for me. To try and distil all that wisdom would have extended this book to a thousand pages, and you wouldn't want to wade through all that! So I have done my best to pick the best bits and aim you in the right direction by highlighting more authors and titles for you to explore.

I should also say that I have only written about the kind of ideas I know about. I am not qualified to write about science, or engineering, or medicine, or advanced technology. These are obviously all fields where ideas are as important as research and testing, and where the ability to think laterally and make new connections is just as effective as it is in business, marketing and communications. Nor have I attempted to tell stories and draw parallels from the other creative industries, where my knowledge is only that of a consumer or audience member. What I sincerely hope is that others – with intimate experience of these worlds – will be attracted by Idea Economics, and that they will be inspired to explain how the Idea Brain works there, whether it be in music, architecture, food technology – or indeed cosmology! I am also confident that the clarion cry of this book 'Ideas for all, by all' deserves to be heard in every area of human endeavour.

There are two superheroes in this book – the mighty idea itself, and you, the reader who believes in your ability to be happier and more successful through a love of ideas.

Originals (about original thinkers) by Adam Grant, a Professor at Wharton, is one of the most impressive books I read while doing my research, and I will share some of his thinking later on. His core thesis is that original thinkers fantasise about a better future, have a vision, and want to change the status quo. But more importantly, they take actual steps towards making it happen. I couldn't have summed up my own goals better.

I wrote the blog below for The Marketing Society to inspire readers to become idea enthusiasts, and not to be put off by missing out sometimes. Children don't learn to walk by standing up. They learn from falling over. In the field of ideas, as in the rest of life, we learn from our mistakes.

What's the best idea you never had?

I am fascinated by how we come up with ideas, how we share them by thinking together, how we develop them, and how we use them to achieve the outcomes and successes that business continually challenges us to achieve. It's a big subject!

I am also fascinated by the other side of the coin – the times when we should have had a great idea but didn't. Also interested in the times we had the germ of a great idea but didn't succeed in selling it or exploiting it. That is why I have asked you the question in the headline. Can you think of occasions when your business or personal life might have been transformed if only you'd had a killer idea or successfully pitched it? What went wrong? Was it your fault – or someone else's? Was there anything more – or different – that you could have done?

If love is what makes the world go round, ideas are truly what enable us to understand it and change it. We live in a world of big money, big numbers and big data. Yet individuals – even very powerful ones – can't have much influence over the money, the numbers and the data.

How very different with ideas! We can't solve problems (or even understand them) without ideas. We cannot appreciate opportunities, let alone realise them, without ideas. We need ideas to take to meetings. In the meetings we have to contribute to the refinement and finessing of ideas. When we are part of a decision making team we must treat ideas as the raw material for solutions, outcomes and transformations.

There is an urban myth that only some of us are capable of coming up with any ideas, let alone great, game-changing ones. I have been extensively researching and trawling for insights among academics, business gurus, philosophers and psychologists. I believe strongly that we all can be idea generators, idea sharers, idea developers, and idea communicators. We just have to have confidence and take some tips on board – the most important of which is that thinking together in a team is just as valuable a skill as dreaming up original ideas in the bath.

A lifetime in advertising has given me a deep respect

for ideas, without which marketers can't make their brands successful and competitive. But admen use the idea word both for ingredients (the 'big idea' in a pitch) and the finished dish. There is usually a lot of hard work in between the eureka moment and the awards ceremony. To become a true idea-meister we need put the same priority on the plated dish as on the promising ingredient. We also need to have as much respect for your idea and their idea as 'my idea'.

And there is invaluable learning for us all from the missed opportunities, the botched decisions and the ideas we never had.

Contents of *The Very Idea*

I. IDEAS ARE THE MOST VALUABLE RESOURCE IN THE WORLD

Many books are written about the contributors to business success. Investment, cost control, sales, marketing, talent, the use of technology – and especially leadership – come up time and again. But for me ideas are the #1 factor behind progress, growth, and ultimately profit. Above all, ideas enhance competitiveness, which is such a vital ingredient in success. In this first chapter I draw upon the wisdom of experts in creativity to analyse what ideas are, where they come from, the role of individuals and teams, and how sometimes (but rarely) they lead to those landmark ideas we call inventions. We also look at how we describe ideas – big/small, good/bad, powerful/weak. Value judgments. All subjective. Yet if ideas are so important economically, they deserve objective assessment, and quantification. Ideas are valuable in their own right.

2. WELCOME TO THE IDEA ECONOMY

In the movie Cabaret, Lisa Minelli sang, 'Money makes the world go round'. We now know that it doesn't. It is actually ideas that make the world go round. This is a moment in time when I believe we should recognise not just that we are living in the Age of the Idea, but that we are living and working in something called The Idea Economy. Almost half-a-century ago Peter Drucker popularised the term Knowledge Economy. Given the rate and scale of change in every field, it doesn't seem unreasonable to recognise that we are now living in a new era, where we are influenced not only by the present and recent past (which is what knowledge, data and short term financials offer), but also the vision of the future which can only come from valuable ideas and the changes they can bring about. The name 'Idea Economy' appropriately reflects this change in emphasis from present to future, and the power of ideas to be the driving force in the new economy.

3. THE CHALLENGE: TACKLING THE IDEAS DEFICIT

I believe that in too many organisations there are not enough people producing ideas, and even the ones that do, produce not enough ideas, and in particular, not enough great – potentially valuable – ideas. This chapter is a plea. It's an appeal to organisations to put a high priority on encouraging their workforce to be at the very least idea positive, and preferably idea active. Also a direct encouragement to everyone in the workplace to become at least idea developers, and if possible idea generators.

In the World Economic Forum report 'The Future of Jobs' published in 2016, it was predicted that by 2020, the three most important *individual* skills for workers will be as follows:

1. Complex problem solving
2. Critical thinking
3. Creativity

To quote from the Report, 'Change won't wait for us: business leaders, educators and governments all need to be proactive in up-skilling and retraining people so everyone can benefit from the Fourth Industrial Revolution'. Business often seems to be obsessed by money and process. Yet all change, growth and progress comes from people and their ideas.

Many commentators have warned of the dangers of a toxic office environment, bedevilled by the 'super busy' culture and wall-to-wall meetings. If there's no time to think, there is no time to come up with ideas.

Ideas are hugely valuable. Ideas are essential for identifying and realising opportunities, and solving problems. Ideas are the source of innovation and invention. Ideas are what we rely on to communicate, to persuade, and to influence behaviour. Ability with ideas will increasingly become the crucial ingredient in personal success as well as corporately. Everyone wants to realise their full potential, and I urge companies to liberate their people to play a more creative role, and all my readers to take it as a personal responsibility. Apart from anything else, the robots ARE coming. They will threaten executive jobs as well as those on the factory floor. The most potent antidote? Your idea capability.

4. MAKING VALUABLE IDEAS

I have spent a business lifetime in advertising and marketing, where the idea is king. It is a dynamic and fast-evolving world – and super-competitive. Initially I was an interested spectator and commentator for three years as a Nielsen presenter. Then I spent 20 years in ad agencies in London, Southern Europe and SE Asia – 15 of those years pitching for my life as an agency leader. For the last 30 years I have been an adviser to some of the world's biggest companies organising pitches and managing the evaluation of multi-million pound client/agency relationships. I have taken advantage of the access this has given me to adland's most talented creatives and strategists to share with my readers a privileged view of how the biggest ideas come about, and how they are developed. Unfortunately – but maybe not surprisingly – advertising isn't the most admired profession. But I believe there is much we can learn from it. Ideas in marketing communications have to pass three stringent tests to become valuable:

a. Is this idea good enough to satisfy our very demanding

clients, who always have the option of going to one of our rivals?

b. Is this idea powerful and persuasive enough to drive behaviour change among our target consumers?

c. Is this idea the very best we can do in terms of dressing our own shop window to attract new clients?

Making valuable ideas is an absolute must for advertisers, their agencies, and everyone involved in the business. It is where I have learned everything I know about the value and power of ideas. I think it provides us with an excellent model.

5. IDEA ECONOMICS – MAKING IDEAS VALUABLE

The Idea Economy requires a philosophy, a set of rules, and an operating system, called Idea Economics, which shows us how to makes ideas not just effective and persuasive, but valuable as well.

Idea Economics is a significant new branch of economics that works synergistically alongside Financial Economics, Market Economics and Organisational Economics, without seeking to take their place. Ideas need capital investment – the finance that can amplify a thought and turn it into a success. Ideas cannot become strong unless they have been forged in a competitive market environment. Ideas can't flourish unless they are managed in a well-organised business structure. Equally ideas will not become valuable unless they are rooted in the human reality of behavioural economics.

Above all no economic system can deliver growth and progress without creativity and the original and innovative thinking which we call an idea. Idea Economics will emerge as the organising ecosystem of mathematics and creativity that quantifies both inputs and outcomes of ideas.

Idea Economics is a new descriptor. But the essential principle – that the best ideas are worth a fortune – is far from new and was established with the invention of the patent system in the C15th. Trade marks were established and gave protection in most countries from the C19th.

In the marketing and advertising field, Effectiveness Awards have recognised marketplace success since 1968, initially in the US, but now in all major markets. In recent years, papers have been accompanied with supporting evidence in the shape of econometrics – so quantifying just how valuable the garlanded ideas have been. My 'day job' for many years has centred on the advertising pitch – a process which firmly established the principle that ideas are not just the tie-breaker for choosing a winning agency. In the majority of cases, the client went to pitch in pursuit of an idea that would be valuable for their business.

The book contains numerous examples of the maths behind Idea Economics, explained by our own in-house Idea Economist. It is not enough to know that original ideas are stronger than imitations, or that you have to produce multiple ideas to make one really valuable one. Understanding the mathematics is crucial to success. Equally there are counter-intuitive facets of Idea Economics. For example we all know that taking risks with ideas is...well, risky. What is far less obvious is that developing mediocre ideas is risky as well. The numbers explain why.

6. THE VITAL ROLE OF THE IDEA ECONOMIST

Our tame Idea Economist

Like any branch of economics, Idea Economics needs its own sages and gurus – people that American author and entrepreneur James Altucher calls 'idea machines using their idea muscle'. I call them highly numerate idea people with idea brains, or Idea Economists. Working for many years in advertising I have encountered some outstanding strategists with this mathematical capability.

Jon Leach, formerly a strategist with highly creative agencies HHCL and Chime, is an old friend from the pitch circuit. He accepted my invitation to become a valued contributor to *The Very Idea*. A few years ago he wrote a paper called The Mathematics of Creativity, and he has done further development work on several of the concepts from that project to illustrate and endorse theories and claims in this book. I am very grateful to Jon. Throughout the book, you will find his contributions under the nom de plume: 'The Idea Economist'. Naturally Idea Economists, in fact if not in name, are also to be found in other activities and industries where ideas for the future are valuable. Amongst others this list embraces politics, the media, academia, think tanks, entertainment, and sport. I can envisage a short-term future when every organisation has its own Idea Economist – an exciting career opportunity for talented individuals with both a flair for creativity and a head for numbers.

7. HOW WE VALUE IDEAS

To introduce money into the equation we need a valuation approach which tells us what an idea is worth now, and what the future earning potential of that idea might be. Having a viable Idea Valuator system is a crucial aspect of Idea Economics. The system I recommend resembles the various Brand Valuation formulae, but is less complicated. We also need to be able to calculate in advance the value an idea needs to deliver. The ad agency BBH, uses a concept called Idea Lifetime Value, which allows for objective evaluation of value over time, rather than the extremely short term impact assessments used by many companies.

8. USING YOUR IDEA BRAIN TO THE FULL

We all have an Idea Brain. It has five core functions: Input; Store; Connect; Compose; Output. Later, The Idea Economist shows how each of these corresponds to a mathematical symbol. There are teachable and learnable techniques to help us use the Idea Brain better. These tips are like any others (for instance, those for public speaking, golf and cooking). The simple ones work, and work fast, but not necessarily for everyone and in the same way. The more nuanced ones may help to make us expert, but may require more practice. Get to know your brain better, and in particular its ability to connect new stimuli with what you have filed away. My tips and suggestions can't turn you into an award winner or garlanded inventor overnight. It doesn't work that way. But what I can do is share with you suggestions and tools that you can start using right away. A key factor is the 'autopilot' setting we unconsciously adopt for large parts of most days. No one can generate new and valuable ideas on autopilot. The setting allows us to carry out regular tasks without thinking too deeply about them. To think, to imagine, to ideate, to be creative we need to turn off the autopilot and switch on the Idea Brain. The sequence of tips starts in this chapter.

9. TEAMWORK – DEVELOPING IDEAS TOGETHER

Working with ideas is not all about coming up with them.

Teamwork – sharing ideas, picking the winners, polishing, presenting, selling and executing them – is just as important. Dealing constructively with other people's ideas is arguably as great a skill as hatching them in the first place. Good process – rooted in my 'Mote' methodology for meetings – is vital. Being a creative contributor is a high order life and business skill. The development process is often a prelude to pitching – and hopefully selling – an idea upwards within an organisation, or externally to clients or customers. When we do this, it has less to do with what we think about the idea, and everything to do with how the idea is going to impact on the intended audience. Sadly many great ideas have been delivered in ultra-fast broadband, but received on a crackly landline.

10. FINDING THE VERY! IDEA AND BECOMING AN IDEA HERO

Now that we have sharpened up the use of our Idea Brain and used the Mote system to facilitate the creative development process, it's time – taking advice from the Idea Economist – to look for valuable ideas, and in particular for that one in a hundred Very! Idea that ticks all the boxes. The digital era has changed the world of ideas in two massive respects. First, the internet has delivered uber-encyclopaedic knowledge for research and referencing at a mouse-click. Secondly social media has made broadcasters and pundits of us all. But of itself instant access to limitless data and information doesn't make us better at ideas. Nor does our ability to reach bigger audiences more rapidly. To be valuable, the idea still has to be well made to make a big impact. Technology has not diminished the importance of valuable ideas. It is a tool, not a substitute for thinking. Idea Heroes – the stars of the Idea Economy – will rely just as much on creative thinking and understanding the numbers.

I very much hope that when you have read *The Very Idea* you will in some way be personally motivated to become a more skilled and prolific idea-maker and creative contributor. At the back of the book you will find a self-administered questionnaire to complete for your own satisfaction. The result will give you an idea about where you stand now and indicate the areas in which you might look to progress.

Chapter 1

IDEAS ARE THE MOST VALUABLE RESOURCE IN THE WORLD

**I love the human desire to do things better.
Self-improvement has been the vital driver and motivator
behind every advance in history.**

I can't dance, but I'm inspired by Strictly Come Dancing.

I can't cook, but I'm hooked on Masterchef.

I have played golf since I was a boy, but I'm still a sucker for lessons and YouTube videos.

Having spent my working life rubbing shoulders with talented creatives and appreciating their ability to create something out of nothing, I'm in awe of ideas – every one of which starts in the brain of just one person.

My experience tells me that there are millions of us who want to be able to create for ourselves. My ambition is to help as many as possible of us become idea people and make a creative contribution to valuable ideas.

This book is about idea economics – the new world where ideas, not money, are the currency of growth, progress and change.

So many business books have been written about leadership, and its contribution to business success. The shelves also groan under titles on business models, marketing, investment, teamwork, motivation, turnarounds, cost control, sales, talent, technology, IT and so on.

But in the list of the 50 best-selling management books of all time, how surprising is it that there are only five on ideas and innovation, despite ideas being the #1 factor behind progress, growth, and ultimately profit. Above all, ideas enhance competitiveness, which is such a vital ingredient in success.

In this first chapter I draw upon the wisdom of experts in creativity to analyse what ideas are, where they come from, the role of individuals and teams, and how sometimes (but rarely) they lead to those landmark ideas we call inventions. We also look at how we describe ideas – big/small, good/bad, powerful/weak. Value judgments. All subjective. Yet if ideas are so important economically, they deserve objective assessment, and quantification.

Ideas are also a huge motivator – both to the generators and beneficiaries of ideas. As Dan Dennett, the American philosopher put it, 'humans are unique in being able to put ideas ahead of our biological needs'.

Put me down as a transformer

I have always believed that changing people was a much better idea than changing the people. But it's a hire and fire culture out there. Perform or you're out. We don't have time to bring you up to speed, so we have found someone else.

It is such a limited view of the world, and completely at variance with everything we have learned in marketing and advertising – where persuasion is the fundamental model. Why would the techniques that work with consumers not work with employees? There would be very little point in talking about behavioural change, much less recommending it, if people can't or won't change. Yet there is a strongly held view that leopards cannot change their spots, or as they say in France, 'Chassez le naturel, il revient au galop'.

There's a vast training and coaching industry that says how wrong that view is. Training is built on the same principles as the educational experience that has shaped every one of us.

I don't know. I listen. I watch. I learn. I try it out. I do. I succeed.

Training and coaching are dynamic and transformative. Had you ever wondered why both words imply speed and travelling together? In ambitious companies changing behaviour has to be achieved quickly and in teams.

Before starting this book, I had already written two designed to help people change behaviour for the better – *Decide* about making better decisions in a better way, and *Mote* about a radical reinvention of the traditional (and deeply flawed) business meeting. For the last 30 years I have worked with some of the world's biggest companies, helping them make important decisions about which agencies to appoint, and how to work with them. This has involved sitting through many hundreds of meetings, helping my clients make some important decisions, and seeing literally thousands of ideas.

What have been my most important learnings?

1. Even the biggest decisions – maybe I should say *especially* the biggest decisions – are based on gut feel as much as on iterative, deductive logic. Slavish adherence to criteria and sub-criteria quite simply won't work.

2. Big meetings are normally hopelessly unproductive, partly because people behave badly when they don't get enough airtime, and partly because increasing numbers around the table exponentially increase distracting interactions. But *orchestrated* meetings, as for example in a pitch process where both sides want a successful outcome, can work very well.

3. My take after over a quarter of a century of managing pitches? Don't assume that firing your agency and hiring a 'better' one will work. It may be better to put the effort into improving the partnership you have. My focus is increasingly on relationship evaluation and enhancement.

4. But ideas are the X Factor, the game-changer. Ideas can be quite extraordinarily powerful and exciting. There is nothing humans produce which is so impressive, so progressive, or so transformational as an idea. That's why ideas fascinate us. That's why we have such respect for people who are good at generating and developing ideas.

That's also why my third book had to be about ideas – and specifically about encouraging everyone to join in. Changing people (and in this case, both the way we think and the way we work together) will be more effective than changing the people, or leaving it to 'someone else' to come up with all those ideas we need.

In selecting content for *The Very Idea* (and you cannot imagine how much of quality and interest has been written about ideas) I have concentrated on the most relevant, sharable, added value thoughts. As an inveterate collector of business books, I distinguish between fascinating books, full of mind-opening facts and conclusions (I call this genre 'wow, isn't that amazing!'), and ones that you can learn and benefit from, and start using tomorrow. This is one of the latter.

To develop the thought, here's a recent blog I wrote for The Marketing Society, whose membership is drawn from across the industry.

Whatever happened to the learning culture?

A PLEA TO ALL MEMBERS:

- To marketers and other business people, don't become so caught up in your busy lives that you stop learning about the world outside your brands and your market place. You have a career to think about, and future employers and partners will be impressed by wide experience and wide knowledge, over and above what skills are transferable from what you were doing last

- To agency folk, don't dedicate yourselves exclusively to knowing about the brands you are working on, and other people's brands that you are pitching for.
- To consultants, don't risk running on empty. The consulting canvas that has served you well for the last few years probably needs refreshing, and if you have been successful as an adviser on a, b and c; who knows how well you could do in future, having expanded your remit to include e, f and g.
- To all of you, please don't resent me pointing this out.

Why do I say this? There are two main reasons. First, there can never have been a time when the juxtaposition of academia and the practice of marketing has produced such a cornucopia of new scholarship, new insights, and new theories. I am a glutton for new papers and new books on a wealth of subjects from neuromarketing to how creativity impacts differently in social media as compared to conventional channels. The sheer profusion of new knowledge dazzles and bewilders like the breakfast buffet in a five star resort!

Secondly, I am staggered at the apparent lack of interest in all this from so many of the clever, well educated, high earning people I meet around our industry.

If you are one of the glorious minority, my entreaty is not aimed at you. But do me a favour and take up the cause of campaigning to reactivate a learning culture. We used not to know too much about how marketing and communications really work. Now there's no excuse. And the more we know, the more successful we will be.

Then there's the fun of it all – working in a quite fascinating business that embraces philosophy, psychology, neurology, technology, and lots more besides. The next time you are sitting in a meeting that is going nowhere, bored and frustrated, remember that there IS something you can do about it. Go Googling, and just see how many new things you can learn in a week!

While researching this book I conducted more than twenty interviews and read numerous books and papers on ideas and creativity. I will share highlights, soundbites and longer passages in this and the chapters that follow. Here is a brief selection of comments on what an idea is to start with.

Putting Ideas into Words

Coming up with ideas is essentially a specialised branch of thinking.

When Descartes wrote 'Je pense, donc je suis' ('I think therefore I am'), he was laying down a marker as an ideas person, as well as proving that he was around in 1637! Thinking and being are pre-requisites of each other for our species, although sceptics – and I am one – would argue that in this confusing, super-busy, over-messaged world, being is actually well ahead of thinking for many of our fellow-humans. And when it comes to solving problems and realising opportunities, that is a big problem.

Descartes was two hundred years too early to be an Existentialist, but I sense he would have warmed to the insistence of Kierkegaard, Nietzsche and their 20th century followers that we should concentrate on our subjective individual experience, rather than the objective truths of maths and science.

But why should we have to choose? In **The Very Idea** I will share with you a strong argument for treating ideas both subjectively and objectively – both as the inspiration for our creativity and valuing the ones we generate and develop. This book is also about the overriding importance of ideas in our lives, because of the potential value of those ideas – particular ideas and ideas in general – and their extraordinary power to transform. Julian Smith (one of the many talented colleagues from the world of advertising and marketing that I have interviewed for this book) puts it like this, 'every idea is essentially a proposal for change'.

The Existentialists were right about the primacy of the individual. Every reader of this book will hopefully be personally motivated to become a more skilled and prolific creative contributor.

In this book I am talking mainly about three kinds of ideas:

- those that make us think differently about an existing activity or involvement.
- those that earn us extra interest or dividends on things we do now.

- ideas that gain us entry into a new source of business or revenue stream.

Ideas are essential for identifying and realising opportunities and solving problems. Ideas are the source of innovation and invention. Ideas are what we rely on to communicate, to persuade, and to influence behaviour. Ideas will increasingly become the crucial ingredients in personal and corporate success.

Not all ideas are the same

Ideas come in many forms. There are three classic dictionary definitions. Let's use Brexit as a vehicle for demonstrating how they differ:

i. Philosophy or belief. eg 'Brexit: our IDEA is that Britain should leave the EU'.
ii. Plan of action. eg 'The IDEA is for us to hold a referendum asking the British people whether they want us to leave the EU'.
iii. A pure concept / organising thought. eg 'Independence from foreign influence and control is a very important IDEA for us'.

But in usage 'Idea' can also mean slightly different things...

iv. A unit of creativity. eg 'We are working on three IDEAS'.
v. 'Something interesting in my head'. eg 'An IDEA occurred to me when I woke up this morning'.
vi. Innovation or invention. eg 'John Logie Baird is

recognised as the first person to make the IDEA of television work'.

Having spent a business lifetime alongside marketers and marketing organisations, I know just how vital ideas are to success in the marketplace, to the value of brands and to the companies that nurture and develop them.

I see ideas as performing the same function in my world as 'upstream' in the oil business (exploration and production of crude oil and gas).

So, what is an idea? How does it come about? All the experts agree that ideas come from people making connections – usually by bringing together elements that were previously unconnected.

In our brains there is a massive storage tank of memory, which is not particularly well organised. A new input or stimulus can jog something in that memory, and it is generally the connection made between the new element and what was there already that stimulates the idea. Heather Andrew of Neuro-Insight told me, 'memory is not just a record of the past. It is plasticine for the future'. Richard Storey of M&C Saatchi made the same point in a slightly different way, 'an idea is like sticky tape. You can attach things to it. You have to remember that ideas aren't born whole and ready to use'.

American psychiatrist Albert Rothenberg calls the process 'homospatial thinking' – actively conceiving two or more discrete entities leading to the articulation of new identities. This sounds more formal than it usually is. Once our imagination takes over (in dreams for instance), it's quite common to have odd bedfellows swimming round in our subconscious. In Chapter 8 I am going to reintroduce you to your Idea Brain, and there are a lot of tips there for sparking the 'cerebral speed dating' that seems to do the trick in terms of matching the two or more ingredients that make a powerful idea. All the experts agree that there are so many different ways of getting there. Will Collin, one of the founders of Naked, now at Karmarama, told me, 'sometimes you make an idea classically by reading widely and exposing yourself to cultures, other times the idea just finds you'. David Droga, founder of Droga5, says, 'ideas creep up on you'.

Lucas Peon the Argentine-born ECD of JWT in London said, 'an idea is a thought than can be turned into an idea to solve a business problem'. When I asked Fergus Hay, CEO of Leagas Delaney, he said to me, 'it isn't an idea unless it changes the business'. There may be no such thing as a wholly original idea, any more than there are completely original ways of getting ideas. But there is such a thing as a unique combination, and everyone recognises that that's what makes a great idea. And we all know that great ideas work. In Chapter 10 (Finding the VERY! Idea), there are some suggestions for making particularly potent connections and combinations.

Ideas come from more than three separate cognitive processes

Tanner Christensen, who is a Product Designer at Facebook, is the author of *The Creativity Challenge*.

He believes that we use three different mental processes in coming up with ideas:

- Imagination – seeing the impossible or unreal.
- Creativity – using imagination to unleash the potential of existing ideas in order to create new and valuable ones.
- Innovation – taking existing, reliable systems and ideas and improving them.

He explains that it is easy to confuse the three, and writes, 'When solving a novel problem, we rely on creativity to generate an answer or idea for overcoming the problem. We might know what the problem entails, but we can only solve it by combining ideas or diverging from our focus in order to see what we couldn't see before. Creativity very much deals with reality, but the solutions we generate as a result of creativity are difficult to measure. Innovation is what takes place when we look at an existing system or process and find a way to improve it, often utilising both imagination and creativity.'

He believes that it is all a question of focus:

- *Imagination* – focus is on things that are unreal or impossible. 'Dreams at night are a type of imaginative thinking; what you see when you dream isn't really happening, and in most instances what you dream cannot physically happen. A great example of this is a recurring dream I have, where a blue-coloured cat teaches me how to fly'.

- *Creativity* – focus is on things that *might* be possible, but we can't be sure until we explore them further. 'Where imagination simply requires that we have *some* context from which to envision an idea, creativity requires that we have knowledge of the idea, motivation and freedom to explore and tinker, intelligence to see what makes the convergence of any set of ideas possible, and then the energy to see the process through'.
- *Innovation* – focus is on what is right in front of us, something that can be measurably improved in the here and now.' Innovation takes both creativity and imagination further, focusing on existing systems or ideas that can be evolved naturally'.

Christensen sums it up like this, 'It's important to know the differences, and to know when you're using one mode of thinking as opposed to the other, and what the context is for that reasoning. Where imagination can tell a remarkable story, creativity can make imagination possible. Innovation uses imagination and the power of creativity to measurable improve on what exists today. If you're trying to improve a process or idea, you should focus on thinking with innovation in mind. Innovation is the way to see how something might work in the future. If, alternatively, you're looking to generate a new way to solve a problem in your life, utilising creative thinking is the way to go. Be sure, in those instances, you have everything you need to think creatively. Lastly, if you want to see things from an entirely different perspective, work to build your imagination.'

I think Christensen has made a good contribution by breaking down ideation into three, although there's obviously considerable overlap, and we don't necessarily have the precise terminology to avoid confusion. I'm not sure I would restrict the term 'creativity' to just one of the processes. Imagination is probably the purest form. We can give our brain the freedom to explore. Innovation is the tightest brief, 'this is how we do things now – is there a way we could do them differently and better?' Somewhere in between is what I would call bespoke creativity (almost certainly to a brief). Here's where the creator is looking for an idea which effectively connects the new stimulus (the brief, the problem, the opportunity) to one or more of the myriad elements stored in his/her hard drive. David Ogilvy wrote, 'big ideas come from the unconscious – but your unconscious has to be well-informed. If at first you don't succeed, don't try exactly the same thing again'. US philosopher Dan Dennett told us, 'there's simply no polite way to tell people they've dedicated their lives to an illusion. What you can imagine depends on what you know, and the conscious mind is an illusion'.

Present and Future Ideas

Idea is a funny word. It's not until you start looking up dictionary definitions that you realise that we use idea in two fundamentally different time frames, and we use them interchangeably.

There are 'present' ideas and 'future' ideas.

Present ideas are thoughts, concepts, impressions or notions relating to now, as in 'she has some strange ideas on bringing up children', or 'the idea that Trump is speaking for America...', or 'the idea of Behavioural Economics has caught on'.

Future ideas, on the other hand, are thoughts or suggestions as to a possible course of action, as in, 'we've had the idea of starting a separate digital agency', or 'the idea is to use Amal Clooney as our spokesperson'.

But nothing is straightforward. Take a phrase like 'she's always full of new ideas', which is a commentary on an ongoing (present) situation that also looks to the future.

Christensen was writing about future ideas, and that is definitely what this book is about. From a background in advertising, it comes naturally to me to look to future ideas, which are also the ones that innovators and inventors are seeking to come up with. I called the book *The Very Idea* in an allusion to how complicated and confusing ideas are, and how the world of ideas is dramatically unstraightforward. I could say, 'my ideas on ideas are likely to be controversial', and believe I was talking about future ideas. Whereas a critic could pick up a synopsis of the book, and say, 'Wethey's ideas about ideas are so predictable', so dismissing my ideas as tired old present ideas. The very idea, indeed!

Have we all got the idea gene in us?

Facility with ideas, as in 'Leonardo was the ideas man of all time', or, 'can you believe how full of ideas Marie Curie must have been to win two Nobel Prizes?' is a quality we all admire. But it is also a quality many of us tend to be over-modest about. Not many people will admit to being poor parents or bad drivers, but my experience is that friends and colleagues claiming above average ideas skills are very much in the minority.

Yet we are all wired to come up with ideas, share ideas, and develop ideas. How else would we be able to navigate our complicated lives over many years? How could we solve problems and spot opportunities? How could we think laterally, and surprise family and friends? It is the facility that each of us have to produce and embrace ideas that makes us what we are. It is a skill we all have – both to create, and to work with others to make them better. Adam Grant in *Originals* says that anyone can have great ideas, but warns that when we've developed an idea, we're typically too close to our own tastes and too far from the audience's tastes to evaluate it accurately. He writes that the biggest barrier to originality is not idea generation. It's idea selection.

In her book, *In Your Creative Element*, Claire Bridges asked, 'Can anyone work in a creative role or does it take a natural talent?' Her book offers detailed training in creativity, and she concludes, 'Perhaps creativity isn't necessarily a gift that you either possess or do not, but rather something that can be developed and expanded, can be instilled in teams and departments, and can be developed to drive businesses to further success'. I have written this book to convince my readers that each of you has built-in idea skills, which can be significantly enhanced by inspiration, training and experience. It is an urban myth that being an 'ideas person' is a highly differentiated ability, confined to very few people. Having been researching the amazing world of ideas for some time now for this book, I am convinced it is untrue.

Michael Michalko in *Cracking Creativity* agrees, 'if you have the intention of becoming more creative in your work and personal life and apply the thinking strategies in this book, you will become more creative. You may not become another da Vinci or Einstein, but you will become much more creative than someone without the intention or knowledge. There is no way of knowing how far these things can take you. We live in a world that offers no guarantees, only opportunities'. He was talking about the strategies in his book. But hopefully the optimistic hope applies to the ones in *The Very Idea* as well.

Every idea starts with one person

There may be no 'I' in team, as the cliché goes. But when it comes to thinking and being creative, to start with at least, it's just me and my brain. Every one of us is an 'I' – however hard sometimes it is to believe it, when our individuality seems to be marginalised by the pressures of the world of work.

Given this, is it a coincidence that idea starts with an 'I'? Probably, but it seems strangely appropriate.

It is not just 'idea' that begins with I. Surprisingly so do so many of the words associated with generating and developing ideas, for example:

- Imagination, inspiration, innovation and invention.
- Insight, intuition, intelligence and inclination.
- Immersion, inclusion, introspection and interpretation.
- Inversion, intervention and intrusion.
- Infusion, immersion and implosion.
- Illusion, impression and illustration.

There are more. It's almost uncanny.

But two heads are better than one for taking ideas forward

Having said all of this, two heads ARE better than one, as we will see in Chapter 9. Two people is the human world's most effective as well as blissful coupling. Just imagine. Double that idea capacity. Double all those other 'I' abilities. When have you ever shared an idea with a colleague, partner and friend, and not been stimulated and inspired to look at this aspect differently, to see more potential in that one?

But that doesn't mean five or six heads are necessarily better than one. Frequently having more people in a meeting results in more egos, more hot air, less clarity and less progress. The *Mote* system developed in my 2015 book of the same name is ideal for the creative development process. *Mote* is about system, planning and training meeting professionals in a lean, agile culture. If the meeting hasn't delivered, go back to you and your brain, get the ideas flowing, use some of the 'I' words, and when you are ready, add a friend and his/her brain. You won't go far wrong! More in Chapter 9.

Future ideas need to be powerful enough to make a lasting impact.

There is a phrase I came across recently to dramatise this, from an unlikely source – a Spanish train.

Alta Velocidad Española (**AVE**) is a high-speed train operated by Renfe, the Spanish national railway company. Alta Velocidad Española translates as 'Spanish High Speed' (the train runs at speeds of up to 193 mph), but the initials are also a play on the word **ave**, meaning 'bird'. The train was launched in 1992. Twenty five years later in 2017 RENFE ran a famous TV campaign, created by Madrid ad agency Shackleton celebrating the anniversary by claiming that the Ave had been well ahead of its time. The campaign line was "El futuro ya tiene recuerdos"; in English, "The future already has memories".

This is a book about valuable ideas, and the fact that they are indispensable for progress, growth, change, and indeed the future. I have spent my life in one creative industry – advertising – but there are many more; architecture, art, crafts, design, fashion, film, music, performing arts, publishing, software, TV, radio, and video games. In all these industries practitioners seek to go far beyond functionality, by innovating and pushing frontiers in such a way as to make an impact and catch the public imagination. Engineering (as in train design for example) is a parallel field. I wonder if *The Future already has Memories* is as close as we are going to get to a way of describing the effect on the imagination of an idea which has made a telling impact.

Advertising and ideas

It would be quite wrong for me to make it sound as if advertising is the only place where people have ideas. It's neither helpful nor true. But that world is the one where I have worked for over 50 years – so there's some bias there! And I hope you will indulge me now and in the next few chapter where I have collected my best learning from being an adman for twenty years and working as a client-side consultant with agencies for thirty. It is also the case that marketing and advertising is an ideal environment to study the idea development process in particular. Food companies sell food, health companies sell medicines. Ad agencies sell ideas. Because of that their attitude to ideas and their aptitude for developing them is positive and polished.

I came into a vibrant advertising industry in the late 1960's. At that time clients and agencies enjoyed partnerships *averaging* seven years, I can compare that to the frantic turnover of relationships we see today. Agencies used to concentrate their creative firepower on coming up with more executions in an existing campaign for their long-term clients, with a new campaign or a launch every now and then. How different now, when new business is the imperative, and effectively the default setting for creativity. Ideas are even more important for revenue and growth. Time frames are shorter. Adrenaline has replaced long lunches as the stimulus. Cricket lovers would draw a parallel between five day test matches and T20, and they would be right. It's quite simply a different game now.

Anna Qvennerstedt is Chairman of one of the world's most highly rated creative agencies, Forsman and Bodenfors – and a famous copywriter. She told me, 'In the digital era we have to come up with ideas that people want to be part of. It's more challenging than life in the interruption model. And also more interesting'. Forsman and Bodenfors is based in the city of Gothenburg on the west coast of Sweden, not in New York City or London. Yet clients from all over Europe, the US and Asia beat a path to their door, such is their reputation for making ideas that transform brands. They are also still retained by their founder client Göteborgs-Posten, the local newspaper. My conversation with Anna was dominated by her stories about the results achieved for their clients. All the great advertising creatives are focused on business success.

Dealing with sceptics

I have taken flak over my decision to write this book. For example:

'Why have you decided to write about ideas? You are a suit, not a creative or strategist.'

'What are you trying to achieve? Not everyone can be creative. What makes you think that your book will make any difference?'

'Only 10-20% of people have it in them to become full-blown idea creators.'

'There are so many real problems in the world / in this company / for people like us. What makes you think that anyone other than you is concerned that there's a shortage of ideas?'

'I'm in Poland for the whole of next week. And before I go, I have got to write two big reports, and do my budgets. Do you imagine I have time to read some theoretical stuff about ideas?'

Then there's more organised opposition

Mark Wnek is a famous British advertising creative, who now works and lives in the US. Here is a blog post he published on 27th December 2017:

Everybody is creative – The Big Lie That's Killing Mad Ave

Overheard at a Mad Ave function the other day:

'I'm sorry but I HATE the word 'creatives' – as if it's something reserved for the anointed few. At our agency we believe **everybody is creative**.'

Three words that creatives come across a lot these days.

Every time I hear them, it's like spit in my face.

A passable sentiment in a toddlers' art class, perhaps; in a professional setting it's so deeply insulting.

Some of us have spent most of our lives working hard to transform what creativity we may have been lucky enough to be born with into a scarce and hard-won skill.

Yes, everyone has the capacity for creativity.

Just as everyone has the capacity to sing, too.

But while few of us would compare our efforts in the shower to Adele, it seems that in the field of creative advertising everybody is Adele.

Imagine anybody in any other occupation getting away with such an idea.

'We've completely changed out the chef and staff. They were getting so precious about every little detail. I mean it's just food. It all ends up in the same place, right?'

'No, he isn't a qualified surgeon, but he has real healing powers. Ok, relax: here comes the general anaesthetic...'

'Steven Spielberg was asking for too much money so we got Steven Spilkus'.

Ludicrous, right?

Not as far as marketing services are concerned, it seems.

I'm not alone in believing that the 'everybody's creative' refrain gets you the Kendall Jenner Pepsi spot [a notorious 'turkey'].

Or that it gets you that nice, personable young bureaucrat as your 'creative director' (you can tell (s)he's creative because (s)he wears jeans and a tee shirt in the office) and the umpteenth anodyne campaign featuring a car driving along a road to music; or two homemakers in a kitchen discussing the finer points of their bleach/detergent/vacuum cleaner by name; or people eating/chewing/drinking something cool and everything around them frosting up; or young people jumping about to music and close-ups of sneakers/clothes/ cellphones/candy; or middle-aged people talking to camera about computers/insurance/banking/pensions/healthcare; or beer/trucks/restaurants described by Sam Elliott; and so on and on ad infinitum.

The 'everybody's creative' refrain has also led directly to the canning of the *actually creative* – such an obvious, glaring, massive, critical problem in a Mad Ave in apparent meltdown, that I and many, many others are stunned it isn't THE conversation in the ad industry right now.

Nothing – digitisation, automation, Big Data, blockchain – nothing matters, no delivery system is worth a damn if what's being delivered stinks.

Everybody is absolutely NOT creative in any sense that helps brands, products and services stand out and engage people and make people love them.

In fact very, very, very few people are creative in that true sense. And the bigger the talent, the rarer it is – and the more expensive.

Just like it is in every single pursuit and occupation from sports to silversmithing.

Every day we read stories about how Mad Ave is failing – none bother to explore the obvious link between this and the dearth/exodus of true creative talent.

Every conversation revolves around the next big thing, none on the critical need to focus on what never changes. (Like Jeff Bezos, whose focus on the old-fangled low prices/ fast delivery/vast choice trifecta recently made him the world's richest man.)

For some time now, Mad Ave's most senior executives have got away with the 'everybody's creative' lunacy. It has allowed them to take millions upon millions of dollars-worth of so-called top creatives off their payrolls and, with nobody going to the wall for quality (i.e. 'This Kendall Jenner spot blows, bring me a good idea'), countless time off the production process.

The niceness of your agency's staff, the brilliance of your strategists, the newest new technology, the sharpness of your tailoring/dentistry, the exclusivity of your golf club – none of this matters if the work is poor.

Superb strategy is meaningless without executional excellence. It's hot air, fog. It's big talk. It's Mike Tyson's catchphrase: 'Everybody has a strategy until they get hit in the face'.

The continued exciting advances in digital technology have given the digerati and their followers first-mover advantage. This always happens at the start of every social revolution. And, as throughout human history, the 'new' is rapidly ingested by all until it's nothing but the norm.

Right now and for a brief while yet, the scientists, the digerati rule – the poets, the creatives, and everything else that's been around forever are deemed run-of-the-mill, or better yet 'traditional'.

'Traditional' stuff like creativity being pushed to the bottom of the totem pole makes it seem accessible by all. Hence smart young people, clever with laptops, have become the new creatives.

Easy to see how tiny a hop it is from there to 'everybody's creative'.

But all science and no poetry makes the world a dull place: driving home the other day listening to sports talk ESPN on 98.7 FM, former Steelers and Jets lineman Willie Colón set to discuss the Jets' quarterback problem, suddenly piped up out of the blue with:

'By the way, we watch a lot of tv in the holidays. What happened to the advertising? When did it get so boring? What happened to stuff like 'Wassuuup?' and 'Where's the beef?' I had about 50 over for Christmas and everybody agreed how bad today's ads are.'

Everybody is NOT creative in any way that is commercially viable – unless quality is merely a nice-to-have.

At their very best, advertising creatives are artists and poets because they engage people's feelings.

Here's how one of America's greatest ever poets, EE Cummings, put it on accepting the Academy of American Poets annual fellowship in 1949:

'A poet is somebody who feels, and who expresses his feeling through words. This may sound easy. It isn't. A lot of people think or believe or know they feel – but that's thinking or believing or knowing; not feeling. And poetry is feeling – not knowing or believing or thinking.

Almost anybody can learn to think or believe or know, but not a single human being can be taught to feel. Why? Because whenever you think or believe or know, you're a lot of other people: but the moment you feel, you're nobody-but-yourself.

To be nobody-but-yourself – in a world which is doing its best, night and day, to make you everybody else – means to fight the hardest battle which any human being can fight; and never stop fighting.

As for expressing nobody-but-yourself in words, that means working just a little harder than anybody who isn't a poet can possibly imagine. Why? Because nothing is quite as easy as using words like somebody else. We all of us do exactly this nearly all of the time – and whenever we do it, we're not poets.'

Every senior ad agency business leader will experience a spike of familiar dread on reading Cummings' fighting talk.

Ideas like 'fighting' and 'battling' and 'hard work' will spark the muscle memory, past confrontations with highly-paid creatives refusing to compromise their work and demanding instead that clients be made to understand how much worse and less effective the work will be if the clients' whims are acted upon.

Creatives who have made extraordinary leaps from brief to idea believing that their account handler colleagues should make similarly extraordinary leaps in 'selling' the work to clients.

Thank goodness, thinks the account handler. that the world has moved beyond this traditional dynamic where different wings of the agency had to support each other.

Thank goodness we're in charge. Goodbye the old 'creative bottleneck', hello frictionless digital.

No surprise then that the majority of advertising entails little/nothing more than getting the marketing strategy on film: it's the logical conclusion to the 'everybody's creative' philosophy.

Obviously this necessitates Mad Ave fees getting slashed: if 'everybody's creative' then why pay a premium to an ad agency?

Which is just one tiny, frictionless step from doing away with ad agencies altogether.

I don't agree with Wnek...
...nor did several readers of his blog

Another creative, RT Herwig, disagreed and posted back:

'As a Creative Director I do take issue with his stance on everyone not being creative (including clients and suits) because I believe the responsibility lies on our shoulders as creative leaders. I responded to him with the reply below. He said my reply was not a reply, but my own article and to go write it on my own page. So here I am, on my own page:

So, Mark, what do you suggest as a solution? The responsibility falls on the shoulders of today's Creative

Directors and CCOs. Everyone (in an agency) is capable of creative thought and coming up with ideas (including input from the client)—it's not just the jurisdiction of a select group/type/department. The fantasy that not everyone is creative (although romantic) is dangerous & outdated. Because as our industry gets faster and more complex, we need to come up with new ideas quicker and it takes different kinds of thinking from different disciplines to come together to solve today's briefs.

Creativity MUST blossom throughout the agency and it's up to creative leadership to nurture/foster creativity with everyone, especially those who work far from the creative department. Instead of telling everyone that they're NOT creative (or that they are to blame for why creative isn't being sold, or that the suits are idiots), the Don Drapers of the world (who romanticise how it used to be) need to venture out of their corner offices and lead by example. The best ones don't bitch about how shitty things are, they adapt. As creative leaders we need to become better teachers/mentors/coaches and help orchestrate and lead collaboration across all disciplines and departments, including the client and his/her expectations.

John Updike said, 'Any activity becomes creative when the doer cares about doing it right or better'.

I get it. The bean counters, the data-miners and the suits are raining on our creative parade. As Creative Directors and CCO's it's up to us to get everyone to care (as much as we do) and to do it better (including our clients). When the work sucks, or when Kendall Jenner ends up in a spot a client produces, we only have ourselves to blame for not being responsible shepherds of our agency / client's work.

Like I tell the creatives that work for me—it's up to you to put your best self and best work on that wall every day. Regardless of politics, or history, or taste. At the end of the day you are the work you sell, or don't sell to your client. Once you start down the road of jaded creative, it's tough to find your way back.

Ideas can go down as well as up

Researching the world of ideas and creativity has been a fascinating experience. I think we've all worked out that only a small minority of people in business are what you would call natural and consistent idea generators. My goal in writing the book is to encourage far more executives and managers to liberate their inner creativity, rather than fall back on the brief / feedback / micro-manage / approve routine. I have really enjoyed interviewing the planners, creatives and inventors who come up with the great ideas that drive change and progress. There are some brilliant tips to pass on, and I have every confidence that many of my readers will rise to the challenge and become consistent and prolific ideas people.

There is a 'but' however. Not all ideas – even ideas that we think are big ideas – are good and valuable. The same mental process – making connections between what we know already and what we have recently learned from looking at a problem or brief – that triggers powerful, game-changing ideas, can also produce bad and dangerous ideas. That's why we need the filters and litmus tests that colleagues provide to scotch potentially disastrous flights of fancy. It is no good my egging on everyone to dream up more and more ideas if we have no mechanism for spotting the dangers of a rogue when we still have time to abort and go back to the drawing board.

A popular myth is that there is safety in numbers, in terms of making sure that contentious ideas are exposed to a lot of people to make sure that they won't lead to disaster.

How different the world would be if that were true!

How much less hazardous life would be if the democratic process (you know elections, referendums and so on) saved us from truly awe-inspiring mistakes like Brexit, Trump or a hung parliament with the balance held by the DUP. There are obviously myriad examples of one-off bad ideas. But what intrigues me is the bad idea that just gets worse as it plays out and triggers ever worse consequences and side effects.

Take Brexit for instance. The Referendum simply asked voters to decide whether to leave the European Union or remain within it. 'Brexit' had a ring to it (much more of a rallying clarion than 'Remain') and the behaviouralists tell us that positive action is instinctively more motivating than just carrying on doing the same old thing. 51.9% voted for Brexit. It's probably fair to say that the vast majority did not understand what the Brexit idea meant (other than a vague Rule Britannia feeling), or what the short and long-term consequences were likely to be. Suffice it to say that no divorce in history was ever so protracted, complicated or expensive. And worse still, Britain doesn't even have someone else to sleep with.

Ideas are like jokes and gifts. The joke teller and the present giver are the last people to decide whether the joke is funny or the gift hits the spot. Only the recipient can do that. We have all worked out that idea generators are full of ideas. The first one off the production line is pretty unlikely to be the best we can do. We need a reasonable level of choice, and the time to look at pros and cons. Assessing reward and risk are essential to good decision making. Nearly all the politicians campaigning before the Referendum wanted the good bits of Europe without the bits that hacked us all off. The Referendum campaigns on both sides were badly planned and run, with no indication that a vote for Leave would turn into a bungee jump without the bungee.

So why do we allow ourselves to fall for politicians with daft ideas? Is it ignorance, or apathy? Is it the feeling we can't make a difference? Or as in the case of the EU referendum or the US Presidential Election, is it simply that a choice between just two unattractive options is not really a valid choice at all – unless at least one of the ideas is well articulated?

Both being directly critical and sitting on the fence have a bad name. We are always being urged to make a positive choice – this idea, this candidate. But the next time you are asked to vote for an idea or a person that smells wrong now and could smell a lot worse down the line, tell it as it is, and stay on the fence (eg vote Remain) till something better comes along!

Inventions

We are all fascinated by inventions. Having the kind of mind, let alone the scientific or technological ability, to think of or actually make something new and wonderful is universally admired. Also inventions are rare. There is – and has to be – innovation everywhere. But to have the idea that leads to actually inventing something...

I researched inventions from a relatively superficial level of knowledge. This was where I started from:

- Galileo invented the telescope
- James Watt invented the steam engine
- Henry Ford the automobile and the assembly line
- The Wright Brothers invented manned flight
- Thomas Crapper the flush toilet
- George Washington Carver peanut butter
- Marconi invented radio
- Alexander Graham Bell the telephone
- Apple engineers the iPod
- Edison invented a whole clutch of things from the light bulb to X-Ray photography, moving pictures and recorded audio
- Al Gore created the internet

I had already worked out for myself that Gore's claim wasn't true! The real inventors were Vinton Cerf, Leonard Kleinrock, Robert Kahn and Lawrence Roberts. But, as it turns out, none of the other names above should have been credited with the inventions they are coupled with. Here are the 'real' inventors:

- Hans Lippershey invented the telescope
- Either Thomas Savery or Thomas Newcomen (according to who you speak to) the steam engine. Although the Ancient Greeks in Alexandria came up with a similar concept 2000 years before!
- Karl Benz the automobile, and the Chinese in the time of the First Emperor the assembly line (to produce the Terracotta Army)
- Richard Pearse the aeroplane
- The Chinese again the flush toilet (but sadly not toilet paper!)
- The Incas Peanut Butter in 950BC
- Either David Hughes or Nikola Tesla radio (also AC transmission. But he is now best known for something he didn't invent, but was named after him – the Tesla all-electric car)
- Antonio Meucci the telephone in 1871 vs 1876 for Bell
- Kane Kramer something very like the iPod and took out a worldwide patent

And if we are talking about Edison...

- Sir Humphrey Davy the light bulb

- Wilhelm Roentgen X-Ray photography
- De Martinville recorded audio
- Louis Le Prince moving pictures

You will like the splendidly named *Stigler's Law of Eponymy*, which says that no scientific discovery was named after the individual who actually discovered it!

It turns out that we can only be sure of one thing: the old proverb – 'Success has many fathers, but failure is an orphan' – which was one of President Washington's bon mots, as we all know. Well, actually it was not. Stigler's Law again. The original quote was in Italian by Count Ciano, Mussolini's son in law, and it was repurposed by President Kennedy during the Bay of Pigs stand-off!

But the weird and wonderful world of inventions holds more mystery still. Not only is it sometimes hard to know who invented what, equally inventors don't always know what they are going to invent!

Roentgen wasn't actually trying to invent X-Ray photography. He was conducting an experiment with a glass gas bulb when he noticed that a ray was penetrating heavy paper. He was just one of the 'accidental' inventors. That list also includes:

- Daguerre – photography
- Goodyear – vulcanised rubber for tyres
- Fleming – Penicillin
- Greatbatch – Pacemaker
- An unknown engineer at Canon – Inkjet Printer

- Art Fry at 3M – Post-it notes
- Constantin Fahlberg – artificial sweetener
- John Pemberton – Cola
- George Crum – potato crisps (presumably they turned out bigger than what he had been working on!)

To return to who invented what, A Professor of Law at Stanford University, Mark Lemley wrote an important paper called *The Myth of the Sole Inventor*. As an expert in Intellectual Property and Patent Law, Lemley made three crucial points.

First, as the title of his paper says, there are very few sole inventors. It is exceedingly rare that one individual comes up with an invention without support from a team or colleagues. Also it has happened frequently that rivals arrive more or less simultaneously at the same or a similar conclusion. Account Planning in advertising had just been invented by Stanley Pollitt at PWP (my first agency), when I joined it in April 1968. It so happened that Stephen King at JWT made the same breakthrough at almost exactly the same time. Not collaborating. Not competing.

Secondly, history conflicts with traditional patent theory and most patent law around the world, which is based on the assumption that inventors operate alone and need protection from rivals or imitators.

Thirdly pioneering inventions (the momentous ones) are not usually the result of an eureka moment. Invention is actually more of an iterative process, almost certainly involving others.

Jonah Lehrer published *Imagine: How Creativity Works* in 2012. Shortly afterwards Lehrer was caught up in a scandal, when he was accused of plagiarism and making up quotes. His publishers in both US and UK withdrew the book from sale. It was a great shame, as there is so much to admire in the book, and I make no apologies for referring to Lehrer's work at various points in this book, including here on inventions. He quoted a study done by Ben Jones of the Kellogg Business School. Jones investigated scientific production over the past 50 years by looking at both patents and peer-reviewed papers. What Jones found is that successful patents and papers are increasingly coming from group efforts, and that these groups are growing in size, 'with the average team increasing by about 20 percent per decade'.

The increasing size of groups here is more than just a trend, it is an indication that only collective efforts are strong enough to produce successful patents and papers, and that the size of the networks needed to produce these successes has been growing over time. For Lehrer, the reason why this is the case is simple. It has to do with the fact that 'the biggest problems we need to solve now require the expertise of people from different backgrounds who bridge the gaps between disciplines. Unless we learn to share our ideas with others, we will be stuck with a world of seemingly impossible problems. We can either all work together or fail alone'.

Maybe the last word should go to Mark Twain. He's

become retrospectively controversial, but surely he got it right on inventions: 'It takes a thousand men to invent a telegraph, or a steam engine, or a phonograph, or a photograph, or a telephone or any other important thing— and the last man gets the credit and we forget the others. He added his little mite — that is all he did. These object lessons should teach us that ninety-nine parts of all things that proceed from the intellect are plagiarisms, pure and simple; and the lesson ought to make us modest. But nothing can do that.'

Talking of polymaths, we must remember de Bono

DE BONO

The now 85 year old Edward de Bono is one of my true heroes. In **Decide** I dedicated a piece of doggerel to de Bono, who I met when I was up at Oxford and he was a young don at Cambridge.

de Bono – the Maltese Eagle*

A small tribute to a philosopher with a mighty wingspan
I've embarked on a serious mission
To raise the humble decision
From just one of the things we can
To a towering achievement for man

The prophet who showed me the way
Wore hats, but none of them grey

He is the thinking man's thinker from Malta
de Bono: the lateral exhorter
Schoemaker gave us the rules
And Belbin told us the roles
But de Bono allowed us to learn
By playing each role in turn

Wear the red hat for passion
And the black one for trashin'
Yellow hat says you are sunny
And green that you are creative and funny

But the cleverest hats are the blue and the white
White hat means you only say what's right
No editor's gloss on conversation
Just unvarnished truth and information

Blue is the smartest hat of all
You're the conductor in the hall
Fusing the sounds the hats are making
By thinking, solving, decision making
(Wethey, 2011)

de Bono has an extraordinary range of interests and areas of expertise. He went to university at 15, qualified as a doctor at 21, matriculated as a Rhodes Scholar at Oxford at 22. He has degrees from 5 universities including Oxford, Cambridge, London and Harvard, yet rejected academia. He was a passionate enthusiast for changing the laws of football, a prolific game inventor, a charismatic and extremely highly paid speaker, and an entrepreneur who built a highly successful company. Oh yes, and he invented Lateral Thinking, Parallel Thinking (the Six Thinking Hats), and built a remarkable educational system in CoRT. He has consulted for numerous organisations – governmental and corporate. He has played a hand in many of the geopolitical issues during his life. He has travelled, advised and spoken all over the world. He has met most of the great men of three generations, and famously moderated a meeting of Nobel prizewinners. To me the most impressive measure of the man is his legacy. The thinking is as fresh and relevant today when he wrote his 82 books.

His credo has been to challenge logic and orthodoxy. He explains that outside mathematics we as a culture have done nothing about thinking for millennia. What he calls our 'traditional thinking software' was developed 2400 years ago by the GG3 (the 'Greek Gang of Three': Socrates, Plato and Aristotle) and is in grave need of revision. He says the situation is a 'bigger and more urgent danger than climate change', rightly asserting that most problems are the result of poor thinking.

'And poor thinking will only continue to create problems – conflicts, wars, persecutions and so on. So we not only need better thinking to deal with climate change itself, but to solve international antagonisms and inequalities.'

His views on ideas are legion. Let me pick out just some of his more memorable soundbites.

From *Lateral Thinking*:

- He invented the Lateral Thinking word PO as an escape from the confrontational dichotomy of YES and NO. He described PO as the intermediate impossible. So he uses PO to argue that the answer to traffic congestion in cities is to make cars with square wheels. And that giving away all food free would remove the problem of thefts from supermarkets. 'Faced with an idea', he writes, 'one rushes to judge whether it is correct or incorrect. If it is correct one accepts it and proceeds. If it is incorrect one throws it out and proceeds in a different direction. PO provides a third alternative which lies somewhere between acceptance and rejection. PO is not concerned with an idea's validity, but with its value in setting off further ideas. Thus an idea that would otherwise have been rejected at once may be saved for a while longer by the use of PO.

- 'In a time of rapid change brought about by technology, education, communication and developing attitudes, one needs creativity more than ever and the ability to develop new ideas'. He wrote this in 1971, 46 years ago. Does it sound familiar?

- 'Since everyone uses ideas, creativity is everyone's business.'

From *Simplicity*:

- 'The first idea that comes to mind may not be so interesting. But the second and third ideas that flow

from it may be very interesting. Wishful thinking –
'wouldn't it be nice if...'

- 'In Lateral Thinking 'wishful thinking should be an extreme fantasy. In the simplification process wishful thinking can be more realistic. Why can't we use this ideal approach?'
- 'Wishful thinking does have to go beyond a known alternative. It is not just a matter of suggesting an alternative approach. The thought must lead reality forward.'

Learnings from one of the most talented people whom I interviewed for this book

BALDER ONARHEIM – 'IT HELPS TO BE PROLIFIC, AND A POLYMATH'

At Advertising Europe in March 2017 I was most impressed with a presentation on ideas by a Danish academic, Balder Onarheim, Associate Professor of NeuroCreativity at the Technical University of Copenhagen. I subsequently conducted two interviews with him. I learned a lot from Balder. We discussed the connection between being prolific and lasting fame. It is already well known that being prolific is a significant factor in fame. Within the sub-universe of top flight performers in the arts for instance, the more paintings an artist paints, the more works an author, playwright or composer writes, the more likely it is that at least some examples of their output are going to be sufficiently outstanding to make the creator famous. It is largely a function of numbers – the more plays, symphonies etc you write, it is inevitable that some will be of relatively modest quality. On the other hand, the shorter the odds on some of them being first class!

One of his most interesting findings is the high correlation between creativity and being a polymath The polymath factor is a different dynamic altogether. I do not think enough is written about polymaths. Balder's theory is that for someone to be a brilliant in business, and a talented sportsman, or a best-selling author and also skilled at playing an instrument, is not twice as good as one dimensional success, it's about five times as good, because it's unexpected. I also feel that one of the reasons that polymaths are not celebrated enough is that they make people jealous. Even intelligent academics, commentators, journalists and so forth resent it. Isn't it enough for them to be brilliant at this, why do they have to show us up by being brilliant at that as well!

Balder told me about a client of his, the composer Daniel Rosenfeld (who wrote the music and sound effects for Minecraft). 'Daniel is probably the only creative person I know, who actually makes a living from being creative. He is a guitar player, who has pioneered playing the instrument on his lap like a Dulcimer, he is an excellent magician, a most accomplished juggler, and also a successful entrepreneur. Most of the other extremely creative people I know excel at everything from consulting to mathematics and physics. Idea-rich people have a constant flow of good ideas in a wide spread of areas. These are not cliché creatives on a big motorcycle, with crazy hair and swearing a lot. The creative polymaths I know are also good cooks, and they also know how to fix a motorcycle engine without reading a book about it. Daniel is also a constant streamer of ideas. Daniel has more the classical sort of creative type of ideas. While you're talking to him he suddenly gets a tune in his head and he'll note it down. It's more impulsive and artistic. Daniel is also notably prolific. He seems to have this never-ending stream of ideas where, nine out of ten might not be useful at all, but he will still have them, and present them and try them out.'

Balder also told me about his neurobiologist colleague Morten. 'He would spend his weekends building a system for using his swimming pool as a heat reserve in winter time even though every expert on heat told him it's impossible. Morten is a tangible example of how these people are not just creative in one aspect of life. A neurologist shouldn't be spending his time on energy storage if you look at his education, but his brain can't help coming up with those kinds of ideas, all the time. He's probably the most idea-rich person I know. He won't go a single day without him calling me or texting me about this new brilliant idea he has. And they're all completely unrelated to what we do. Morten's brain has a tendency to mature ideas. So when he has an idea, it's normally quite concrete and technical.'

'If you look at a lot of famous Nobel Prize winners,' Balder told me, 'they were also great musicians, great dancers, they wrote poems. The other thing about these people who are crazy skilled in completely different areas, they're also super humble about it. It's just what they do. They never thought about it as being anything particular. They happened to be great cellists, great singers and also the best mathematicians. That's just who they are.'

More from Balder Onarheim

CREATIVITY TRAINING

It's only a step from analysing what makes a polymath to working out how the ability to generate and develop ideas can be enhanced. Balder again, 'Is there such a thing as creativity training? We need to try and find the most simple, effective ways of improving people's creativity through as little face time as possible. Can we sit down with people and work with them for say 12 or 24 hours, and then they will exit and be provably more creative. But not necessarily in exactly the area you might imagine. Two or three years ago we did one of our creativity training programmes with some IT people, and in the feedback form one of the participants wrote that it was a really good course, he really enjoyed it and it also helped him to understand his wife better.'

Balder told me, 'that's where I am now. You can be in charge of how you develop your brain and your way of thinking and use that skill to also understand others. The way your brain is, and how you think, is a result of all the training that you've done. Understanding that concept makes you more willing and interested to change your own brain. It also helps you understand why other people are the way they are.'

He told that earlier that morning, he had had a meeting with Dr BJ Fogg, the inventor of the Tiny Habits methodology. Dr Fogg helps people to change behaviour by adopting small new habits. He finds the smallest thing they could do to change something and that could be getting to bed at a certain point of time or, doing one push-up each day, or making lists when you're not a list-maker. Then he would help them to keep doing that for such a long time that they actually groove their ability to change behaviour.

On Balder's creativity course, once people can feel themselves changing into more creative people, they suddenly realise that they can actually choose to change things in another domain. A lot of his former students went on and did other types of course, so they suddenly had the courage to learn to tango, or whatever else they wanted to be better at.

Are the idea and the communication of that idea the same thing? In advertising, yes. In other areas of creativity, not necessarily. Take cookery for instance. Recipes and menus are quite different things. We start with the concept, the ingredients and the preparation and cooking instructions. The dish obviously needs a name. Then there's the taste, the texture, the look of it, the smell of it, the accompaniments, and possibly too, with the Heston Blumenthal's of this world, the theatre. The idea is actually a series of ideas, or an idea with multiple dimensions, like music or movies.

TIPS ON IDEAS

- Ideas are a fundamental human skill and the way to success
- Ideas are a subset of creativity
- Creativity is about putting two or more concepts together in a useful way
- Lowest filtering is the key to creativity
- Defining problems too tightly limits the solution
- Ideas take up a lot of working memory. Write them down immediately in the parking lot. Don't let the brain be overloaded
- Intense physicality can stimulate creativity
- Use sleep as a structured method
- Use daydreaming as a technique
- Analyse your dreams
- We're very bad at randomness
- Take risks

ON HAPPINESS

Another of Balder's discoveries is the link between being happy and a prolific generator of ideas. 'Some of the happiest people I know and work with, they love coming up with ideas. They do it all the time.' Elaine Fox made the same point in Rainy Brain, Sunny Brain: 'if you want a successful brainstorming session get people into a happy and relaxed mood first.'

In discussion with me Balder agreed with me that so many executives in big companies are not happy. They are living frustrated, unfulfilled, unproductive lives. 'We're wasting human capital', he said. 'It is not just of interest to academics that people are educated and trained to do one thing, and end up working like passive robots. It then becomes a much bigger issue. It's certainly a human capital issue. It's also a serious social issue. It's a cultural issue.'

'Some cause happiness wherever they go; others whenever they go.'

I wrote a blog about happiness using the well-known Oscar Wilde quote above.

When he said it, he might have had business meetings in mind.

Haven't we all suffered in conference rooms at the hands of people who try to dominate, to interrupt, and to be generally contrary and uncooperative? We also know too many meeting participants who are, well, miserable...

In these circumstances it is only natural to celebrate quietly when they have to make a premature departure!

Happiness is one of those words we don't readily associate with business. But that is almost certainly a mistake. There was an interesting study published last year by economists at the University of Warwick, and publicised by Damian Symons of the M&C Saatchi Group agency Clear at the Saatchi Institute event at the London Business School on 24th November 2016. Symons reported that happiness led to a 12% spike in productivity, while unhappy workers proved 10% less productive. As the research team put it, 'we find that human happiness has large and positive causal effects on productivity. Positive emotions appear to invigorate human beings.'

Nor is it really about money. Financial incentives aren't enough to make for highly productive employees. Professor Andrew Oswald, one of three researchers who led the study, said companies that invest in employee support and satisfaction tend to succeed in generating happier workers. At Google, employee satisfaction rose 37% as a result of those initiatives — suggesting that financial incentives aren't enough to make for highly productive employees.

Shawn Anchor, author of *The Happiness Advantage*, has found that the brain works much better when a person is feeling positive. At those times, individuals tend to be more creative and better at solving problems. And additional research has shown that when workers are happy they're more effective collaborators working toward common goals.

Symons referenced another study – this time a paper published by the American Psychological Society in 1985 – in which three researchers at the University of Maryland (Isen, Daubman and Nowicki) demonstrated through four linked experiments that happiness stimulates creativity. As the paper concludes, 'the impact of positive affect on creative problem solving is that good feelings increase the tendency to combine material in new ways and to see relatedness between divergent stimuli. We hypothesise that this occurs because the large amount of cognitive material cued by the positive affective state results in defocused attention, and the more complex cognitive context thus experienced by persons who are feeling happy allows them a greater number and range of interpretations'.

In other words happy people are likely to out-perform people who are miserable in a challenging area like creative problem solving.

When I introduced my 'Mote' system for improved meeting culture in organisations I wasn't aware of these studies. But I was very influenced by Tony Crabbe (who wrote **Busy**), and Roman Krznaric (the author of **Empathy**). Crabbe is passionate about the need to liberate successful business people from being 'crazy-busy' and feeling that at all times they must tell everyone how busy they are. Drastically reducing the amount of time they spend in largely unproductive meetings, will make these high-flyers not only far more effective, but also happier and better partners, parents and friends.

Krznaric's book is a plea to us all to try and feel how it would be to be in the other guy's shoes. In his view, not only enlightenment, but also happiness, stems from not being dismissive, prejudiced and arrogant.

My own experience of a business lifetime spent in conference rooms was quite sufficient to be able to identify the negative and corrosive behaviours that make everyone, including the perpetrators, feel unhappy. All of us have grown up in a business world built on the left brain pillars of efficiency, productivity and power. It is refreshing – to me at least – to realise that right brain values like happiness and consideration can prove just as potent.

MYTH: There are far more important considerations than ideas – ie money and short term financial performance.

REALITY: The world depends on change and innovation for its future. In the business world, half the biggest companies in the country will probably not be in existence in their current form by 2025. Lack of commitment to innovation is one major reason. Many corporations are stuck in traditional business models, manufacturing and distributing products that are similar to what can be easily produced in economies with lower overheads and wage bills. Or they are retailing at diminishing margins while being undercut by online competitors. Or providing services in hyper-competitive markets.

We narrow our focus to exclude anything but the short term at our peril.

CHAPTER 2

WELCOME TO THE IDEA ECONOMY

Transitioning from the Knowledge Economy to the Idea Economy

The trouble with history is that we can explain the past, but we are not always accurate at defining where we are.

Most commentators agree that our current economic era is The Knowledge Economy. The phrase was coined by Fritz Machlup in 1962, and then popularised by Peter Drucker in his book *The Age of Discontinuity* (1968). Blogger Charles Hugh Smith described Drucker's analysis, which was amplified and updated in his subsequent book *Post-Capitalist Society* (1993), in the following terms:

> The transition from the industrial economy to the knowledge economy is the modern-day equivalent of the Industrial Revolution, which transformed an agrarian social order to an industrial one of factories, workers, and large-scale concentrations of capital and wealth. These major transitions are disruptive and unpredictable, as the existing social and financial orders are replaced by new, rapidly evolving arrangements. As Drucker put it, the person coming of age at the end of the transitional period cannot imagine the life

led by his/her grandparents – the dominant social organisations that everyone previously took for granted have changed.

Following in the footsteps of historian Fernand Braudel, Drucker identified four key transitions in the global economy: in the 1300s, from a feudal, agrarian economy to modern capitalism and the nation-state; in the late 1700s and 1800s, the Industrial Revolution of steam power and factories; in the 20th century, a Productivity Revolution as management of work and processes boosted the productivity of labour, transforming the proletariat into the middle class; and since the 1990s, the emergence of the Knowledge Economy.

In Drucker's view, knowledge, not industry or finance, is now the dominant basis of wealth creation, and this transformation requires new social structures. The old industrial-era worldview of 'labour versus capital' no longer describes the key social relations or realities of the knowledge economy. In a knowledge economy, the primary asset – knowledge – is 'owned' by the worker and cannot be taken from him/her. Knowledge is a form of mobile human capital. Drucker suggested that our great transformation would be completed by 2010 or 2020.

Well, that's where we are now. And although knowledge is now supplemented by more 'Big Data' and short term financial information than we can either cope with or interpret, I am convinced that it is high time to usher in a new era – an era focused not on the present and immediate past (which is what knowledge, data and short term financials offer), but on the future.

We should recognise that we are living in the Age of the Idea. We are also working in something called The Idea Economy, which is driven not by any old ideas, but by *valuable* ones and the changes they can bring about. I call it The Idea Economy, because it is 'looking-forward knowledge' we need, and that can only come from ideas. But we need numbers too, and they are 'the world's most prevalent language', as we learned from **Sapiens: A Brief History of Humankind** by Yuval Noah Harari. Left-brained leaders will correctly demand quantified proof that ideas are valuable, which means maths. So alongside the Idea Economy we should also welcome Idea Economics (Chapter 5), and the Idea Economist (Chapter 6).

Idea Economics is a significant new branch of economics that works synergistically alongside Financial Economics, Market Economics and Organisational Economics, without seeking to take their place. Ideas need capital investment – the finance that can amplify a thought and turn it into a success. Ideas cannot become strong unless they have been forged in a competitive market environment. Ideas can't flourish unless they are managed in a well-organised business structure. Equally ideas will not become valuable unless they are rooted in the human reality of behavioural economics.

Above all no economic system can deliver growth and progress without the creativity and original and innovative thinking which we call an idea. Idea Economics will emerge as the organising ecosystem of mathematics and creativity that quantifies both inputs and outcomes of ideas.

I asked our very own Idea Economist, Jon Leach, what makes societies and economies prosper. Is it just one thing like access to resources or free markets or a Great Leader (or whatever your economics text book tells you)? Or are there multiple cylinders firing an engine of growth?

The Idea Economist on the Engine of Growth

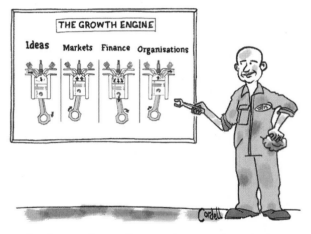

Strangely, for such an Economic question, it is not Karl Marx but his contemporary Charles Darwin that gives us the clearest answer as he set us on the way to answering the more profound question – what makes anything grow and prosper?

Biologists would say that Evolution – the mysterious process where new organisms appear and expand across the natural world – requires four things to happen.

- First, **Variety** is essential. In biological terms this can either be due to genetic mutation or a sexual shuffling of the genes to create a range of types within one species. Either way, Evolution 'needs' variation to avoid each generation of offspring being identical to the last.
- Secondly, **Competition** is needed. There needs to be some sort of 'live or die' selection method that favours one of the new varieties so that winners with a particular characteristic become a new generation subtly different from the previous one. No competition, no distinctive winners, no change.
- Thirdly, **Amplification** is required. By winning the battle for food, light or sexual partners, the survivors get to fill the empty space and become the new majority. It's not just the survival of the fittest. Now everyone else is dead, the fittest get the run of the place too.
- Fourthly, **Codification** needs to happen. Without some reliable 'record keeping' from something like DNA there is no new base line established from which to launch the next round of Variation, Competition and Amplification. But with DNA installed in our cells, nature can code up the 'blueprint' for each new set of winners as the three previous steps spits them out.

And then, as they say in the ads, it's just rinse and repeat.

And after a millennia or so you have a rain forest with millions of different species. But also, over in our more concrete jungles, exactly the same four steps galvanise our advanced economy and society.

- First, we need Variety in the form of new ideas and innovation.
- Next, Competition, where the ideas are tested against each other by the market, to see which of them is most valued.
- Then, the winners will receive Amplification as investment of time and money pour in to back a winner.
- Finally the whole process is Codified as companies record business processes, contracts, patents, software etc. to ensure that the winning idea is kept in its pristine state.

But actually it isn't 'finally'.

Because just as in the Jungle – so too in the human world – the ideas people come calling again and take these pristine bits of 'business as usual', and with their mutant minds and mongrel methods create another wave of innovations to throw in the market, to seek capital, for richer for poorer, for better or worse, for ever and ever. Amen.

And so it goes. And so it grows. Unless one of the four cylinders isn't firing.

Because to maximise the system – remember all four are tightly linked – you need *all four* to be fully functioning to get the best results. Or, as the proverb has it, a chain is only as strong as its weakest link. In mathematical terms if all cylinders are functioning fully – let's say they are set at '1' on some imaginary dial – then the growth output is 1 X 1 X 1 X 1 = 1.

But if any one of them is misfiring – let's say it is running at ½ rate – then the whole engine of growth is restrained as ½ X 1 X 1 X 1 = ½. Or to put it another way, a convoy can only travel at the speed of the slowest ship.

So the first claim of Idea Economics (for the economy and society it serves) is that to thrive it needs well-functioning markets, capital flows and companies *but also* a well-functioning Idea Economy.

The fourth economic discipline of ideas is just as important as the other three – no more, but also, no less. It is our job to make sure that this cylinder has its moment in the sun, as we lift the bonnet on how the whole growth engine works...

The Idea Economy is a new place

The Idea Economy is different. It is the successor to the Knowledge Economy, not an updated version. We are moving from relentless analysis of the past and drilling down into the present to focus on the future and how to shape it.

As Mark Earls said, 'The future is a place that doesn't exist yet. And yet we cling to the impression that by gathering the right numbers together in the right way, we can predict how things will be. We don't need any of that dangerous creativity because we will one day know everything. One day.'

My enthusiasm for The Idea Economy comes from a conviction that the world's problems are not going to be solved by available knowledge, but by new thinking and ideas capable of identifying and realising fresh opportunities.

The internet of course has changed everything by facilitating the availability, speed and spread of both existing and new knowledge and ideas. We have moved from a command and control world where governments, the media, and powerful organisations communicated from on high to a weak and generally deferential populace, to the absolute opposite.

Now almost everyone has the means to communicate and reach out on smartphone, tablet or laptop. Advertisers compete to generate attractive content. Broadcasters provide endless opportunities for audiences to give their opinions. Social media is there for individuals to talk to each other and share content. People used to be constrained by geography and the restrictions of one-to-one communication from interacting with each other. Now social networks are to all intents and purposes infinite. There are no limits to spreading ideas – hence every incentive to come up with them.

We have also witnessed the amazing phenomenon of a US President who not only uses Twitter to disseminate ideas, but also to make policy, and attack his enemies and detractors, or simply be spiteful and rude.

We have also become used to the fusion of news and editorial (is that where 'false news' has come from?), to the relentless spinning of statements from politicians, and leaders of businesses, organisations, and to 'issues' always being promulgated with 'angles'.

We are truly in the era of the Idea Economy.

It is about People, Time and Ideas – as well as Money

People are the only way to produce ideas, but many of the people that are best at generating and developing ideas are crazy-busy at work, and both they and their colleagues who are rather less stretched are over-modest about their ability as idea people. The success of Idea Economics in an organisation depends both on leaders encouraging their best talent to upskill as idea people and creative contributors and liberating them from some of their other duties so that they have the opportunity to both generate and share ideas. People are also vital as raw material in idea development. Creative veteran Reg Starkey says simply, 'Ideas come from talking to people.'

Time is fundamental. It is the opportunity area. If time at work can be freed up for generating and developing ideas without adversely affecting productivity or the efficient running of the organisation, Idea Economics becomes dynamic and profitable. Some people may be released full time to become idea specialists. For others it will be a question of freeing up part of their day. Time and resource is also required to define the necessary skillsets and train them in the techniques and disciplines of creativity and ideas. People clearly use their own time to develop and share ideas on social media, chat shows etc. What could be more beneficial to companies than harnessing this skill and enthusiasm?

Ideas in this system, are inputs, outputs and the currency itself. Also we have to distinguish between ideas in different sectors, eg (and there are many more):

- Brand / Advertising / Communication ideas
- Political ideas
- Entertainment ideas

Elevating the idea from component to driving force in The Idea Economy is a massive promotion. A key requirement of Idea Economics is for there to be a valuation methodology. Here is a first look at what the criteria determining value might be in each case. The full story is in Chapter 7.

Starting with a Brand idea.

CURRENCY = REVENUE / BRAND SHARE / BRAND VALUE

- Development potential
- International potential
- Originality
- Creativity
- Versatility
- Humanity
- Sustainability
- Cultural impact

- Memorability
- Stretch
- Newsworthiness
- Ease of comprehension and communication

+

- Excitement
- Buzz

Let's now look at a political idea:

CURRENCY = POLLING / VOTES

- 'Fit' with party positioning
- News impact
- Voter appeal
- Longevity
- Competitive strength
- Originality
- Creativity
- Versatility
- Humanity
- Sustainability
- Cultural impact
- Memorability
- Stretch
- Ease of comprehension and communication

+

- Excitement
- Buzz

Next an entertainment idea (eg a potential box set):

CURRENCY = VIEWING FIGURES / REVENUE

- Audience appeal
- Competitive strength
- Originality
- Creativity
- Cultural impact
- Memorability
- Promotability
- Second/subsequent series potential

+

- Excitement
- Buzz

IDEAS: MAKING THE RIGHT CONNECTIONS IS CRUCIAL

In Chapter 1 we said that all the experts agree that ideas come from people making connections – usually by bringing together elements that were previously unconnected. So connections are the vital engine of idea making.

But arguably it is not as easy as that. Here is the Idea Economist's explanation of why we cannot assume that every connection is going to make a valuable idea.

The Idea Economist on the Connections Conundrum – 'not every Connection is a Ley Line'

Ley lines are the geographical phenomenon whereby certain 'places of power' like standing circles, ancient churches or cross roads line up in straight lines when examined from the air. For some, these reveal strange mystical and magical lines radiating across the landscape; lines that our ancient forebears could sense and thus mark them with their most sacred constructions.

Vortices appear to be points of power or energy on the Earth, and ley lines are the relationships between those points. An analogy might be that the vortices are acupressure points, and the ley lines between them are meridians on the skin of the body of Mother Earth.

For others Ley Lines are no more than statistical co-incidences that occur naturally. These killjoys say they can be created with no more than standard human endeavour and do not require you to get in touch with your Inner Druid.

Now creative ideas can also have an intimidating and rather mystical nature. Are they a rather magical thing; the product of a mysterious alchemy only knowable by a few mystical savants? Do creative people have in-built neuronal Ley Lines in their brains upon which magical ideas alight?

Or can any educated person turn base metal into gold if they understand the chemical engineering of the human creative brain?

I suspect it is the latter. And – apart from overly secretive keepers of the sacred creative brain – this is probably a Good Thing.

But first let us come back to Ley Lines and what we might term the Hippy vs Statistician dispute. Sceptics have noted that human beings are inveterate pattern spotters and will ascribe 'agency' to what may be a random occurrence. Just because three things have formed a straight line doesn't mean that someone or something planned it this way.

So Ley Lines with their spooky straightness and the clear significance of the objects lining up do seem to resonate with most of us. Sometimes you even get four or five artefacts in a row!

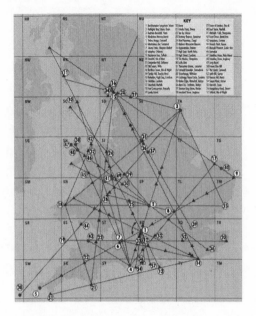

But statisticians have observed that if you throw enough beans on a tray (say about 20) at least three of them will line up just by chance, especially if you are not over fussy about what counts as 'straight'.

Now this is just the sort of party pooper comment that you would expect from a soulless statistician. To drive the point home a young statistician who went on to become a famous name in advertising, Simon Broadbent, found a way of proving that Ley Lines were extremely likely to be natural co-incidences not mystical artefacts.

The way he did it is by observing that straight lines made up of three points were really just a sub-set of triangles, namely very flat triangles.

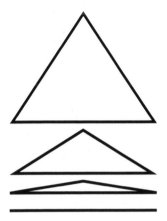

He argued that on a flat surface, whether a mystical Celtic landscape or a tray for bean chucking, when you scatter objects across it (obelisks or beans) by definition, when you draw in the lines, they produce triangles of various shapes and sizes.

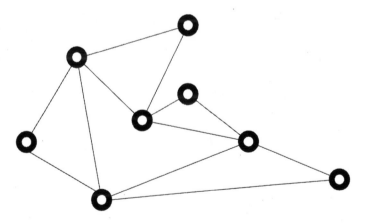

So, he observed, given your view on how flat those triangles have to be in order to count as a 'straight' line, it was only a matter of adding more and more obelisks/dots (and hence creating more and more triangles) before a Ley Line emerged.

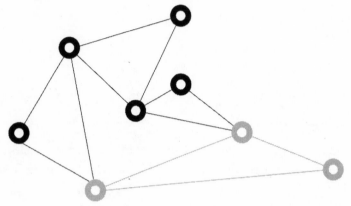

For the average bean chucker (or obelisk mapper) it was very long odds that just three points would make one of those rare ultra-flat triangles.

Think of it this way: with two points awaiting in the landing zone, the new one has a narrow zone to land in to create a flat triangle.

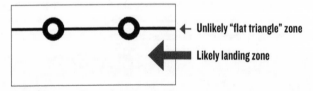

← Unlikely "flat triangle" zone

Likely landing zone

But suppose the first new stone (the 3rd in total) drops in and misses. Now there are three lines for the next stone to drop in on and make that flat triangle.

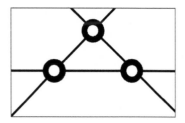

Put another way, as the fourth stone arrives it creates four possible triangles (the original one and the three potential new ones). As more and more stones arrive from the heavens they generate more and more potential triangles to try their luck with the Ley Line gods.

With five points on the map there are now 8 triangles, six points gives us 13 triangles and so on...

Points	Prior Triangles	New triangles	Total triangles
1			
2			
3	0	1	1
4	1	3	4
5	4	4	8
6	8	5	13
7	13	6	19

...and so on

So in the county of Cornwall, which Broadbent used as his real life study example, there were dozens of standing stones that you could use as reference points. There is obviously a debate about where definite Obelisks stop and random-debris-in-a-vertical-position starts, but if you take a relatively low cut off at 30, you still find that there are 433 triangles. And depending on how hard you squint, an awful lot of those are flat. Or Ley Lines if you still insist.

As the table above shows, even 16 stones will give you more than 100 triangles.

The point is that the more objects you are playing with the greater the chance that they will form a meaningful pattern.

People who are interested in lots of different things tend to have interesting ideas

This is very important for creativity, and the Idea Economy. So many of the experts that I have spoken to, and also the authors of several of the best books on the creative process, emphasise the – pretty obvious – link between having extensive general knowledge, and a wide range of interests and the ability to make connections at will. As I said in the Introduction, I write for people who are inquisitive.

We saw in the previous chapter how Balder Onarheim took this a stage further with his identification of polymaths with creativity (not just being interested in lots of things, but being good at them).

Mark Earls reminded us earlier in this chapter that in the Idea Economy the desire and capability of making the connections that show us the future are vital attributes.

This is the Idea Economist's take on the phenomenon.

The Idea Economist on the Ley Lines of the Creative Mind

You often find with creative people is that they are interested in many, many things. Often quite obscure, unrelated topics. And more to the point they are always filling up their brains with new ideas that are unrelated to their immediate creative challenge. I once had lunch with a Creative Director of a top advertising agency and ended up discussing his interests in unreconstructed Tory philosophy, midnight blogging, statistics in Direct Marketing, the merits of German Camper vans over US ones, and the secret of good Indian food.

This section is based on the learning from the numbers in the section above.

A creative idea can be defined as the point of connection in one person's mind of two previously unrelated ideas in a way that is recognised and valued by other people.

So for example, Damien Hirst combines 1) human skulls with 2) diamond encrusted bling and we get 3) the Diamond Skull and an object that is much discussed and photographed (and as proof of its creativity is more valuable than the sum of its two components).

Now the trick here is not just to put together any random ideas to create a third; that just gives you a common or garden triangle.

It's a bit like with jokes. Linking two things together is the core trick with humour. But it depends how you do it. For example if you combine 'Reindeer' with the use of the homophone word 'Dear' as a term of affection, you get the common joke 'You are very 'deer' to me'. Sadly it isn't very funny. It's a triangle. It doesn't line up. It hasn't been passed around much. Better ideas are more famous.

So just as a good Ley Line stops being just three random points, so a good creative idea, (or joke or piece of art) occurs when a new 'line' is formed in the creator's mind and then in other people's. The new thing aligns perfectly with the two other things to make a very flat triangle – a line.

But what do we mean by 'a line in a mind'? Certainly this is more of a metaphor than a neurological claim (although neurones do form lines). So an idea is 'right' in the sense that it feels aligned and proper. Or shoots off into the distance in a clear, purposeful direction (watch people's eyes as they grasp an idea. As they look away they are seeing it stretch off into the distance).

For those of you of a more musical disposition a good idea may 'resonate' or 'sound right'. The analogy here is with a musical chord where the frequencies of the three notes have clear and simple mathematical relationships to each other like 2 to 1 or 3 to 2.

Just as human hairs in the cochlea resonate when the right frequency touches them, so a great creative idea makes the hair on the back of your neck stand up. It just feels right.

So the art (or craft) of being creative is to create straight lines between disparate ideas. In a world full of unremarkable triangles, it is the very flat ones that stand out.

Now as Steve Martin has observed, 'some people have a way with words, and other people....oh..huh... not have way.' So a writer like Nabokov can give us this creative metaphor:

> 'Shadow of the waxwing slain by the false
> azure of the window pane.'

Where clumsier talents will give us:

> 'The ballerina rose gracefully en pointe and extended one
> slender leg behind her, like a dog at a fire hydrant.'

Two metaphors, one ugly and misshapen the other perfectly, achingly straight.

Clearly great artists have the ability to pluck Ley Lines out of their minds. Where does this leave the rest of us?

The first skill we can hone is the recognition of straight lines i.e. good creative ideas. For some this may be an innate skill but is also one that can be acquired with practice.

Creative directors in advertising or design agencies (the editors of an agency's output) will often review a hundred creative concepts a day. Even allowing for a few days down at Cannes, they may well see 10,000 triangles year and must get very good at spotting the straight lines amongst the crooked chaff.

Similarly a young creative team will be generating 100's of lumpen triangles a week and be told which of them might just be straight enough to work. And so they learn their craft.

So apart from working in a creative agency the advice would be to see and consume a huge amount of creative work (on TV, in annuals, in galleries, on shelves). Rather than force them to explain why something is good/straight, let the experts give you the benefit of their intuition. Just let it wash over you until you pick it up.

So it may seem annoying that creative directors often divide creative ideas into 'brilliant' and 'crap' with nothing in between. But in a world of multiple triangles, perhaps there is something to be said for having a culture where straight lines are worshipped and anything that is slightly bent is despised. It's part of the craft culture.

The lack of structure and focus in the creative milieu can be annoying to more mechanical minds. But to the hunters of the Ley Lines of the human mind, being told to stay focused on the problem at hand is like asking them to move heavy obelisks around to make straight lines: too much like hard work. They would rather wander off into the glades, find a few new obelisks and conjure up a new line of thinking that way.

What can the rest of us learn from this?

- More mechanically-minded companies should continue to employ outside agencies to work on their creative problems. Not only will a creative agency bring fresh pairs of eyes. It also brings people who work on problems outside the category. Applying lessons from seeming unrelated categories can often solve the problem. In fact it makes it hard not to.
- And on a personal level the task is to be an interesting person. The best advice on how to be interesting is to be interested.
- So by all means become a specialist in your industry or category. But also move around a bit. Change

companies, or at least projects regularly. Live in a different country.

- And finally, also nurture and develop interests in other things in the world however uncommercial or lateral.

These are not just your hobbies or indulgences but valuable personal obelisks you can place upon your own mental plain. And perhaps one day, when you get that mystical feeling of a strange power coursing through you, three of them will have aligned and you too will have a perfect Ley Line in your mind.

Indeed, it's a statistical inevitability.

MYTH: The Knowledge Economy is with us to stay. Big Data is what matters. We have almost infinite knowledge and information at our disposal. The issue is mainly about processing and applying it.

REALITY: We know plenty about the present and immediate past – and that is what all our financial data is based upon. We desperately need to have more insight into what the future holds, and we need ideas to help us get there. The most successful and fastest growing companies are those who are best equipped to generate ideas and make it possible for their customers and account holders to do so (Apple, Microsoft, Google, Facebook, Twitter et al). We don't have to justify the arrival of The Idea Economy. It's patently already with us, and there is so much material for us all to be imaginative, innovative, and makers of promising connections.

Chapter 3

THE CHALLENGE: TACKLING THE IDEAS DEFICIT

What do I mean by Ideas Deficit?

I believe that in too many organisations there are not enough people producing ideas, and even the ones that do, produce not enough ideas, and in particular, not enough great – potentially valuable – ideas. Given the pivotal importance of ideas set out in Chapter 1, and the fact, explained in Chapter 2, that we are now living in the Idea Economy, ideas have never been so vital for our growth and progress. Yet ideas and creativity are far from the top of the agenda. Business is overwhelmingly left-brained. Short term financial management rules. Life in offices – even for high-fliers and the most talented – is relentlessly crazy-busy. Action is prioritised over thinking, meetings over planning and managing change, caution over risk, saving money over making it, answers over questions, problems over opportunities. Significantly the use of consultants and outside experts has proliferated. Bought-in thinking and ideation has literally and figuratively replaced the suggestions box.

This chapter makes the case for us all working on our ability to come up with ideas and collaborate with others to develop them.

Also why it is in every organisation's interest to make the office an incubator for ideas.

But today most workplaces are not incubators for ideas.

It wasn't always like that

If I go back to my very early days in business, when I started work at Nielsen in 1965, I can remember the names of the clients that I worked with. They had time. They were interesting people. They wanted lunch, not because they were lushes, but because they had lots to talk about, and they had views on things. They were interested in life. They were interested in what was changing. They were interested in politics. They were interested in sport. They wanted to talk about all these things. And so, when you then moved with those same people into a discussion on something sensitive like loss of brand share, or the effect of advertising, they were great people to talk to, because they were open-minded, by and large. They might have really strong points of view, but they were prepared to debate them. And they had time to debate them. And they had their own ability to come up with ideas.

But problems at work go back a long way

This debate isn't exactly new. C. Northcote Parkinson wrote

Parkinson's Law (work expands to fit the time available) in 1957. Laurence Peter published **The Peter Principle** (people rise to their level of incompetence) in 1969, and at more or less the same time de Bono was developing his CoRT system for teaching children to think. (It was subsequently extended into adult education with positive results). So from the late 50's (say ten years after the end of WW2) through to the late 60's (by which time I was happily toiling in adland), it was being recognised that transferring military hierarchy and organisation to the office didn't actually work very well. Yet for the most part the problem wasn't recognised, and nothing much changed except the relentless march of technology – computers for all, no secretaries, instant access to everyone, look it all up on the internet.

I've worked with clients for over 50 years now, and I have started to really worry about office workers in big companies (directors, managers and executives) and the life they lead. I think they're too busy, they're spending their time in the long, largely unproductive meetings that I wrote about in **Mote**. Most don't get much of a chance to make decisions because they may be there when a decision is taken but they're not making it. And sure as hell they're not the source of ideas. They seem to have abdicated thinking to 'experts', other people, and they don't seem capable of coming up with ideas or doing their thinking. There's a feeling that it has to be based on research which has got to be based on something else. They don't seem to want to contribute. So the book is for them really. Apart from anything else, it's a plea to people to use what I call their idea brain. And not to feel that thinking and creativity has always got to be done by someone else. We can do it. You can do it. We're all capable of it.

The Busyness of Business is a big problem

Are you busy?

After 'how are you?' it's probably the commonest greeting these days. I guess we all want to be busy, and we want to be seen to be busy. So we encourage our business friends to tell us how busy they are too.

Greg McKeown (author of **Essentialism**), says, 'We don't have the space or time to think.'

Being busy is obviously desirable economically (busy means money coming in), socially (no-one wants to be caught out watching daytime TV), and career-wise (difficult to move to a really busy job without a track record of being busy).

But let's stop to think whether it is a really good idea to be so busy. Or if being slightly busy or quite busy might not be better than very busy. Let's look at what being very busy means. It is having a responsible job – hopefully with salary to match. It is doing well, in terms of being promoted or being hired by another company. It is also about being respected. So far all good. But are there downsides?

Unfortunately, yes. Work/life balance can get out of kilter. It is difficult to prioritise at both work and home, and you can miss out on important aspects of life with family and friends, with pressure on evenings, weekends and holidays. Health is threatened with less time to relax and sleep. You sit in meeting after meeting, you can't think straight, and inevitably you'll make more mistakes.

The experts are very critical of what happens in offices

Dave Coplin (*Business Reimagined* and *Return of the Humans),* Tony Crabbe (*Busy*) and other experts on the workplace more qualified than me have written eloquently about the dysfunctionality of what most people would call 'life at the office'. I have made my contribution with *Decide* and *Mote* suggesting respectively a more robust way of making decisions and a radical solution to the plaintive cry of 'Sorry, I'm in a meeting' several times a day.

In *Business Reimagined,* Coplin coined the phrase 'Intellectual Ambling' to describe the moments when our brain is given licence to wander and explore. Or rather not – in today's office. 'Our current workplaces', he writes, 'which prioritise activity over thought, reaction over reflection make intellectual ambling counter-cultural. Even more significantly, the noise and distractions make listening for insights extremely difficult either from the chaos of meeting after meeting, or the incessant flow of email after email, or the office chatter going on around us. We have effectively created insight-preventing workplaces'. Coplin criticises the principle of 'Group Think' on the grounds that genuinely new thinking (let's say ideas) 'is going to happen much less often with people who see the world the same way as you.'

That has been one of the unintended consequences of the much-vaunted open-plan office. Coplin says that to come up with ideas we need what he calls Deep Thinking. 'Yet the chances of finding 15 contiguous minutes in our current working environments without interruption from meetings, emails or other distractions are so rare that we are unlikely to ever harness this incredible power'. Dave's fundamental thesis is that while technological advancements have been well adopted / embraced in our personal lives, the workplace hasn't yet been affected enough. Our model of 'work' and 'the office' is still rooted in bygone eras, and actually we have the opportunity to fundamentally re-think how we do work and run businesses.

In the book Dave talks about the problem with being too focused on productivity. Most of our products and services are good enough now. Driving for more productivity isn't going to bring us to the next level of marketplace advantage. For that you need creativity and innovation, capabilities our organizations aren't set up to facilitate.

Coplin is a big fan of flexible working, in the sense of not being tied to the office. But there are cultural changes needed for flexible work to work. It shouldn't be an individual's perk. It needs to be a deep-seated organisational change. Theoretically working from home at least for part of the time should free office workers from many distractions, and not commuting every day gives them time back to think. But it doesn't always work. Trust is a critical attribute to get right. Coplin says that the reason we still cram ourselves into crowded commuter trains and endure traffic jams isn't so much that bosses think workers won't be hard working and committed when they work away from the office. The biggest problem is apparently that we believe our peers will think we're slacking off — because we're sure we would slack off themselves if we aren't at our office desk. So many people who do take up flexible working often overwork and burn themselves out trying to convince everyone they're really working. Coplin thinks that too many employees have been disconnected with the outcomes of the organisation and are treated as cogs in a process. This is disempowering, disengaging ... and very damaging to motivation.

Business psychologist Crabbe agrees. 'The ability to respond to new challenges with genuinely novel and useful solutions will be crucial. Businesses need people to step back, imagine fresh possibilities for their businesses and create entirely new solutions. In short, they need people to think. Businesses will need people to look up from their to-do lists, to identify and solve new problems, to create disruptive solutions. The problem is, taking the time to think and imagine is the last thing that's likely to happen among a frantically busy workforce.'

In *Busy* Crabbe outlines a unique three-step approach to stopping the cycle of 'Overly Busy'. How did they do it before? It's a question many of us ask, as we stay glued to our laptops or our phone, always present, always working, always trying to be 'productive' at all hours of the day. And yet, we can't keep up. Which leads to that question: How did they (which, for those of us of a certain age, means 'we') do it before?

Crabbe offers a succinct answer: because we are trying to resolve information-age problems with industrial-age solutions. We try to be more productive, we try to 'manage time' — when the problem, according to Crabbe, is not that we have too little time to do what we have to do. The problem of the information age is that we give ourselves too much to do. Busy is not just a burden. It has become a badge of honour. One brags about how busy one is. Stopping this cycle of being over-busy and never actually catching up — which, despite our bravado, just makes us exhausted and frustrated — begins with understanding what Crabbe calls 'the three faces of busy'. Each of the three faces refers to a different way in which we relate to busyness:

- *The first face of busy* sees 'busy as an experience'. This is the busyness, that keeps us harried and overwhelmed, the busyness that makes us feel that we don't know how to manage our time.
- *The second face* is, 'busy as a success strategy'. In this case, we believe that success comes by being more productive, by always striving to do more and more. Unfortunately, this type of busyness leaves us little time to do the 'big stuff', such as taking the time to think creatively.
- Finally, *the third face* is 'busy as an approach to

happiness'. This busyness face, writes Crabbe, refers to the goal of having more and more — more stuff, more popularity, more status. Values, relationships and our health are put on hold during a relentless acquisition frenzy.

In his book, Crabbe offers three distinct strategies to battle each of the faces of busyness.

- *The first strategy*, aimed at getting beyond busyness as an experience, is a strategy of mastery. The goal is to become masters of our lives, Crabbe writes. It means to stop trying to get everything done through more efficient organization and start, instead, to make tough choices about what to eliminate. Mastery also involves, Crabbe writes, 'shifting our focus from managing time to managing attention'.

- *The second strategy* is to differentiate. This strategy is aimed at getting beyond busyness as a success strategy. As noted above, if we only focus on being more productive, we don't take time to reflect or be creative — the keys to standing out in our overcrowded world. In this section of the book, Crabbe urges his readers to focus on innovation, not productivity of more of the same. He also argues that too many people see busyness as an effective brand, when all it really does is convey your lack of mastery. A truly effective brand is a simple summary of what makes you unique (for example, one of his clients had 'no problem!' as his brand, which is the nickname he had been given in his business for his can-do attitude.)

- Crabbe's *third strategy*, engagement, is designed to overcome busyness as an approach to happiness (the 'having more makes me happy!' attitude). The three steps in this strategy are let your values define your meaning of success; develop deeper relationships with fewer people instead of piling up the number of connections; and replace the addiction to shallow buzz ('I'm flying from meeting to meeting.' 'I've taken up this new hobby.' 'I'm a player!') with the joy of flow — Mihaly Csikszentmihaltyi's famous term for losing oneself in a task and not realizing the time flying by.

Keith McCambridge, a Management Consultant (now with Oliver Wyman), gave me some useful perspectives. He highlighted resistance to change as a core weakness and related it to risk aversion. He felt that both inhibited ideas – bottom up, as well as top down.

He told me that in several of the corporates he had worked with 'individuals are actively discouraged from having ideas'. He went on to say, 'this is a particular problem when the people at the top are out of touch, and ideas are so important. I believe that the role of leaders is to create the right environment for the children to play'. What a refreshing contrast to the highly dirigiste, micro-managing culture found in so many companies. Active encouragement of ideas is not a nice to have in a world where speed is crucial.

It is essential to be agile and move quickly, when as Keith explained to me, Amazon can now test in four hours what it takes a High Street retailer four months to work through. That takes ideas – and a profusion of them.

Discontent – new research evidence

Busyness and dysfunctionality aren't the only problems. Discontent is a problem as well. Former Waitrose CEO, Mark Price, did some research on the mindset of workers in tech companies, where one might surmise that morale was relatively high. Not so, it seems.

Highlights of his report (*Tech in Focus*) on attitudes and morale in tech vs non-tech industries were published in the *Daily Telegraph* on 2nd Feb 2018, as follows:

- When asked 'Do you feel you're being developed', less than half tech and non-tech workers said, 'yes'.
- Less than half workers in the tech sector said they feel happy at work, and only just over half of those in the non-tech sector.
- Equally less than half of workers in tech felt that their employers care for their well-being.
- There were three key areas where workers in tech are less positive than their counterparts in non-tech companies:
  - Being empowered to make decisions
  - Feeling that their views are heard at work
  - Feeling that their doing something worthwhile in an organisation they can feel proud of

- Significantly managers in tech companies on nine out of 12 'engagement' questions score lower than the people they are managing.
- Management employees in tech feel less happy at work than management employees in non-tech industries.
- When asked what would improve their workplace happiness, techies prioritise mind over money; 16% indicate that (more) money would make them happier at work, whereas 28% indicate development is a key factor. This is a notable difference from employee in non-tech industries, where the proportion is 26% and 20% for money and development, respectively.

It is a puzzling and worrying report.

Too many meetings don't help people develop

Cutting back on meetings is one possible action area. Let's put some questions:

- What percentage of our working week is spent in meetings?
- Is that more than last year or three years ago?
- How useful are the meetings I attend?
- What would happen if I ruthlessly pruned my meeting schedule? How much time could I liberate – every day, week, and month? What would I be able to do with the time?
    - Work more?
    - Work better?

- – Think better and more?
- – Put more time into personal life and family/friends?

Sounding good, isn't it? Maybe being very busy – for hundreds of thousands if not millions of people – is a reflection of the extent to which all our working lives are dominated by meetings. And that aspect of busyness is not rewarding (financially, socially or in terms of career). Nor is it likely to help the very organisation that presides over the meeting regime in which you are caught up – your company.

My book *MOTE: The Super Meeting* is dedicated to helping to make meetings more effective and productive, and offers a radical new approach. If we succeed in pruning the meeting tree, and giving it a giant haircut, I believe there will be many beneficiaries:

- Companies whose directors, executives and managers will be freed up to do more actual *work*
- Those same staff members will be able to get their lives back in balance and work better and live more happily
- Their families. The list goes on...

So what's stopping us? I'll give you a couple of behavioural phenomena: Loss Aversion and Sunk Cost. Loss Aversion is the state of finding it difficult to give things up. Pundits call it FOMO (the fear of missing out). We are worried about what we might miss by not being at this meeting or that. Sunk Cost relates to the huge time investment we have made by attending hundreds of meetings. Does it make sense to stop now?

Here is another behavioural thought – taking control of your life. We know it would make sense to have the time to think better, work better and live better. If it's only meetings standing in the way of freeing up that valuable time, let's join the movement for fewer, better, more effective meetings with less people tied up in them. If time was as valuable as power sources – and it is – freeing up huge units of people's time would be the equivalent of a massive conversion to sustainable and affordable energy.

Meeters are suffering – and creativity can become the casualty

I wonder whether some of the people that I'm talking about, the 'meeters', as I call them, stuck in meetings day after day, week after week, have actually turned off the part of their brain that does ideas, and is receptive to them. From my work in client/agency relationship management, it is clear that many executives can't really understand where the advertising Johnnies are coming from, because to the clients they just seem so strange. If you spend your working days in a relentlessly logical and rational environment, creative and lateral thinking can come across as alien. If somebody says, have you ever thought about taking this brand outside this very tight positioning? No, they haven't because that wasn't in their remit. It wasn't in their capability.

But we do all have the ability to think and have ideas. The meeters were all kids once, and they've probably had a decent education and led interesting lives. And their partners and families have interesting lives too. But when they come to work, they're in super-duper button-down, unsmiling, transactional mode. They're not in the spirit of the thing. And my conclusion has been, from having seen the relationships when I was 20 years in advertising and when I've been doing the relationship monitoring, compared to the pitch bit, the pitch bit liberates people. If you have a client team on a good pitch, an interesting pitch, for a good brand, they have a lot of fun. It's like an away day that lasts two months. They really become lively people again. And they go off auto pilot. And they start thinking. So, that's what this book's about.

I went on to explain that you see the problem particularly in briefs. You see it in hugely unimaginative and over-directive briefing. Clients impact the creative process at different points in the cycle. First, they are the goal setter and specifier at briefing stage. The decline in the standard of briefing in many companies is shocking. There are people who are writing briefs who shouldn't be allowed to write briefs, because they have, to my mind, not the slightest comprehension of the creative process. Often they are way too junior and inexperienced.

They really don't understand. They think that if you force agencies down a narrow corridor of no choice, and you have to have this, and you have to have that, and this is a must, you will get precisely what you want. The reverse is true. You will get terrible stuff back. Which they inevitably criticise for being terrible. In any commercial creativity situation, briefing, in my view, demands as much creative consideration as the response. If you want great ideas back, you simply have to put great ideas in. I'm not talking about either being dictatorial or doing the creatives' jobs for them. I am simply advocating putting time and thought into the ideas that ask for ideas back.

Micro-managing the creative process doesn't work. You see it in feedback, where people don't even realise that, to an agency, non-aligned feedback is pointless. Most of my work is with global brands, and you can't have people at different levels, and in different countries, giving feedback which is radically different, because they can't be bothered to think together. They simply don't seem to understand that just saying 'no' a lot is not really what they're there for. What they're there for is to say 'yes' as often as possible, because they're using professionals, in the same way that people don't second guess their lawyers or their accountants. They accept them as professionals and experts. But in matters creative everyone is an expert! Feedback is another crucial contact point. Client briefs. Agency responds. Client looks at the agency's recommendation and feeds back. As pointed out above, this feedback needs to be aligned. However complicated the client's structure, the response needs to be clear. Also fair, and in keeping with sympathetic understanding of the creative process. There are rules. Respect the ideas presented. Give yourself time to think and consult. Resist at all cost the temptation to rubbish creative work while it is still warm. There's a priceless cartoon in Luke Sullivan's book *Hey Whipple Squeeze this – a guide to great advertising* where the junior member of the client team asks his boss immediately the agency's presentation is done, 'CJ, can I be the first to say why we don't like it?'

Accentuate the positive, but if you don't like an idea and it is never going to fly, you save everyone's time and temper by making it clear. The sole purpose of feedback is to get great ideas out of good ones. In de Bono's words, 'the first idea that comes to mind may not be so interesting. But the second and third ideas that flow from it may be very interesting'.

Finally there's the approval stage, which in an iterative (and hopefully collaborative) process is not going to be dramatic. In creative areas like film, theatre, music, architecture, design and advertising, not only is the devil in the detail, but the core idea itself is going to finesse and develop. Formal approval is never going to be a once-off moment. It is going to be a question of progressive development and agreement.

I have worked closely with clients, first as an agency guy, then in the cauldron of the pitch circuit, and most recently as a counsellor to both sides within ongoing relationships, and I've seen an enormous change in the way clients contribute or don't to the creative process. When I started out they were fascinated by it, really involved in it, hugely supportive. Since then they seem much busier and more distracted, and spend far more time in meetings, spend far more time in travelling, much less on ideas and creative work.

Interestingly – and not at all surprisingly – clients who have chosen to work with successful creative agencies are far less likely to behave like meeters. You can see this in the next chapter from BBH's respect for their client partners. Anna Qvennerstedt of Forsman and Bodenfors was also at pains to tell me how ambitious, visionary (and receptive) are their clients in Gothenburg and beyond.

The Pitch is a different world

A successful pitch process delivers a good team-building experience and liberates everyone to enter into the spirit of the ideas game. Pitches also get marketers out of their offices, which helps.

Before they even get into meeting agencies, there is a 'discover and interrogate' phase. What kind of a company are we? What is our culture as it relates to marketing communications? What are our brands all about? Where do our priorities lie? What has gone well, and what less well with agencies over the last three years? How are we doing in transitioning from a largely traditional media model to using technology and digital platforms? They meet a selection of agencies, each of whom brings something interesting and distinctive to the table – and importantly asks good questions.

Clients have often told me that they value the strategic inputs from the pitch process, almost as much as the creative recommendations. Agencies are astute strategically and have the priceless advantage of experience across a multiplicity of other clients. They also tend to be proactive, rather than reactive when there is the prospect of an account to be won.

Agencies flourish on pitches, and afterwards when they are winning an account is, they are in their element. What I admire most is the combination of expertise and flair the best agencies show. It usually has a dynamic effect on the clients, who become lively people again. They go off auto pilot. And start thinking, and become receptive to ideas.

Sir John Hegarty told me about his experience with Levi's, 'Levi's was the beginning of a number of things that came together, about youthfulness, rebellion, individuality, irreverence. How could you capture for Levi's all of those things that are represented by jeans? Other brands could have articulated this, but it was authentic for Levi's, because Levi's was the original one. And that was where the campaign grew from. It grew from the belief that, somehow, the idea had to capture everything that jeans represented to a young audience. And then gradually the idea grows in your head, and you are adding the bits and pieces to it to give it flesh.'

This is not a mechanical, left brain approach. It is the authentic voice of creativity, explaining where a big, valuable idea came from, and why that idea worked – spectacularly well – and over a long period of time.

I took the decision in 2012 to change my stance on speculative creative work – and in particular pitch briefs from clients that mandated that each finalist agency should have to spend hundreds of thousands of pounds of their money putting forward ideas. I didn't invent the pitch, so I don't blame myself for all the speculative creative I directly or indirectly commissioned! As an agency executive, I operated within the new tradition, and made scores of pitches on an increasingly elaborate stage. During the course of the thirty years from 1980 (the year as it happens that I set up my own agency Wethey Scott Pocock with a number of colleagues), pitches gradually changed from what we might call 'competitive interviews with some spontaneous ideas' to a free for all, with agencies offering and clients demanding not just more and more creative for free, but also full-blown plans and recommendations. The terms of trade can best be described as winner take all, losers give it away.

In 1988, I set up AAI as the first client-side consulting firm, organising pitches on a 'headhunter model' with the clients paying, and the agencies as candidates, in competition with the long-established AAR, who then had a business model largely based on representing agencies.

Interestingly BBH followed Collett Dickenson Pearce and Partners (CDP) in standing aside from the industry convention in not offering speculative work in pitches. Both agencies had a market-leading creative reputation, which allowed them to take this stance, and not suffer. In the next chapter, the BBH staffers I interviewed explained the advantages of this policy. If there was a downside, it did sometimes take BBH longer to get new campaigns up and running, by comparison with agencies who had been cooking creative work through the process.

But by 2012, I knew I wanted to work in a new – less exploitative – way. My new policy on pitches was called 'Mutual Decision', a different kind of process that I trademarked. It was based on the premise that the end of the pitch process wasn't simply the client deciding which agency to appoint – *'Bloggo picks ABC agency'*, as the headline goes. There was an equal and opposite decision to be made – *'ABC to work with Bloggo'*. With Mutual Decision, either we agreed a different selection methodology (rather like the way other professional service providers are chosen – credentials, experience, fit, chemistry etc), or the client undertook to pay fees for creative work, if that was going to be a requirement. Honestly? It led to a cut in the numbers of pitches we managed, but paved the way for the move into a business based on relationship evaluation, and other premium added value services, which was my long term aim in any case. I don't regret the years of dramatic pitches – mostly with a big reveal at the end. In any case agencies with creative work are a bit like horses at Cheltenham with jumps. It's something they are good at, and want to do. But I certainly don't regret calling time on it. It was the right thing to do.

Ideas can make a huge difference

At AAI the most exciting thing in the 'glory days' was to sit in conference room after conference room, and watch the reality of ideas being sold – and now and then, bought. During the couple of days when the final presentations were being made, all the agencies would be offering ideas – developed to specific briefs – that simply had not been there before. It is a thrilling moment for a client team (particularly on a global brand, where people don't meet that often) to see shiny new ideas for *their* brand. Most of us dream of finding opportunities where there used to be a problem. To meet for the first time an opportunity in the shape of an idea makes all the late nights and travel worthwhile.

I think that we are in a situation where we are putting people through repetitive meeting torture. It has taken an awful lot of the oomph out of them. Many of these people have been educated well, promoted regularly, and paid handsomely – but they are not in any sense offering creatively or delivering ideas.

And this book is really designed to get people to want to come up with ideas. Because I think people who want to come up with ideas are going to be more sympathetic to professionally produced ideas from elsewhere.

So, that's my mission. It's not just confined to advertising. It just so happens that, for me, the advertising world is an absolutely brilliant example of commercial creativity in action when it happens. When it's doing well. And also an awful example of how bad it can be, when the spark is extinguished. Watch TV most nights, and you see the tragedy. Not even the most enthusiastic apologist for the industry could say that this is a vintage period, or that the output is even acceptable. Why? Lack of quality ideas and good thinking, in my opinion.

Ideas are the way forward – also our best form of defence against the robots

We have already seen from the World Economic Forum report *'The Future of Work'* that the three most important *individual* skills for workers will be:

1. Complex problem solving
2. Critical thinking
3. Creativity

The imagination to come up with original ideas, and the related ability to work collaboratively in teams to make these ideas happen are integral to all three of the top skills. Ideas are the not only the world's most valuable commodity. They have already become the crucial ingredients in personal and corporate success.

On 10th May 2017 I attended a fascinating presentation about **THE FUTURE OF WORK** at Ogilvy, from their consulting division RED. The lead story is that AI (*Artificial Intelligence*, but to IBM who were also part of the platform team *Augmented Intelligence*, on the grounds that you still need people to tell the computers what to do!) is going to have a profound effect on employment among highly paid management and service people. The lead speaker was Ogilvy's 'Chief Futurist' an American lady called Jess Kimball. She quoted an Oxford Martin study that predicts that 80-100% of what are currently the highest paid jobs in the US (representing 47% of all the US work force) will disappear to be replaced by computers and robots *in the next ten years*. So this isn't Trump worrying about coal miners in West Virginia. The people whose jobs are threatened work in shiny offices across the 50 states, including Wall Street, Cincinnati and New Jersey. She also explained that the two countries where the impact of executive level job losses will be highest are USA and UK. My reaction – apart from healthy scepticism on the lines of 'surely not in Slough' – is that encouraging Meeters to become Creative Contributors might not only make them more productive and improve their quality of life, but actually keep them in work while their colleagues with no idea or creative skills are being made redundant. It's quite a thought.

I learned five key things at the Ogilvy event:

1. The new age thinkers and creatives will have to crunch data and synthesise research as well as generate ideas and develop strategies.

2. We are currently training millions of millennials for jobs that won't exist. Repetitive jobs are bound to disappear, but new types of work will emerge.

3. The Fortune 500 will become the Five: Alphabet, Apple, Amazon, Facebook and Microsoft.
4. The only defence for companies is to constantly acquire knowledge.
5. All communications (external, internal, marketing, advertising, PR, HR) will come together.

The Undercover Economist thinks the robots are coming – but it might take longer than we thought

TIM HARFORD 'THE UNDERCOVER ECONOMIST' WRITING IN THE *FINANCIAL TIMES* 22ND OF DECEMBER, 2017

To adapt a 30-year-old quip from the great economist Robert Solow: you can see the robots everywhere except in the productivity statistics. This fact has been puzzling me for a few years now. Productivity growth is disappointing — especially but not only in the UK — and it has been for years. Unemployment is near record lows, and employment is high. All this is the opposite of what one would expect if the robot job apocalypse was upon us.

Yet there is no denying the remarkable advances in various branches of artificial intelligence. The most talked-about example is the self-driving car. This technology has come a long way in a short time, which is more than one can say for the original participants in the 2004 Darpa Grand Challenge, a race sponsored by the US military. With large cash prizes for the first autonomous vehicle to complete a 150-mile course in the Mojave desert, the best effort foundered after just seven miles. The contest became a punchline. Just 13 years later, nobody is laughing about autonomous vehicles.

Then there are deep-learning technologies such as AlphaGo Zero, which took just 72 hours to teach itself to become seemingly invincible at the formidable board game, Go.

Alexa, Cortana, Google Assistant and Siri have made voice recognition an everyday miracle. Strides are being made in image recognition, medical diagnosis and translation. There are behind-the-scenes triumphs: deep learning is optimising power-hungry cooling in server farms.

All of this makes the puzzle of high employment and low productivity even more puzzling. Yet there are several ways to resolve it. A simple explanation is that the robot talk is all hype. Computer scientists have been over-optimistic before. Nobel laureate Herbert Simon predicted in 1957 that a computer would beat the world chess champion within 10 years; it took 40. In 1970 Marvin Minsky predicted that computers would have human-like general intelligence 'within three to eight years', a prediction even more inaccurate than Mr Simon's.

A more encouraging story is that we are understating productivity, for example, by undervaluing the output of services in general and the digital economy in particular, much of which is free and therefore invisible to normal measures of economic output.

A third possibility is that — to borrow an idea from the

writer William Gibson — the future has already arrived, but it is unevenly distributed. Perhaps the zero-sum scramble to dominate winner-takes-all markets is simply squandering most of the potential gains.

Researchers argue that the productivity slowdown is real. It may feel plausible to suggest our data simply are not good enough to recognise that productivity is growing strongly, but the story seems off in a number of ways — most obviously that the productivity shortfall is just too large to be a statistical illusion. Something similar can be said for the zero-sum fight for corporate dominance: it may well be happening, but is it really so wasteful that huge productivity gains simply evaporate?

How, then, to resolve the puzzle? In the simplest way possible: to say, 'just wait'. There is no contradiction between disappointing productivity growth now and spectacular productivity growth in the near future.

This is true in the narrow statistical sense that productivity growth tends to bounce around: a bad decade may be followed by another bad decade, or by a good one, and today's productivity growth tells us little about tomorrow's.

But it is also true that there tends to be a delay between a technical breakthrough and a productivity surge. The most famous case in point is the electric motor, which seemed poised to transform American manufacturing in the 1890s, but did not realise that potential until the 1920s. To take advantage of the new technology, factory owners had to turn their organisations upside down, with new architecture, processes and training. Prof Brynjolfsson's early research in the 1990s found companies saw little benefit from investing in computers unless they also reorganised.

If the benefits of today's new ideas are real but delayed, that may also explain the productivity slowdown itself. Consider the self-driving car: right now it is a research expense, all cost and no benefit. Later, it will start to displace traditional cars, the traditional car industry, and many related businesses from parking garages to automotive repair. Finally, perhaps decades after a self-driving car becomes feasible, the full benefits are likely to be apparent. One does not simply invent a new machine: economic progress requires much more than that.

Perhaps, then, this is a brief lull before an explosion of new technology that will radically reshape the world around us. Or perhaps we are due for another decade or two of disappointment. Either scenario seems possible — and both of them promise an uncomfortable ride.

The Jim Stengel interview

I much enjoyed sharing a platform in London with Jim Stengel, who used to head up marketing at the world's most famous client marketing organisation – Procter & Gamble, and booked him for an interview. I wasn't disappointed!

I asked Jim whether he thought it right to encourage people who are not called creative this and creative that to be full of ideas and to be enthusiastic about involving themselves and putting themselves forward instead of leaving everything to those crazy agency folk? I also told him about the 'E' for excitement in the VERY! Idea (see Chapter 10), and the importance of creating ideas that excite consumers, as well as ourselves.

Jim replied, 'Yes David, I think you are right and I think you're on to something. So cheers for this project. I think it's great. Just getting this topic on the table with people in a way they can speak about it with openness and alertness will be half the battle. You've framed it in a way that I think people could have that discussion. So I love that. You know, I think you're right to look at excitement. I think it's excitement inside and outside. If people aren't excited inside with the idea itself then forget it. So I think excitement is a good area.

I think of my life at P&G and the eight years since. When I went to Cincinnati to take up the CMO role, I discovered that we were suffering from an epidemic of people not creating the conditions for ideas and creativity. As a company we were very activity focused. To be creatively orientated, you deliberately need to create those conditions.

Physically, spiritually and emotionally and we just weren't doing it. It takes someone to call time out and to set different expectations for our work. You need different goals, different aspirations and then to encourage people to think how it affects their work. That's a leader's job and I find that there are people who do that. It's coachable. It's teachable. But the leader has to be self-aware enough to say if my organisation is not conceptual, creative or eliciting creativity then let's do something about it. We conducted a large study early in my tenure as global marketing officer. The results were really disappointing. We weren't reaching our potential as a company. Our market shares were down on 70% of our categories. Our innovation was pretty terrible. So the CTO and I, said let's put our heads together on this and assemble a group of people who we think are really terrific and diverse – coming from engineering and chemistry as well as marketing. Let's say to them, that we're only reaching our goal on about a third of what we put into the market. So what's going on, because we're better than that?'

Jim sent the group off to look at everything, and gave them total access. One of the most important conclusions they came back with was the company just wasn't creating the conditions for creativity and conceptual breakthroughs. And that involved everything from moving people around too much, and being focused activity and not thinking.

'We simply didn't have the right people working upstream on new ideas,' Jim told me. 'We didn't have the physical surroundings that were conducive to creativity. We took these findings to senior management, and we made the changes. In particular our innovation accelerated like crazy that decade, and we had a good run.

If I had a legacy at P&G, one of the symbolic acts was going to Cannes many years ago, 2003 was our first one. In the first instance it was the idea of Bob Isherwood at Saatchi and Saatchi. He's actually a lovely guy with lots of ideas. I held an off-site early in my tenure at P&G where I asked my CEO AG Lafley if he would come with me. I said let's rent some place in the country and invite the CEOs and creative heads of our most important media and creative agencies.

The brief on that meeting was we were the most important client for all of these agencies and we're getting the worst work. So what gives? It's not money. So what I asked my CEO to do was just be unplugged. 'I don't want PowerPoint, I just want you to stand in front of them and say what are you trying to do, and what are you happy about, what are you frustrated about, what's your job like, and just talk. And they're smart enough to take it in interesting directions'. And I did the same. I told them I am embarking upon a massive cultural renewal at P&G. I'm looking at the work people do, I'm looking at the culture we create, I'm looking at what we reward, I'm looking at processes, I'm looking at how we recruit and I just want this place to be much more energetic and optimistic. I want us to be more creative, more results-oriented, and more accountable.

I said, now let's get your best ideas. How can you help? Because what you all share here is P&G's success. Isherwood hardly said anything the entire two-day meeting. Then he came up to me and he said I think you should take a contingent to Cannes. And this was despite the fact that P&G had historically said there's no way in the world we'll ever go to that festival. Waste of time, money, blah blah blah. He said I just think it will shake you up. It will send a big message to your people and to your agencies. You will be forever changed because of that. After the off-site I booked a meeting with him and asked him to tell me more about this, how would we do it, and so forth.

We decided to go ahead, and in the first year we took 20 or 30 people. We partnered them with their agencies and we did it very P&G-like. You know, with notebooks, an outline, and objectives.

We met on the final Saturday for breakfast in a room in The Majestic with a lot of flip-charts and with no agency people, just P&G. I asked my colleagues what blew us away this week, who'd you met, how'd they impress you, what did you hear and what are we going to do differently when we go home? And that breakfast went into lunch. So much energy, ideas, commitments. And so that began, it was one part of what became a real revolution in that culture. And then when we went back so we didn't lose that energy we booked meetings every three months. We got everyone together and said well how's it going?

We were trying to do something larger than us. We were setting different goals, we were setting different standards. I actually hired Wieden and Kennedy coming out of that. And that led of course to the famous Olympics work and the Old Spice campaign. It shook up our current agencies. One of them came to me after we hired Wieden and Kennedy and they said boy we sure know the game has changed. This is not the old P&G.'

Martin Riley's view

Martin was my client at Pernod Ricard from 2002 until he retired from the business in 2014 as Global CMO. He was also President of the World Federation of Advertisers.

'I think it actually starts with what we might call instinct. Something that one feels inside, whether it's in your head or your heart. To me instinct is partly who you are – the core of you as an individual and your accumulated experiences which combine to say I feel this or I think this, or I react to something in a certain way. Often you don't know, you're not rationalising it, it's thinking fast and slow again. It's encouraging people to trust their instincts. You know in previous roles that's something I've tried to encourage teams with whom I've worked or who've worked for me to do. To tell me why they believe this thing would work, this new product idea, advertising idea, even the way of organising ourselves or organising meetings.

That's why as a manager, it's very important that you have one to one meetings with your direct report as well as a team meeting. Because the dynamics are quite different. On a one to one you can explore different parameters of the idea. Nobody's getting embarrassed about it in front of other people.

Managers need to be receptive and must not cut off people's ideas too early. One of the techniques that I try to use is just to stop myself interrupting – however enthusiastic or maybe negative I feel about the idea. It's almost a conscious thing to say hold on, bite your tongue, grip your fist and let the person finish. You may be so enthusiastic you want to just say wow, what about this, what about that. Or you may think I'm not sure. It's not for us. There may be reasons why not. It's been done before. But let them finish. Let them finish.'

MARTIN
David, if you had to make a very short shopping list of the things – say three things – that agencies excel at and those they are poor at, what would they be?

DAVID
What agencies are really good at is taking you out of your immediate comfort zone and your immediate context.

For a marketer it's important to know what business you're in. You don't want to get stale and you don't want to get narrowed, so you need somebody to bring you out of that. The real thing they can bring is a knowledge of what is happening out there in terms of consumer trends, what other brands in different categories are doing, how people are living. There is a tendency for marketers to think that the only thing that matters to people is your brand.

The second thing that they contribute is strong strategies. They can paint the landscape in which you operate in terms of consumer trends and how people live. They need to be able to come up with some sort of insight shared with you. Or you brief them as to where you and your brand could fit in with these trends, and how your brand's attributes make it relevant to the landscape you're now operating in. In other words, you don't go back into your historical perspective, your authenticity or whatever. That's all great. But how are you going to package it so it's relevant to the people you are trying to influence. They do that very well.

The third thing of course is creativity. They have very creative people.

What they do less well is concentration, focus and longevity. And you might say longevity's not always their fault and I would agree with you. But I think they need to do those things well and they don't always do. Not applying their efforts, time and people to these three things is part of their downfall.

They also have a fixation with new business.

MARTIN
Overall, I think we're all capable of ideas. I don't think there are ideas people and non-ideas people. I think there might be people who can articulate their ideas better, more easily and effectively than others. But teasing ideas out of people who may not be as extrovert let's say as others, or as articulate, is part of the challenge of being a manager.

Mark Earls and other pundits on ideas for all and ideas from all

Let's hear once more from Mark Earls, author, commentator, consultant, and someone who has been a highly supportive collaborator.

He says that the apologetic remark, 'I'm not very creative' cannot be true. 'All of us are creative', he says, 'It's what makes us human.'

He explained to me that neuroscientists have discovered that creativity (the mental skill of holding a concept in attention while amending details so that something new is created) is a more recent evolution in the human than straightforward rationality. Creativity – not rationality is the icing on the human evolutionary cake.

Nor should left brain leaders worry about spending more time with creative people and trusting them. He says, 'Being truly creative doesn't make you unreliable, flaky or difficult. We just see things that aren't there. We question things. We want to make something that hasn't been made before.'

Howard Gardner, Harvard Professor of Psychology and the pioneer of Multiple Intelligences, agrees:

'Creative geniuses don't start as prodigies. Creative types are not antisocial loners. They are inspired one-offs who just know what to do. It's much easier for major corporations to accept the rules and pay a fortune to outsiders to do their creative thinking for them. But all of us have to use our creative powers. You are creative. You can do it yourself. Indeed, you must do it yourself.'

Being negative or over-modest about one's creative ability is what the psychologists call a cognitive distortion. We shouldn't allow colleagues who are capable of coming up with ideas and developing them to put themselves down. The demand for ideas is at an all-time high, and will continue to grow. There's a famous Bill Gates quote about shifting people into thinking work.

Balder Onarheim told me, 'I wrote a piece called The Creativity Battle. You have a lot of people who make a living from selling being the only one that can do that. And it's in their interest to protect it as something that no one else can do. So if you are the creative director at an ad agency you have to protect the concept of creativity and make sure that your finance people or client people don't think they're creative because then you're actually jeopardising your own position. Creatives constantly try to reserve creativity as something they do. But talk to academics and scientists who have studied creativity from a biological or psychological perspective, and the first thing they will say is that it is one of the most inherent human capabilities.'

When I conducted one of my interviews with Balder, I asked him whether being creative and being good at ideas is the same thing?

'It's not the same thing. I would say coming up with ideas is one way of utilising your creativity. So when I teach creativity I'm very focused on getting away from only the notion of an idea. A lot of people think that creativity is about coming up with the idea and then executing it, while to me creativity is about all the things you do in the process of making something new. That could be running out of ink in your pen, and finding a solution to that problem which is not the same as anyone else would come up with. That's also creativity.'

If managements don't think straight, and run out of ideas – bad things can happen

For this masterpiece on deeply flawed corporate decision making I'm indebted to the scatological talents of Daniel Gryniewicz – to be found on *www.fprintf.net*. It was a popular blog when I shared it with my readers:

The Plan

In the beginning was the plan.
And then came the Assumptions.
And the Assumptions were without form.
And the Plan was without substance.
And darkness was upon the face of the Workers.
And they spoke among themselves, saying,
"It is a crock of shit, and it stinketh."
And the Workers went unto their Supervisors and said,
"It is a pail of dung, and none may abide the odor thereof."
And the Supervisors went unto their Managers, saying,
"It is a container of excrement, and it is very strong,
such that none may abide by it."

And the Managers went unto their Directors, saying,
"It is a vessel of fertiliser, and none may abide its strength."
And the Directors spoke amongst themselves, saying
one to another,
"It contains that which aids plant growth, and it is
very strong."
And the Directors then went unto the Vice-Presidents,
saying unto them,
"It promotes growth, and it is very powerful."
And the Vice-Presidents went unto the President,
saying unto him,
"This new plan will actively promote the growth
and vigour
of the company, with powerful effects."
And the President Looked upon the Plan, and saw that it
was good.
And the Plan became Policy.
This is how Shit Happens

MYTH: Most companies believe their people are given every opportunity to come up with ideas, and that there are plenty of ideas to go round.

REALITY: It simply isn't true. There's too much emphasis on being acquisitive, and too little on being inquisitive; too much on transaction, and too little on transformation. Too many meetings, not enough time for people to do their real work. Poor life work balance. Too little time for self-improvement. Too little time to think. The world of work is highly imperfect, and crying out for major change. Arguably it is the relentless assault on reason which has focused attention on the need for problem solving, critical thinking and creativity – all of which heavily rely on ideas.

Chapter 4

MAKING VALUABLE IDEAS

Cavatina

'Cavatina' is an Italian word meaning a short, solo melody.

An English film composer called Stanley Myers used the term as the title for a piece of music he wrote for a long-forgotten 1970 film 'The Walking Stick', starring Samantha Eggar (with walking stick) and David Hemmings (without). Eight years later Cavatina was repurposed for a far-better known film about the Vietnam War called 'The Deer Hunter' directed by Michael Cimino and starring Robert De Niro. I remember Cavatina well for different reasons. I arrived in Portugal in 1973 to head up the McCann-Erickson office in Lisbon. The business was a joint venture with six prominent clients. There was a part state-owned liquid gas company called Gaz Cidla, and the best spot on the 'local' end of the agency showreel was a pretty decent corporate ad, using Cavatina on the soundtrack. I had never seen The Walking Stick, The Deer Hunter wasn't yet thought of, so the music meant Gaz Cidla to me.

Forty years on Cavatina is a staple in the repertoire of every competent busker with a guitar. Yet almost no one on the Tube escalator can put a name to the haunting refrain. If the name doesn't ring a bell, Google it. I guarantee it will be very familiar to you.

In many ways Cavatina is symbolic of successful ideas and inventions in general: memorable, long lasting, but with obscure, confused or contested origins. Myers is largely unknown today, while everyone has heard of John Williams, who made a brilliant recording of the piece. I'm sure most people would say that Williams wrote Cavatina. And a maximum of one per cent of movie fans know it was recycled for The Deer Hunter, rather than composed specially for it.

Why do I start with it? Quite simply, it's because of my weakness for dreadful puns. De Niro was one of the deer hunters. I am crazy about ideas. I am an ideas addict. I am an idea hunter!

It is the result of 20 years working in advertising, and 30 organising pitches and watching talented agencies presenting amazing ideas (as well as some ordinary and distinctly dodgy ones) to global clients desperate for the spark of genius creative that can transform the fortunes of their brand.

It has been a privilege to commission ideas and watch competing teams respond. Also to see raw ideas develop into valuable creative properties.

Ideas are made as well as born

There is some tentative language around ideas:

- Generating ideas

- Coming up with ideas
- Thinking of an idea
- Developing an idea

I like 'making an idea', which embraces the imagining, the gestation, and the teamwork needed to bring it to fruition.

A remarkable book on advertising ideas – from nearly 80 years ago

JAMES WEBB YOUNG: A TECHNIQUE FOR PRODUCING IDEAS

There is probably an academic syndrome or theory describing the experience we have all had, when within a short space of time, several people recommend you meet the same person, get tickets to see the same show, dine at the same restaurant, choose the same resort.......or read the same book. I now have my own name for it – the James Webb Young phenomenon.

Mr Young lived from 1886 to 1973. He was an advertising man, when that profession was in its early days. But his contemporaries felt his talents could have taken him into almost any profession.

He joined J Walter Thompson in Cincinnati in 1912 as a copywriter, and retired from JWT only in 1964, having built the agency's international network, and led both The Advertising Council and the 4A's. But it is as an expert on ideas and creativity that he deserves to be remembered. His book *A Technique for Producing Ideas* was recommended to me by several good judges, and they were all absolutely on the money. The book is extraordinarily insightful, useful, and fresh today.

The book is still available on Amazon, and I strongly recommend it. It's very concise, beautifully written, and seminal. There can be few books – and this is little more than a pamphlet – which so acutely tell you how to do something which other 'experts' would prefer to leave in the land of mystique.

Although it was written to help people in the advertising industry, I think it works across the spectrum of ideas.

Here are just a few of Young's words of wisdom. He suggests that there are five stages in the process:

1. Gathering raw material
2. Digesting the material
3. Unconscious processing
4. The A-Ha moment
5. Idea meets reality

And two principles:

1. An idea is nothing more nor less than a combination of old elements.
2. The capacity to bring old elements into new combinations depends largely on the ability to see relationships.

GATHERING RAW MATERIAL

Not just the specific information about the market, the product, the consumer etc.

Also a fund of general material.

'Gathering raw material in a real way is not as simple as it sounds.' Young writes, 'It is such a terrible chore that we are constantly trying to dodge it. The time that ought to be spent in material gathering is spent in wool gathering. Instead of working systematically at the job of gathering raw material we sit around hoping for inspiration to strike us. When we do that we are trying to get the mind to take the fourth step in the idea-producing process while we dodge the preceding steps.

Every really good creative person whom I have ever known has always had two noticeable characteristics. First, there was no subject under the sun in which he could not easily get interested — from, say, Egyptian burial customs to modern art. Every facet of life had fascination for him. Second, he was an extensive browser in all sorts of fields of information. For it is with the advertising man as with the cow: no browsing, no milk.'

In his introduction to a later edition, Young wrote, 'I would put greater emphasis on [building] the store of general materials in the idea-producer's reservoir. You gather this vicarious experience best, not when you are boning up on it for an immediate purpose, but when you are pursuing it as an end in itself.'

DIGESTING THE MATERIAL

This part of the process is harder to describe in concrete terms because it goes on entirely in your head.

a. You take one fact, turn it this way and that, look at it in different lights, and feel for the meaning of it.

b. You bring two facts together and see how they fit. What you are seeking now is the relationship, a synthesis where everything will come together in a neat combination, like a jig-saw puzzle.

c. Facts sometimes yield up their meaning quicker when you do not scan them too directly.

d. Little partial ideas will come to you. Put these on paper. These are foreshadowing of the real idea that is to come

e. You will get tired of trying to fit your puzzle together. [Don't] get tired too soon. The mind, too, has a second wind.

Unconscious processing

- Make no effort of a direct nature.
- Turn the problem over to your unconscious mind and let it work while you sleep.
- Drop the problem completely, and turn to whatever stimulates your emotions. Sherlock Holmes used to stop right in the middle of the case and drag Watson off to a concert.
- You have gathered your food....and masticated it well. Now the digestive process is on.

The A-Ha moment

- Out of nowhere the idea will appear.
- It will come to you when you least expect it.
- It may waken you in the middle of the night.

Idea meets reality

- Take your little idea out into the world of reality.
- Many good ideas are lost. The idea man, like the inventor, is often not patient enough to go through this adapting path of the process. But it has to be done.
- Do not [hold] your idea close to your chest. Submit it to the criticism of the judicious.
- A surprising thing will happen.
- A good idea has self-expanding qualities. It stimulates those who see it to add to it.
- Possibilities in it which you have overlooked will come to light.

Developing ideas individually vs brainstorming

It is impossible to have any discussion on where ideas come from without getting into the brainstorming debate.

Lehrer in *Imagine: How Creativity Works* mentions studies comparing brainstorming with an alternative strategy where group members are required to come up with ideas on their own. The results of the studies are clear, according to Lehrer. He quotes Keith Sawyer, a psychologist at Washington University, 'Decades of research have consistently shown that brainstorming groups think of far fewer ideas than the same number of people who work alone and later pool their ideas'. The same research also showed that the quality of ideas produced in brainstorming sessions is inferior to that produced by individuals working on their own. Not only did the solo students come up with twice as many solutions as the brainstorming groups but their solutions were deemed more 'feasible' and 'effective' by a panel of judges.

The main problem with brainstorming, according to Lehrer, is that the very lack of criticism that is meant to allow creative ideas to bloom and flourish, actually ends up doing just the opposite. Indeed, it appears that a healthy measure of criticism is actually an integral component in contributing to the best ideas. So, why is it that criticism encourages creativity, while the lack thereof stifles it?

Lehrer puts forward two reasons:

- First, when we are encouraged to criticise others' ideas we listen more intently to, and are more engaged with them. We also strive to improve their ideas with our own: 'we think about their concepts because we want to improve them; it's the imperfection that leads us to really listen. By contrast, when criticism is discouraged there is less room to engage with other people's ideas, and so less room to build upon them'. As Lehrer explains, 'when everybody is 'right'—when all new ideas are equally useful, as in a brainstorming session—we stay within ourselves. There is no incentive to think about someone else's thoughts or embrace unfamiliar possibilities.'
- The second reason why criticism encourages creativity appears to be because the act of dissent in itself entices us to think outside the box.

BBH – Profile of an Idea Factory

James Webb Young's prescription for coming up with great
ideas has been put into practice – successfully, and not so
well – by thousands of agencies and hundreds of thousands
of practitioners. Countless brand owners have benefited
and grown rich as a result of these techniques, whether
they were consciously or instinctively followed. Millions
of people have had their lives enhanced by buying and
believing these messages.

My life at AAI has given me the opportunity to work
for some great clients and with some stellar agencies. I am
familiar with some outstanding case histories – some at
extremely close quarters. It is invidious to pick the 'best'
ideas and the 'best' agencies. I thought the most useful way
of sharing an idea hunter's tale would be to pick one agency,
one culture, and one set of key players, in order to see where
great ideas come from, and how they turn into valuable
assets over time.

Bartle Bogle Hegarty (universally known as BBH except
by Private Eye, who insisted in calling it Bogelby Hargell
and Pratt!) is an advertising agency that has been extremely
successful since its foundation by John Bartle, Sir Nigel
Bogle and Sir John Hegarty in 1982. This is the mantra
carved into the reception desk of their UK office and world
HQ in Kingly Street just off London's Regent Street.

IS IT TRUE? DOES IT STAND OUT LIKE
THE DOG'S PROVERBIALS?
WILL IT START A CONVERSATION?
A TREND? A MOVEMENT? IS IT SOLID
LOGIC – OR INSPIRED MAGIC?
IS IT NEWS? BIG ENOUGH FOR PEOPLE
TO DIGG, DOWNLOAD, BOOKMARK OR
EVEN 'LIKE'? WILL PEOPLE SHARE IT?
WOUD YOU? HAS IT MADE THAT LEAP
FROM GOOD TO GREAT? ARE YOU
EXCITED BY IT?
DOES IT FEEL FRESH? RARE? BLOODY?
DOES IT KICK STAUS QUO
IN THE TEETH, HOOF CONVENTION IN
THE NADS & POKE ORDINARY SHAPLY
IN BOTH EYES? IS IT SIMPLE? CAN YOU
PHONE TWEET IT IN?
WOULD IT PLAY BETTER AS A GAME?
MAKE THINGS 'APPEN AS AN APP?
COULD IT RING TRUE ON
MOBILE? SHINE ON RADIO? ZING AS
A JINGLE? STAND OUT IN 3D?
IS IT FUNNY? LOL OR A FULL ROTFLMAO?
WOULD A DIRECTOR KILL TO SHOOT IT?
A CONSUMER KILL TO TAKE PART
IN IT? COULD IT SURPRISE MORE AS
ANIMATION? SHOT ON A CAMERA PHONE? STARRING
GLOVE

PUPPETS? DRAWN BY KIDS? WILL IT MAKE
PEOPLE LAUGH? CRY? GASP? BUY?
COUD IT STILL BE BETTER? WHAT
IF IT WERE SHORTER? OR LONGER?
WHAT IF YOU DROPPED THE HEADLINE?
CUT THE VISUAL? WHAT IF YOU
SWAPPED THEM ROUND? IS THE
LOGO TOO BIG? TOO SMALL?
IS THE LOGO SUPERFLUOUS? WILL IT
MAKE THE BRAND FAMOUS? OR ONLY
YOU? IS IT DESIGNED TO DOMINATE
AN AWARDS BOOK OR POPULAR
CULTURE? DOES IT HONOR THE BRAND?
OR IS IT PURE SCAM WANK?
WHAT IF YOU TOLD THE STORY
IN ESREVER? COULD A MUSIC 360 MAKE
IT AMAZING? COULD SILENCE? WOULD
IT WORK BETTER IN 90 SECONDS?
10? OR 2? COULD IT BE VIRAL? WHAT
THE FUCK IS VIRAL? WOULD IT BE BETTER
IF THE AUDIENCE MADE IT? DOES IT
LOOK LIKE AN AD? DOES IT SAY
ANYTHING NEW? IS IT HONEST?
IS IT HONESTLY AS GOOD AS IT
COULD GET? IS IT CREDIBLE? IS IT
INCREDIBLE? HAVE YOU LET SOMEONE
RIP IT APART? HAVE YOU PUT IN THE
CRAFT & FINESSED THE CRAFT? DOES

IT TRAVEL? ACROSS BOUNDARIES,
COUNTRIES, LANGUAGES AND CULTURES?
CAN IT LIVE, BREATHE AND KICK ASS
IN EVERY CHANNEL? DOES
IT INTEGREAT!? IS IT A LITTLE SCARY?
WILL IT MAKE ANYONE SAY-FUCK WISH
I'D DONE THAT!? DOES IT HAVE A
DIFFERENCE? WILL IT MAKE A
DIFFERENCE? WHEN THE REST OF THE
WORLD ZIGS, DOES IT ZAG

BBH have been very helpful to me in writing this book, and I am most grateful to the six current and former staffers who agreed to be interviewed by me, and to London MD Adam Arnold and particularly to Managing Partner, Effectiveness Tom Roach and Executive Assistant Jo Smith, who kindly made all the arrangements.

Historically the Holy Grail for ambitious clients and their ad agencies has been to develop long-running campaigns delivering success over many years. For this to happen at one agency requires three things: good agency management delivering great people consistently over time, big (we should now say valuable) ideas, trusting relationships, precise goal-setting and data capture. I have been fortunate enough to know the agency and its principals over 35 years, and this one agency in London has produced the following legendary campaigns:

- 'When the world zigs, zag' for Levi's
- 'Vorsprung durch Technik' for Audi
- 'The Lynx Effect'
- 'Keep Walking' for Johnnie Walker
- 'Cream of Manchester' for Boddingtons
- 'Dedicated to Pleasure' for Haagen Dazs
- 'To fly. To serve' for British Airways

There have been many other clients and more excellent advertising ideas, but I want to concentrate on these seven ultra-valuable ideas, and share with you the accounts of Sir John Hegarty, Sir Nigel Bogle, Neil Munn, Ben Fennell, Nick Kendall and Jim Carroll on making ideas at BBH, and how the success stories came about.

Here's John Hegarty's take on ideas.

Hegarty on Making Ideas

'I feel is that an idea is only a theory until it's actually executed. An idea exists, really, in your head. It's the germ of something, and as you work with that idea, you begin to develop it, you begin to give it shape and form. I always say to male creators, this is the closest you ever get to giving birth. We talk about the germ of an idea, but actually, what happens is like the child within the womb, it begins to grow and, eventually, you give birth to it and everybody can see it.

So until people can see it, you can explain it, you can say it's going to be like this, it's going to be like that, but actually, it's not until it's born and everybody can share it, that it actually becomes THE idea.

Art without an idea is just decoration. Whatever anybody is doing when they are looking for an idea, be it a book, be it a painting, be it a piece of architecture, they're trying to touch your soul in some way. They're trying to capture that inner self, that inner feeling of this is truly significant. Because you're trying to be significant.

That's why I always say we have ideas all the time. Sometimes it could be shall we have pizza or pasta? Like it's hardly going to change the world. So you're trying to capture the inner audience, that sort of soulfulness, that place in your heart, your soul. However, you want to define that something, in your gut that makes you go 'wow'. I think that's what great ideas are as opposed to just ordinary ideas.

You're trying to explain something that you feel, rather than something that is. When you set out on this journey, you never actually really know, David. You didn't know it was going to be that significant. That's where the magic comes in.

The sum of its parts adds up to something much greater than the individual bits. There's almost a religious feeling about it. It's like you've been touched by some sort of spirit.

You often wonder where ideas come from. You are given them, you know. I'm not religious at all, but sometimes you ask yourself why was I given that idea?

As you get older, you get more confident, rather than necessarily better. One of the things that was said to me when I was at art school, and I always remember it, is that if you're not drawing every day, you're not getting better every day.

I think it's a bit like that having ideas. The more ideas you have, the more confidence you gain. There has to be a fearlessness in what you do because you've got to come in every day and have a new idea – and that idea can't be like yesterday's idea. Whereas in lots of jobs, you can go on, basically, repeating in some shape or form what you've done for 30 or 40 years.

Great creativity requires confidence because there are a whole lot of people standing there and you have to tell them what the idea is. There are sceptics out there, but people, in the end, follow the prophets because they believe they've seen the future. A great idea is like telling everybody tomorrow is going to be amazing, if you follow me.

There's a friend of mine who is a poet. He said to me, it's just energy. If an idea has energy at its core, it will attract people to it.'

Hegarty on Creativity and Presenting Work

John   'People say to me, 'where do you get your ideas
        from?' I reply, 'if I knew that, I'd spend an awful lot
        more time there!'

        I think, to be great at ideas, you have to feel
        things, you have to be aware, you have to be
        sensitive. You've got to be in touch with your inner
        soul. You're trying to capture this inner core.'

David   'Can one still do that with new forms of digital
        advertising or is that just such a different medium
        that it's unlikely it's going to be the same?'

John   'It's unlikely. My view is that you've got to understand the audience's relationship with the medium. What's my relationship with it? What do I turn to it for? And if it's Google, I'm in search mode. So I'm not prepared to give it the time, I'm not prepared to sit back and consider.
I think that's the problem with digital.

From very early on, we sat around a campfire and someone told a story. There is a reason why we sat around the fire. You don't really want to do that at 9 o'clock in the morning, but you want it in the evening when you become receptive. Being receptive to storytelling is crucial. And storytelling is so crucial and fundamental to all communication.'

David   'And you need more than a nanosecond to tell the story too.'

John   'And it's WHERE are you receptive? You go into a cinema and the lights are turned down, because it's like this is the campfire, this is the moment. We seek those moments out, we want them. Brands have to learn how they can tell their story at the moment which is applicable to a story being told. Digital's not like that most of the time.'

David   'It's very interesting you should say that. I saw what you wrote in your book about the pitch and what it means to agencies. And having seen hundreds of pitches, it is quite extraordinary when the thing is

going reasonably well, how receptive people are in
that environment, even if the lights aren't out, like
at the cinema.'

John   'Yes. If you think about it, when you're sitting
around a table, with everyone looking at the screen,
the screen becomes the campfire, and people are
receptive.'

David   'I remember a pitch that you and Nigel were doing,
and I forget what it was for now, and you went over
to work the U-matic to show a couple of Levi's
spots, and the client was so receptive that they
said, 'I want one of those'.

I think one of the other clever things you did was
the two-room trick, and you were well ahead of the
game on it.'

John   'Yes, that's right. We went from one room to the
other. There was a moment in the pitch where we
moved them to the other room to reveal what the
idea was. It's a bit like Coptic churches, you know.
During the service in a Coptic church, the priests
come out and they sing some, and then they go
back into an inner sanctum, and hold part of the
service within there. Then they come out, explain
things to the congregation, and go back in again.

That sense of there being two rooms is a
powerful way of presenting. It doesn't all have to
be in one place. It's a bit like a kitchen and a dining
room, isn't it? The meal is cooked in the kitchen,

and then you bring it into the dining room. You can eat in the kitchen, but it's much more casual. But when you have the dining room, this is the place where we all sit round, we celebrate this food, and it's the same principle. It's about creating a mood. As I said, the campfire was that touching moment in prehistoric times, when a fire was lit and a storyteller would begin to tell a story and people were ready. Presenting ideas is about trying to get people to open their minds I suppose.'

David   'Creating a mood is a brilliant way of describing it.'

Kendall on Planners and Ideas

'Last year, I devised a training programme for planners on how people create. I told them that your job isn't to study planning. I gave them the famous John Bartle quote: 'I don't want to be famous for strategy, I want to be famous for ideas'. Nobody will ever see your strategy, they only see the idea.

You must recognise that you are in the business of ideas, so understanding how ideas happen and where they come from is what your muscles should be trained on. Not on logic flows and segmentation studies.

Sometimes planners get confused by that and they spend all their time just looking at planning. We had Grayson Perry talking to them about ideas. There are so many good videos online nowadays of creative people talking about creating and how it happens for them.

Strategy at BBH meant sitting next to John and getting

a direction from him. You realise now that he was the first planner at BBH. The more fresh and interesting the direction, the more the chance I have to give the creatives some magic to work with.'

Carroll talking to David about working at BBH

David   'I want to ask you the eternal Holy Grail question, where do ideas come from?'

Jim   'Before I joined BBH I had seen from the outside the extraordinary execution and polish, dramatic film and print work and so forth, and you imagine the secret is in the execution. A lot of its success did derive from executional excellence, but when you get inside the business you find that a lot of the debate and focus was around ideas – and critical to that was the policy of not doing creative pitches.

In the early pitches I attended you could see that the BBH process was built around the talents of John Hegarty, because not doing creative pitching prompted Nigel and John to do more rigorous strategy than anyone else would do. But the pitch would always culminate in a sort of visionary speech from John. He didn't have any boards or pictures or execution – no scripts or anything like that.

He just had a particular way of painting a picture of the opportunity and where the brand could go and he would take clients with him. It wasn't just nebulous stuff, it would usually be articulated as an idea rather than as an execution, and I think that became critical to BBH. You had to get the idea first, and the idea had to be one that could work across platforms, channels and geographies.

As the agency matured and we got more creative directors, they had to learn how to handle the 'no creative pitching' routine. I think the creative directors who followed John weren't as comfortable just talking. They needed material – a line, some art direction, a mood edit, or a manifesto. And all these specific outputs actually got people into the discipline of developing an idea, not an execution. It was a very particular BBH thing and it was distinctive. It prepared us for the multi-platform digital world because, we were already used to pitching with themes, ideas, big thoughts etc. rather than executions. This was down to Hegarty and the other founders.'

David   'Were there any occasions where not doing creative pitches left you with maybe not enough time to get it together after you'd won?'

Jim   'Inevitably many clients asked for a picture, or a mood edit, as a distillation of the idea. But it wouldn't be a piece of creative communication aimed at getting behavioural change etc. We'd often do a mood edit made out of Hollywood clips, and there would be quite a challenge getting from the pitch idea to the first execution, the second execution, and so on. Clients can fall in love with the mood edit and then it can be difficult working out the actual sequencing of execution from one ad to the next.'

David   'So it's probably no coincidence that some of the campaigns, the legendary campaigns, have lasted a very long time?'

Jim   'Yes. In the modern era, the world of communication has become obsessed with platforms, neuroscience, behavioural economics and so forth. I sometimes feel that the power of the idea to run across platforms and to create behavioural changes, is not prioritised in the way that it used to be.

What was significant about the Levi's campaign was that it was very much art directed. Hegarty was an art director by trade. It quite quickly became a European campaign, so it had to be low on copy and high on music.

So very early in the BBH era you have a defining campaign which is visual, and all about a simple big idea, the original jean. It was fundamentally more about the brand than the consumer. BBH was quite a brand-centric agency. And that was because if you looked at youth in the mid-80's, even in just the UK, but all the way across Europe, you would have seen fragmentation and tribes and there would be no consistency and coherence.

So you had to focus on the brand, and look at big unifying truths. That became a pattern in the agency. We looked slightly more than other agencies to the brand to tell its story, rather than relying on consumers to deliver insights. This didn't happen in every case, but it was our bias. Then you elevated the debate to get to a unifying truth. Because with youth culture you had to talk in terms of sex, rebellion, freedom and individuality. You couldn't talk about some subtle nuanced cultural change that you'd noticed in the nightclubs of Manchester.'

David   'Now has that changed? In your view? With social media and stuff.'

Jim   'There was a period in BBH's history where the world moved a little bit towards us, as you got more multi-platform campaigns, and more international campaigns.

So you had to unify around either big consumer truths or simple brand narrative. You had to move towards campaign ideas that could work across platforms and geography.

I guess in the digital age you might argue that the pendulum has swung a little bit back and that people are looking for localised consumer insight again, and it's slightly more fragmented. But I'd

still argue that a brand is a shared belief. What is
the role of a brand manager if not to define that
belief? So you do need still unifying singular ideas
to pull people together, even if the execution of
them gets more fragmented.'

David   'Right. Do you feel from your experience that
it helped then having clients who were really
engaged and interested in ideas?'

Jim   'Yes. I think that during my time in the industry we
have moved from a period where the cavaliers were
the dominant client force to a period where the
roundheads have taken over.

Looking back, the cavalier marketing director was
a really great champion of the brand and had ideas
that worked. They were usually people who had a
passion for ideas and creativity, who had a curious
enquiring mind, who actually were interested in the
mechanics of the idea and how it worked.'

David   'The ones who went to shoots.'

Jim   'Yes, absolutely. I mean, you know, John and Nigel
would talk about Johnny Mezsaros* being a sort
of a genius of the early Audi days. We worked
with some extraordinary talent at Levi's, people
like Robert Holloway, and on Lynx it would be
Steve Miles, you know, an extraordinary man
who's passionate about ideas and creativity. And
there was Geoffrey Probert over at Unilever. These
were all genuinely cavalier, talented, charismatic

marketing leaders. The modern age has put the roundheads in charge. I feel that we are living in an age where everything is slightly more rational, logical and process driven.'

Bogle on ideas and mediums

One of the things that I feel quite strongly about is creative people coming into the business having been taught to have ideas, as opposed to how to be an art director, or how to be a writer. I find you get a young creative team coming in, and I ask, 'who's the writer, who's the copywriter?' They go, well we spun a coin outside. And I can't draw, and he can't write, but we have ideas.

But in my experience, great creative people express their original thinking through a medium.

Picasso didn't say, 'I've had an idea'. He said, 'have a look at this'.

Digital or no digital, I bemoan the demise of some of the eternal craft skills – the ability to write brilliantly, or art

*Writing in *Campaign* in 2003, Pippa Considine gave this succinct word picture of John Mezsaros – BBH's defining Audi client.

Meszaros is one of the more unusual clients of the past few decades. A Hungarian refugee, who headed the marketing for Volkswagen and Audi, he not only oversaw some of the most famous and effective campaigns of the century but went on to write award-winning advertising himself. Meszaros came to England in the late 50s as a trainee miner and then took an opportunity during a strike to leave his base in Pontypridd and set out for London. In 1968, after spells spent as a hotel porter in Baker Street and plucking chickens in a Sainsbury's store, he took a job at VW cleaning cars. Then he was promoted into an office job and in 1975 was asked if he wanted to do 'a bit of marketing'.

directors who can visualise his own stuff. A lot of art directors now will go to the studio and get a studio person to mock it up for them. They can't do it themselves. If you take our great Boddington's campaign, it was done by a classic art director. The Haagen Dazs launch campaign was done by Rooney Carruthers. John Hegarty did a lot of our early print work. They expressed their thinking and their idea through a medium, and I think this teaching of ideas in isolation leads to people who can't actually nail the execution in fine detail, because they haven't been taught how to do it.'

Munn talking to me about working on the client side and then at BBH

David   'How did you find the contrast between working first client-side and then at BBH?'

Neil   'I think the environment has changed since I was a client. Back then there was more like-mindedness sitting around the table, and generally more fun and energy. What hasn't changed, however, is that for ideas to thrive in an agency/client relationship they need two things: real ownership and real decision making.

      Today the world's become so complicated, and as a consequence of that, there are fewer people prepared to step forward and say, I own this idea, I'm backing it. I'm backing it almost irrespective of the personal consequences. And there's too much marking off, and making sure all the ducks are in line, and making sure that all of the people in the organisation across all of the departments, and the countries, etcetera are satisfied that it's suitable. It just dulls it, and it slows it down, and it looks less sharp when it arrives in the market.

And that's all down to a crisis of confidence as the world has become complex. Clients have to be more accountable than ever. There are more people who feel they have an opinion on what represents a valuable idea based on the data sources they're drawing upon. This is affecting decision making. As decision making slows, energy and confidence recedes. It is therefore critical that there is a leader on the client side who is ready to properly own an idea and to be really decisive in taking it forward. I had a decent run when I was a client. The reason I had some success in Unilever was that I worked out a key dynamic of the organisation. It's an organisation that didn't want to make decisions.

One specific example. I wanted to launch Axe in Italy, and I knew that if I went to the board, or the senior stakeholders, and said I'd like permission to launch Axe in Italy, nothing would ever come back, and it would stall, and there would be no action beyond inertia.

So I just flipped it on its head, and said, I am launching Axe in Italy, unless someone decides no. And of course there was no decision coming back down the tree, so I just ploughed forward, and carried on.'

David   'It's like the TMO in rugby, isn't it? Any reason I shouldn't award a try? Any reason I shouldn't launch Axe in Italy?'

Neil   'Yes, exactly that. Lots of scurrying around but generally people wanting to avoid making decisions.

I feel there are two sicknesses in business at the moment. There's hurry sickness, and there is decision making sickness.

Hurry sickness. Everyone's hurry, hurry, hurry, short term, short term, short term. Feeling they're productive, because they're busy, and obsessed by short term metrics.

The other is decision making sickness because just not enough decisions are being made in business.'

David   'So there is a problem, isn't there, with receptivity to ideas? Marketing people don't have the readiness to believe that an idea could be valuable, could be wonderful. There're all sorts of reasons for saying...whoa, I don't know.'

Neil   'Yes, the readiness is extremely patchy.

Make no mistake, there are some really inspirational, highly capable client leaders out there. But the centre of gravity is orientated today around a kind of systematic decision making, where everybody wants to collect all of the evidence and data, and make sure there's not an iota of uncertainty in the path forward.

Ideas cannot and will not thrive in that context. There is also a natural divide between single brand companies and, multi brand companies. When there's only one brand in a company, everybody's got a point of view on it. It makes the decision making even more multi-layered. Compared to a portfolio company, where you can, if you're a young up and coming brand leader, get hold of a brand, and establish the agenda, and shape your own mini culture within the organisation, and really set an energising vision.

Someone once said to me, it's all right for you guys at BBH. You've got big organising brand ideas. And I said, yes, but do you understand what it takes to get to a big organising brand idea that's got resonance with your target market? You have to commit to it, ahead of really knowing whether it will be an instant success in market. You have to be patient. You have to persevere. And you have to course correct. And after two years, or whatever the time is, you look back, and say, wow, we've got something really powerful, and distinctive, and differentiated in this market place. And we are now going to use that as a real source of competitive advantage going forward. But most marketers don't have the patience to nurture and establish the idea for one to two years, and then to really get the benefit from it.'

David 'Largely because they won't be around at the end of it?'

Neil 'That's the main driver. I think the notion of timeframe is very important in the context of outstanding ideas. Why should I do the two years of hard spade work, envisioning it, carrying the risk, course correcting, when I have a plan to be moving on in two years? That's definitely an issue. I also think the notion of timeframe is very important for us as a business at BBH.

Our future is based around creativity, not advertising. If we can deploy our creativity in smart added value ways that connect with how clients are building their businesses, we should be around in 100 years' time, even with AI and all of the new technologies that are going to unfold.

There is always going to be a need to bring a fresh and different perspective to a challenge. Clients will continually need their own source of sustainable differentiation.

We want to be using our creativity to attack clients' business problems. And we want to be rewarded for doing that and, for the idea that we put on the table. Not paid based on hours deployed but on idea impact.

We all know that the concept of customer

lifetime value is important in a number of our clients' conversations.

I believe that there should be a parallel concept called **brand idea lifetime value.**

It's a challenge for us, finding a better way to articulate how that value is unlocked over a period of time.

We now have all of the impact and effectiveness stories for our current clients on the office walls. It's a cultural evolution for us. We are a creative, emotionally-led business that thrives and gets most excited by the power of the idea, the power of difference. But proving how we make a difference is equally important in today's environment. And we've got to work harder at finding the techniques, tools, and muscles to communicate, clarify, and underpin that.

Procurement might even be enthusiastic about the concept of Idea Economics. Our challenge with procurement is bridging between the emotion of ideas, and the nuts and bolts rationality. Idea economics could provide a very good bridge.'

Bogle, talking about Levi's:

'Levis was a founding client of BBH in 1982. It was the third piece of business we got, and that was in 1982, and pre the 501 campaign. The right time to start talking about it from a case history point of view is when we got to the 501. At that stage, Levis' business was in trouble. It had kind of lost its way. It was trying to be things that it wasn't. It was trying to be overtly young and trendy, and lots of young people dancing around New York. Back in the late '60s, there were a lot of retail brands, like Jean Junction and Jean Machine, and the look was very, very tight fitting.

What we always do with brands is go back to the fundamental truth about the product and explain it in a way that's got an emotional twist to it. So if you look at the 501 campaign over time, it glorifies the product and does it in a way that gives it an emotional fire power.

People liked the idea of '50s and '60s America and rock music and Tamla. They didn't necessarily like America as global policemen. But we were able to take the bits of America that were powerful for the brand and use them, and not get side-tracked by any bad aspects of the United States. So we started with Nick Kamen in 1985. The first two commercials were about going back to the soul of the product, which was shrink to fit and stonewashing. And if you look at that commercial, the first two, the other one was called Bath, and there was a guy actually getting into a bath to shrink his jeans. There's a hell of a lot of detail on the product. You see the way that the guy in the second one crouches to get the comfort of the seams right. The way that the unbuttoning sequence goes in the launderette film. It was all about getting people used to the idea of a jean that didn't look like the very tight jeans that were currently in the market. They took off like a rocket.

We launched around Boxing Day of 1985, and people just started talking about it straightaway. The idea was the 501, not just the Levis brand. Damned if I know why it was called 501, but it was distinctive. The button fly was distinctive. The shrink to fit was distinctive. The loose fitting, relatively loose fitting shape of the jean was distinctive. And then we put it in to this beautifully accurate, cleaned up '50s environment of the launderette. And then there was the use of music. Marvin Gaye. It was that cocktail of things together that worked very, very quickly to get a new generation of jeans wearers to get to the 501. And I think when we launched in the UK, I think literally they were selling 20,000 pairs of 501s in the Spring and the Autumn. So it was like a new product, but it was a new product that was a hundred years old. When we finished the campaign, many years later, they were selling across Europe about 55 million pairs.

And that was the short term downfall of the brand. Because what happened over time was that originally the campaign targeted 16–20 year olds who we were keen to re-engage with, and that worked very, very well. But as the brand grew, so did the purchasing profile of the customer. It started to age, went up to 20–25, 25–30, and more and more of the volume was being bought by people over the age of

30. And gradually, it almost inevitably got to a stage where younger people were going, 501 is now my dad's jeans, therefore I don't want to wear them.

From winning the business to saturation took us into the late '90s, by which time it was beginning to struggle. It was a good run. We must have made about 30 commercials. Essentially what happened was, the NPD was the advertising. So the product never changed, but the advertising did.'

Same story, different perspective from Hegarty

'At that point I can walk into a meeting room, and explain that this guy walks into a launderette, takes his sunglasses off, removes his T-shirt, takes his jeans off, puts them all into a washing machine, sits down and turns to a great, big, fat man. So he's left in his boxer shorts. You're not saying that by itself would transform a whole clothing market and launch boxer shorts, but within your head, you can feel the idea.

I suppose, in a way, that Levi's was that. It was the beginning of a number of things that came together about youthfulness, rebellion, individuality, irreverence. We could capture all those things that jeans represented, because Levi's was the original brand. The idea captured everything that jeans represented to a young audience. When a brand is in trouble, you go back to the roots of what made them great. You have to recapture that moment when this particular garment became symbolic of a whole youth movement.

I'm demonstrating the value of the product and I use almost kind of physical things about it. So in that one, that was obviously shrink to fit. You don't need to do this anymore; you can actually go and now buy them shrink to fit. Each one we did, I took an aspect of the jeans and said I'm going to talk about the originality of this product, the irreverence of this product, particular aspects of the product – so it might be button fly, it might be shrink to fit, it might be the watch pocket, it might be the stitching, whatever it might be. If a campaign is going to work, you've got to have a pathway to follow so each idea builds on the last idea with the product at the centre of it.

That's how that idea came about. That idea of re-establishing this product as being definitive of a moment in time when youth and when music and rebellion were all wound up into one. That was the genesis of that.'

Bogle on Audi

'When we got Audi in 1982, which was our first client, it was talked about as a very bland Euro car. People weren't quite sure where it came from. I guess I would say the nearest equivalent to that would have been Saab. Saab was a kind of interesting car, but nobody quite knew what it was or where it came from. Audi was a car that people were aware of, and it might have come from Belgium or somewhere. It certainly didn't have particularly strong German associations. The brief we put forward in the pitch was to give it German credentials, Germanness in the best sense, and also to feature more about the innovative engineering that comes out of the Audi factory. The head of Audi worldwide at that stage was Dr Ferdinand Piech, who was not a finance man, he was a car designer and engineer. When you went to the factory, it was very clear this was a company run by engineers, and not by marketing or finance people. So, the early advertising we did on Audi was all about the Germans, the Mullers and the Reinhardts, getting to the beach before everyone else. This was taking a slightly light-hearted view about Germanness, but making a serious point about the innovation in the car – the aerodynamics, or four wheel drive, Quattro etc., etc.

And, the ambition was to get into what we called the prestige car club, which we didn't sit in. The prestige car club was, at that stage, Mercedes, BMW, probably Jaguar, and that was about it. Audi was knocking on the door, but didn't have the design credentials at that stage to get in. The way to get into the prestige club is to look very like the other people in the club. So normally, we preach the power of difference to make a difference, but today if you look at a picture of a Mercedes, a BMW and Audi side by side, it would be very hard to tell which one was which if you took the badges off. They all use the same wind tunnels. They look very similar. But the early Audis, in that first 'race to the beach' campaign with those very sleek, aerodynamic bodies, looked rather lightweight. There's a way of folding the metal which looks quite heavy. The car designers deserve the credit for changing the Audi look.

But from an advertising point of view, when John Hegarty came up with Vorsprung durch Technik (advancement through technology) which was a brilliant way of combining the fact they were German with a sense of technical prowess, everybody, including me, said, John, nobody's going to understand what that means. And we can't have an end line that nobody understands what it means. He said, 'yes we can. We should have an end line that says, we're German, and Technik will do the job of implying we've got technical ability'.

And of course, Vorsprung durch Technik entered popular culture and it's now 35 years old. It's chanted on the terraces at Chelsea. Spitting Image did Vorsprung durch Technik, with the Germans in tanks and things.

We were at the factory when we first saw those words, and the Audi people described it to us as a company motto that we don't use anymore, and so we brought that out of retirement.

I think what BMW and Mercedes do differently to Audi, and it's partly because they've been around as a prestige car longer, is they are much more descriptive of the owner. So people have a point of view about Mercedes owners. They're that bit older, I'm going back bit now, golf clubber on the weekend, people who've made it etc., etc. Quite conservative, although Mercedes is changing. BMW is about bankers, slightly more flash, Beemers they used to call them and so on. And Audi did not define its driver as precisely as BMW and Mercedes. Some people say that's a bad thing, but I think that's one of the great strengths of Audi, because I think people who buy Audis don't want to be defined too tightly.

They want to be them, as opposed to, well you're the kind of person who drives a BMW. There is that quite important difference, I think, between Audi and the other two. And of course now, they've gone from when we started working with Audi, I think they sold 17,000 units in the UK, and I think this year's target is like 170,000. Also, the percentage of profit that they supply to the group now. It is amazing. And, you know, they're bloody good cars. They're very well made, the interiors are beautiful. They are absolutely, firmly established in the prestige car club now.'

Fennell on Audi

'The Audi work is as good as it's ever been right now. And at the centre of that work, and at the centre of the work for 35 years, has been Vorsprung durch Technik. It happens to run as an end line, but it's much more than an end line. It's an organising idea.

When BBH is at its best, the Lynx Effect, To Fly. To Serve, Vorsprung durch Technik, those are organising ideas. They happen to sit at the end of the advertising often, but they are also the advertising strategy, the advertising idea, the communications, the template. They're all those things. They're much, much more than an end line. They also probably define the product.

Audi talk now about Vorsprung durch Technik being a component of every car. It's almost like an engineering component. They also talk about it on the balance sheet. It is an asset of the Volkswagen group. It was a set of words on a poster at the Audi factory that John Hegarty spotted. He said, from then on, 'that's the strategy, that's the idea, it's also the line.' And, 35 years later, it couldn't be more central or critical to everything we do, and plan, and say on Audi. It was born of the brand. It wasn't a group of people sitting with a blank piece of paper and saying, what shall we give Audi? It was mining and exploring the brand's history, vocabulary. Iconography in Audi's case was the four rings. And letting the line reveal itself.'

Kendall on Johnnie Walker

'Keep Walking came from a moment, quite late on, when we were talking about walking the walk or something. I said to John O'Keefe that it would be nice if it was more of a call. John said something like Keep Walking and I said that sounds good to me.

Where does an idea come from? Well it comes from a good client. 30-odd years in the business tells me that clients get the ideas they deserve. Ideas also come out of necessity. For us on Johnnie Walker the business necessity was putting right three or four years of decline and allaying the fear that we would lose the top spot and the next generation of drinkers. It's a share thirsty brand and that probably put the whole of Diageo on alert. There's nothing like a burning platform to make people jump and dance.

Alice Avis was the critical client figure, at that time working with Leo Burnett. It was a long-running relationship, and Diageo were only allowed to work with aligned agencies.

Alice was searching for a solution on Johnnie Walker and wasn't happy with what she was getting from Burnett. Fortunately she found out that BBH would be a possibility, given that technically we had become a subsidiary of Burnett. So we were allowed to pitch. In those days BBH wouldn't do speculative creative pitches, and Alice offered to pay for us to work on the pitch for three months.

I wish people would stop thinking pitches are the answer, because the best ideas come from a very collaborative process and iteration, with briefings, and going back and forth and back and forth and so on. People talk about beta testing as if it's something new but the idea of getting a direction from bouncing ideas back and forth is not new

This brief actually came as two briefs, one for Johnnie Walker Black and one for Johnnie Walker Red. The most fundamental questions was 'what is the brand?' Client people would say, 'what do you mean?' And we'd reply, 'you have done a brief for Black and talked about where you think that fits, and also done a brief for Red, and talked about who the target is. But are they the brand, or is Johnnie Walker the brand'? Only then were we able to get to the place where we could start thinking of a bigger idea like Keep Walking.

We agreed there were lots of reasons for the decline including Asian recessions. But the challenge was capturing the next generation. It's almost like whisky is not really putting its best front foot forward versus other categories. So if you are number one, you should be fighting the good fight and leading the category and leading the definition of values in that category. All they had been doing was creating images like the Scotch highlands, over-reverence for the product, dinner suits and the James Bond of Casino Royale kind of feel. You're not really giving a vibrant set of values for people to aspire to in the next generation.

This brand started out in 1820 and is still going strong. The birth of Striding Man in 1907 was key. If you look at the archive, a killer question comes along: 'why is it called the Striding Man?'

Organisations can sometimes lose sight of their history. If I had a client team I'd always have somebody in charge of the brand history, to keep everyone informed, keep it alive, keep it fresh in people's minds, wherever it might be. So it's slightly forgotten why it's called the Striding Man. It wasn't the perambulating jolly bloke or the man in strange trousers with a bulge or anything. It was called the Striding Man because he was the spirit of the company when Tom Browne was given the brief to capture the spirit of the Walker and Sons Company, as part of its attempt to proselytise whisky around the world, which they were doing at the time. So very much a figure of striding forward and progress.

There was a last piece in my head, because we'd got to some work, using the Striding Man as opposed to Red or Black, or their 30-odd malt whiskies. It started as a very visual idea. We were working on 'walk the walk' or something, 'Johnnie Walker since 1820'.

There was a late-night moment when we were trying to

make it more active. John O'Keefe and Hugh Baillie were talking about it, and we all agreed that we really didn't want to go down the route of 'look, here's a bloke who's rich. You can be rich too if you emulate this person by drinking Johnnie Walker'. It's nonsense isn't it? And very old-fashioned more to the point. Nobody believes that kind of thing any more. We realised that the active role of communications is to inspire you to progress rather than say, 'look, this person's progressed, why don't you do it too'.

What we wanted to do was create a modern brand around Keep Walking that could inspire progress in every corner of the world. We produced a whole set of mood films and some print.

That's my memory of the story, but I've probably missed bits out. There is a follow-on where we took it out to research, before they decided on the pitch. We beat Leo Burnett hands down. The message became 'inspires personal progress', to remind everybody of the real story.

So that's the story of how we actually got to the work. We were fortunate to have an organisation willing and capable of taking on an idea. People talk about leadership and increasingly, as I get older, I value followership as well.

So we were invited, as the next step, to present to the newly-formed Johnnie Walker global brand team. This team, and this is relevant as well, was not a series of marketing people, it was a series of managers in each of the countries. Diageo, like a lot of global businesses at that time, was fragmented into power bases in countries, which is where they build their business.

We presented the campaign at four in the afternoon to the general managers and their civil servants, the global marketing team led by Alice. They'd had an exhausting day talking about how to align themselves. And in a way when we came in, we were a gift to them because they suddenly had the symbol of oneness for their brand.

The legend goes that they tore up the rest of the agenda, worked all night about how to get this out as a leadership idea into the markets, and the day after we were talking about how to get it around the world in around 30, 40 days or something. This consisted of going to each region and presenting it and at each of those leadership meetings around the world, somebody from the exec would stand and open the meeting, and somebody from the global exec would also be around to close and say I bless this.

I remember a particular meeting that Nigel and I went to. Nigel told me not to talk too much, because we only had half an hour. He said we'll do 15 minutes on the whole idea, we'll have ten minutes chat and we'll give him five minutes back in his diary. Chairmen and CEOs always like five minutes back in their diary, they'll thank you for life.

So we did the 15 minutes as I was instructed and Nigel closed and said we recommend it to you, this big idea and the Chairman said I agree, it is a big idea. If anybody gets in its way, let me know!

That was it and he gave himself ten minutes, not just five,

by agreeing. It's such a skill to agree to things as opposed to finding problems – and that's the story of Johnnie Walker

We undervalue ideas on the whole. We won the IPA Effectiveness Grand Prix for Keep Walking, and the paper sets out exactly what the campaign delivered. Very few papers in the IPA actually talk about the ability to align an organisation and to galvanise the employees. One of Keep Walking's biggest dividends was the internal one. What really happened is we managed to align an organisation like Diageo and when an organisation like Diageo is aligned, Diageo is good.'

Kendall on Boddington's

'Clients never quite understand that media's part of the creation process, not part of the execution process. Still to this day media is left till last, or just treated as a distribution process. Boddington's is a great example of creating a canvas to paint on.

The brief was to move from being a regional brewer to a national brewer, and how to do that partly in take-home as well as the on-trade, and how to do that without losing the brand. They had a widget in the can that made the product creamy.

I think the interesting thing with Boddington's is how to do things in opposition. I quite like it. I think ideas are oppositional, somehow so to do it in a way that has not been done before by definition is to be creative and I think Boddingtons is a case in point.

At that time the theory was that you had to feature the user in your ads – like John Smith's. Essentially to do a beer ad, you shouldn't talk about the beer. I just found this attitude so mistaken. It actually presented us with a communication opportunity. Everybody else is doing this, what could we do that is different? Well, we could start back at the product again. Boddington's (and this was before craft beers) was a kind of premium session lager. So we had the idea of building a quality image and making sure that as the brand expanded nationwide, it didn't create that situation where it lacked authenticity, it was just one more beer swill etc.

That was the brand challenge. So we started thinking inside the product as opposed to outside. Now again, it didn't start easily in that place because the brief very definitely did say this is a smooth pint, The reason to believe was the creamy head, which is like the Guinness head that they produce with nitrogen. We were supposed to be highlighting a particular type of drinking experience, signalled by the creamy head.

Nonetheless, even though the brief was that, a lot of the early work ended up being kind of jokes and gags about Manchester, the weather etc. I'm a great one for believing people's personal passion should be part of ideas as well, either because of the kind of work they want to make, or even down to personal prejudices! I came from Manchester, and the last thing I wanted was clichés about Manchester.

I didn't want to give in to the clichés. After all Manchester is a vibrant cultural centre, very modern in many ways, with its music scene and so on. So why were we behaving like this? Why is Manchester portrayed like this? Things kept going up on the wall, and I remember feeling the frustration. How you get to ideas is to create opportunities, not complain about what's on the wall!

Kevin Brown, our head of media, created that opportunity.

He came in and said that a lot of the cigarette companies were coming off back covers, and the magazine people are terrified about losing all that ad revenue. 'There's a real opportunity here to do a deal. Would you be interested in back covers? They're almost posters in print'.

He recommended using different back covers to match around ten different segments of the beer audience, and showed how he could hit these segments on quite a low budget, thanks to the deal opportunity.

The Cream of Manchester worked like cigarette ads (Silk Cut etc). That was the big breakthrough in actually getting to the idea. The creatives thought about the canvas that had been painted for them and this opened up a completely different set of possibilities that the words on the brief hadn't quite managed to convey.

That's why I still work with Kevin Brown. I believe thinking about where your idea is going to appear can be a really powerful way of inspiring that idea.'

Hegarty on Boddington's

'Boddington's was a great example of the sum of its parts being greater than the actual thing itself. We had done a print campaign and everybody said now we must go on television and we said all right, okay. And I remember the account man saying we can just sort of put the print ads on TV, can't we? We can just animate them – sort of words on wheels.

But it doesn't work like that. The ads weren't very good. I went back to the client and told him that. They don't have the irreverence and spirit that I think it needs. He said we quite like what you sold us, John. I told him we can do a lot better.

We already had Cream of Manchester, but we came back with face cream!

I wanted to treat the beer and the cream in a very irreverent way. And we came back with face cream, as we called it. It was the girl rubbing cream on her face. On paper, it didn't make sense until I explained it. But it had that funny connection, so it didn't seem to make sense. But it did. Beer is drunk by men, not women, yet here we were showing it being rubbed on a woman's face and being wonderful and spoofing a skincare ad. Actually it was demonstrating how wonderful the cream on the top of a pint of Boddington's was. And, you know, it woke people's imagination in a way. It was a great campaign.'

Fennell on British Airways

'One of the things BBH has done often, and it's true of Walker, true of Audi, true of BA, is when we have shone a light on an asset, an icon, a set of words that the business may have moved on from, or forgotten. And that's definitely the case with To Fly. To Serve. It was not a set of words that BBH invented. It sat on the British Airways crest, which sat on the badge of every pilot's hat. And it was a set of words that they had lost in the archive, or forgotten. A group of people, the BBH team, led by Nigel, and at the client end Kerris Bright and Abby Comber, decided that in that very simple and connected couplet, everything that BA stood for was encapsulated.'

So, absolute flying excellence. The job of a pilot, at its most simple, is to get you safely from A to B. And fabulous service. And, those two things are the high ground of course, literally and metaphorically, in the category. And it felt like, in the face of other challenges, ash clouds, Gate Gourmet, union action, low-cost airlines, BA had lost its way a bit.

The best bit about the BA case study, and there's lots of data to back it up, is that the launch of To Fly. To Serve was all driven inside out. What BA acknowledged, and what we know (and I've used this thinking many times since), is that there is a virtuous circle that you can create when you make colleagues feel very proud. This is forgotten sometimes. There's a critical role of communication which is, if you make colleagues feel proud in a service industry, they serve better, which drives customer satisfaction, which in turn drives customer preference.

So, the data is absolutely empiric, in black and white, on the BA case study. The more proud colleagues felt of the brand and of the communication, the better they served, the more satisfied customers were, and the more customers chose British Airways. And the spike in colleague pride through 2011, 2012, 2013 when To Fly. To Serve was getting the most investment support, when it was most front and centre, led to extraordinary performance all over the business.

Yes. And they did amazing things. There was an iconic move that doesn't get talked about much, based on a pilot being a bit like a surgeon. Neither really think they're in the customer service business. They treat the illness, or they get their passengers there safely. They don't do service. That's not part of their job. But a big part of the To Fly. To Serve programme was a programme called Beyond the Flight Deck, and it was about getting pilots, at the end of the flight, to step out of the flight deck and to say goodbye to their customers.'

Fennell on Lynx

'Lynx is a very different category, a very different target. The brand is called Axe internationally, Lynx in the UK. In 1995 they came to us having built a very successful business. In building that brand what they had really talked about was their fragrance credentials. They were a body spray, but they behaved like a fine fragrance. And actually, the product truth was they had much better quality fragrances than other deodorants.

Lynx was used by young men, as both aftershave and deo, because it smelt great but kept you dry. Or rather, the biology of it lets you sweat, but fragrances your sweat. And, our strategic pivot was, stop talking about how it makes you smell, and that kind of outer directed benefit, and talk much more about how it makes you feel. And essentially we introduced the concept of confidence. Putting Lynx on will make you feel more confident. You will walk a foot taller. You will feel more able to impress, attract, and seduce women. And the most direct telling of that story is to have a situation, spray the product on and show an effect.

We've sort of made the same ad over and over again. The protagonist sprays on the product, and having the product on changes the way he carries himself, which makes him more confident and helps him to become more attractive to the opposite sex. And all over the world, over a very extensive period, that's helped drive amazing growth for Lynx.

In terms of where did the idea come from – we sat in a load of consumer groups, where consumers talked about feeling more confident. Interestingly Emma Cookson was the planner, but it was actually Gwyn Jones [the senior suit] that wrote, 'Lynx is your best first move'.

And it was a really interesting set of words, because it says, first move. It says, you're going to need other moves. But it says it's your first move. And that was taken by the great Paul Silburn, who was working at that stage with Tiger Savage, and they wrote the first script, which finished with the line, the Lynx Effect. It was a film called House Party, which was a very simple before and after construct. Bumbling guy, not very confident, sprays on Lynx, becomes very confident. And that before and after construct is something we kept doing for many years before we kind of evolved the format. But, yes, it was doing a lot of groups, writing a proposition that was about confidence, and then a couple of fabulous creatives making a link.

But times have changed, and Unilever feel very uncomfortable with doing work like that. Nowadays they want to be progressive and diverse. They've moved to much safer territory, probably to the detriment of the brand with 15, 16 and 17 year olds. You could say it was a perfect campaign for the Loaded, FHM type generation of the moment and we hit our stride on talking to that consumer. We live in more complex and nuanced times now, and the brand is probably looking for its next big leap, because what worked then probably doesn't work now.'

Fennell on Tesco

'The final thing I want to talk about wasn't created by BBH, but it's an idea that we've totally embraced, and I think we're investing with more meaning now, is Every Little Helps, for Tesco.

Food Love Stories, is a perfect example of what I think Every Little Helps should stand for. Every week we tell another very personal, very authentic food love story, and the consumer can go instore and buy all the ingredients and get the recipe card for exactly that dish we've just told you on air. We're giving mums and dads who are just cooking the same five, six meals every week wonderful recipe suggestions, with a bit of back story to each, and then giving them the tools, and the recipe, and the ingredients to then go and make it. The stories are very authentic. Very stripped back. Very insightful. And everyone has one. We tell our suppliers stories, we tell colleagues stories, and there are always three protagonists in every story.

There's the cook. There's the dish. And there's Tesco.

The campaign explores the relationship between those three players. What I love is that Every Little Helps had become an end line. I think what we've done (and it began with Dave Lewis) is vest it with much more meaning again.'

Lehrer on the Clustering of Genius (from *Imagine: How Creativity Works*)

(JONAH LEHRER WAS QUOTING FREELY FROM THE WORK OF DAVID BANKS, A STATISTICIAN AT DUKE UNIVERSITY)

'Human geniuses are not spread out evenly over time and space; rather, they tend to arrive in tight, local clusters. An example of this is Athens in the period between 440 BC and 380 BC. As Banks points out, 'the ancient city over that time period was home to an astonishing number of geniuses, including Plato, Socrates, Pericles, Thucydides, Herodotus, Euripides, Sophocles, Aesychulus, Aristophanes, and Xenophon' (Aristotle just narrowly misses this time frame himself, so it would not take much of a stretch to add him too).

Another example here is Florence between 1450 AD and 1490 AD. Lehrer wrote, 'In those few decades, a city of less than fifty thousand people gave rise to a staggering number of immortal artists, including Michaelangelo, Leonardo da Vinci, Ghiberti, Botticelli, and Donatello.'

Lehrer's other example is Shakespeare's London of the 16th century. 'Just consider the list of geniuses who surrounded Shakespeare. There was Marlowe, of course, but also Ben Jonson, John Milton, Sir Walter Raleigh, John Fletcher, Edmund Spenser, Thomas Kyd, Philip Sydney, Thomas Nash, John Donne, and Francis Bacon'.

For Lehrer, the fact that these cities (and others like them) managed to produce a glut of geniuses is no accident. Rather, it has to do with the fact that there were a handful of key cultural conditions that prevailed therein at the time in question. Lehrer points to four of these cultural conditions in particular. They are 1) The accessibility of education; 2) A certain cosmopolitanism; 3) An atmosphere that allows for, and even encourages, risk-taking; and 4) A balance between protecting intellectual property rights, and allowing old ideas to be used for the purposes of new innovations.

Is it stretching too much of a point to say that the BBH story also illustrates the impact of a powerful culture and having outstanding talents intermingling and feeding off each other?

Or that the same argument applies for encouraging the emergence of Idea Economists across a broad front?

MYTH: Advertising is a flaky and indulgent industry, which is not a good role model for business in general.

REALITY: Unfair. My experience of running pitches around the world demonstrates how clever and talented creatives and planners in good agencies can produce valuable ideas in very tight time frames. I have had privileged access – particularly from BBH – to dramatically successful case histories – from an agency that still has a culture you can cut with a knife.

Having multiple ideas to choose from is the key. As the French philosopher Emile Chartier warned, 'Nothing is more dangerous than an idea, when it is the only one you have'. David Droga, founder of Droga5 – a very successful New York-based agency – reassuringly says that ideas creep up on you, and uses pre-printed A3 pads with 100 boxes. He aims to fill in all the boxes as a first step every time the agency receive a brief. Prolific pays. And later on I will share the maths of this with you.

Chapter 5

IDEA ECONOMICS: MAKING IDEAS VALUABLE

Ideas are potentially investments in success

To operate within The Idea Economy we need a philosophy and a set of rules. I call it Idea Economics. Idea Economics is about leveraging the value of ideas to bring about change, progress and growth.

It is a completely new value system for ideas, which I have developed with advice from various experts, including Rory Sutherland, the best known apostle of Behavioural Economics, and the redoubtable Mark Earls. But principally I have worked closely with Jon Leach, our own in-house 'Idea Economist', who has given me invaluable help with the maths in this book. Some years ago Jon authored the ground-breaking paper **The Mathematics of Creativity**, which became the authentication of my original – but only marginally quantified – vision of Idea Economics.

The very high stock market valuation of tech and social media-based companies is evidence of Idea Economics in action. This sector tends to be valued on the basis of future earnings potential of existing ideas and the likelihood of the company having such a creative culture that it is bound to come up with more ideas – and employing people who are very inventive and creative.

All sorts of things are valuable by dint of what they can help us achieve. Investment is a good example. Injecting money, or time, or labour, or brain power – but usually money – can make all the difference to a project or venture. I see the idea-that-makes-the-difference (a valuable idea for short) as an investment in the success we are trying to achieve.

Idea Economics is hardly new. It has been with us since the C15th!

Idea Economics is a new descriptor. But the essential principle – that the best ideas are worth a fortune – is far from new, and was established with the invention of the patent system in the C15th. Patents were originally first granted in the Venetian Republic. In 1474 the Venetian Patent Statute was passed to offer a degree of protection from imitators to inventors and innovators, primarily in the glass industry. The London Patent Office opened just over 500 years ago in 1617 to encourage the publication of new and practical ideas, and to enable inventors to benefit financially for a period of time by having legal protection from being ripped-off. Intellectual Property Law originated even earlier in the late C16th. Ideas can only be protected if they have been executed – for example as a book, a working model. Trade marks were established and gave protection in most countries from the C19th. Why would anyone in past centuries or the present day wish to apply for the grant of a patent or trade mark if they didn't think their idea was valuable?

I entered the world of marketing and advertising at a time when agencies cared a great deal about Creative Awards, and clients didn't. Nowadays there are still a host of Creative Awards schemes around the world, but rather more where creative excellence is a qualifier, but marketplace performance the deciding factor.

These Effectiveness Awards have recognised marketplace success since 1968 in the US, with detailed econometric supporting evidence in recent years – so quantifying just how valuable the garlanded ideas have been. There is a stellar example in Chapter 7.

Econometrics

Econometrics is of course far more than a means of measuring campaign success and return on Investment (ROI) after the event. Companies who are seriously committed to marketing effectiveness pursue medium and long term growth strategies within the framework of tailored econometric models.

In June 2018 the consulting firm Ebiquity, who among other things carry out media audits for many leading advertisers, were signed up by the advertisers' trade body ISBA to improve industry standards in effectiveness and attribution measurement. Ebiquity said the following at the time:

'The technical diagnostics that go with econometrics require a trained statistician to properly interpret but a more common sense interpretation of how the model relates to the real world is just as important. Econometrics is a technical exercise but it should not be just a technical exercise – That way lies madness and spurious correlation in equal measure!

All of which is a shame, because econometrics, properly applied, is a really useful tool to help marketers understand what has worked and what hasn't.

In a world where the lure of the shiny and new is ever more seductive to the enthusiastic marketer, and where marketing accountability is a business imperative, knowing where to invest time and money, rather than relying on the latest spin, is of paramount value. After all, the media agency business model is fundamentally reliant on clients spending more money with them on the media mechanics which deliver the most profit: hard as it may be to believe, these are not necessarily those which are in the best interest of the client.

It is used – and indeed useful – as a means of determining where to concentrate marketing and media investments.

It is increasingly referenced by the Finance function within an organisation as a business case proxy for marketing investment.

Quite simply, econometric modelling is poorly used if it is merely a post-campaign ROI justification tool.

Far better is the use of econometric modelling to identify

diminishing returns and provide the basis for future-facing planning, budget optimisation and forecasting at the strategic planning and the campaign planning stages. Econometrics should be part of a 'Do-Learn-Do' culture of continuous improvement.

Of course, the models therefore need to 'make sense'. For this, you need an experienced modeller, who combines the necessary 'stats' knowledge with sound business/marketing/commercial – and common – sense.

Automated modelling systems do exist and they are attractively priced, with apparently similar outputs. Our experience is that they require significant manual intervention to make the outputs truly accurate, as opposed to apparently accurate.

The Benefits of Econometrics include:

- Empirically informed decision making (not based on 'woolly' metrics)
- Optimised budgets
- Identification of monies which can be diverted to channels with better returns or which can be invested in new initiatives
- Better forecasting
- Higher ROI over time

I believe that for marketers and their agencies there are further benefits in a mutual commitment to econometrics:

- It gives marketing a far more professional image.
- It provides transparency at a time when the media

industry is being challenged on conflict of interest.

- It builds collaboration and partnership – way beyond handshake-based relationships and subjective decision making.
- It allows marketers and agencies to share the same language of numbers with key stakeholders.
- It symbolises a long-term mutual commitment to success.

It is hard to see why brands and their agencies operating within econometric modelling wouldn't welcome a mathematical approach to valuing the ideas that inspire and drive their campaigns. If we can prove the value that campaigns contribute, we can also accept that the ideas that win through are very valuable in themselves.

Idea Economics is a good fit with econometrics.

My own journey in economics and world of marketing and advertising

I graduated from Oxford University in Philosophy, Politics and Economics, and this gave me a lifetime's interest in politics, and a grounding in philosophy, which has helped cushion me from the slings and arrows, as well as seeing the good times in perspective. More importantly economics gave me, a Classicist since the age of 8, a healthy respect for numbers, where the numbers come from, and how to use them.

I learned as a student that there are many definitions

of economics. Most focus on the creation of wealth, and the science of production, distribution and consumption. Macroeconomics surveys the big picture at global, regional or country level. Microeconomics is about our individual and family struggles to make ends meet and if possible move forward.

My first job was in Marketing Research at AC Nielsen, also in Oxford, where I started to understand the connection between the marketing of a brand (and in particular the ideas that went into advertising it) and marketplace results – sales, distribution, brand share etc. I was presenting bimonthly data on sales, brand share, distribution etc to very large FMCG clients. Nielsen was at that time the stand-out brand leader in marketing research, and it was our standard practice to track advertising spend alongside sales.

After three years I moved to London in 1968, and was fortunate to be appointed Account Executive at what was probably the smartest agency in town, Pritchard Wood & Partners. It was an extremely creative shop, but also the agency where Stanley Pollitt invented account planning, and his team (including Bob Jones, Peter, Jones, David Cowan, Creenagh Lodge and David Wilding) relentlessly pre-tested every campaign we developed. Meanwhile across town Stephen King at JWT had more or less simultaneously come up with the same system. *98% Pure Potato* by John Sullivan and Tracy Follows chronicled those heady days. The age of innocence in advertising was over. Art was being channelled by science. Data was looming over the horizon.

Advertising has been much influenced in the last 20 years by Behavioural Economists and their conviction that what might seem perverse and paradoxical consumer behaviour to the classical economists is actually a normal human reaction to an imperfect and asymetric world. Corporate life, and in particular mergers and acquisitions, has shown clearly that the brands that have been built by production, distribution and consumption (and indeed advertising) are much more valuable than conventional company assets.

An area largely neglected by economists has been the added value of ideas and creativity in achieving progress, prosperity and growth at both macro and micro level. American retailer John Wanamaker and English manufacturer Lord Leverhulme are both credited with the aphorism that half their advertising was wasted...if only they knew which half! Perhaps more important is the assumption that both industrialists were happy to accept that half of their advertising spend WAS productive. In my business world, we all know that advertising (more properly 'marketing communications') works. Indeed we are also confident that much innovation, not to mention the genuine inventions that come along rather less often, are productive, profitable and significant contributors to health, wealth and happiness.

So creativity is an important factor in growth, and ideas are vital. We are all familiar with the ecosystem of coming up with ideas and developing them. We readily use value judgements about individual ideas:

- It's a big/small idea
- It's a good/bad idea
- It's a powerful/weak idea

The problem is that we do not have any kind of widely accepted ready reckoner or valuator for valuing them. But all over the world manufacturers and agencies enter Effectiveness Awards, mostly providing econometric analysis to support bold claims of increased sales and marketplace success.

I have been a judge on both the IPA and EACA (European) awards. Both award schemes are widely respected across the industry, as are the Effies (the pioneer initiative that persuaded clients and agencies alike to recognise that creative excellence without success in the marketplace is simply not enough). Judging campaigns on performance as well as creativity is the very best example of Idea Economics in action. That these awards have spread to all corners of the world is testament to the universality of this belief. Donald Gunn also deserves great credit for his single-handed promotion of the connection between work that delights and work that works. The various Gunn Reports are also based on Idea Economics.

I was also for a number of years an advisory board member of the econometrics firm Marketshare, and learned a great deal about the many ways of quantifying the impact of marketing communications, and the ideas they are based upon.

My 'day job' for many years has centred on the advertising pitch – a process which firmly established the principle that ideas are not just the tie-breaker for choosing a winning agency, but intrinsically in the majority of cases valuable, and the reason the client went to pitch. With the emergence of Idea Economics the maths will be available to inform such decisions.

At AAI I have also seen numerous examples of what we might call 'Dove Syndrome' – the positive knock-on effect in terms of new business gained for the agency that has created acknowledged success stories. Valuable ideas that build brands and sell lots of product also stimulate the agency's own revenue stream – organic growth and new clients. These valuable ideas bring benefit all round – to the agencies, as described, but also clearly:

- To the company
- To the individuals and teams responsible – within the company and later on in terms of career enhancement
- To consumers who appreciate successful brands

Yet on the other side ideas are routinely generated, developed and implemented on rough and ready reward/ risk calculations, almost exclusively based on optimistic and internal assumptions. This is a dangerous and illogical way of going about things. Ideas cannot be judged solely by the people who came up with them. That is the fallacy of micro-managed pre testing. An idea is only worth the impact it makes on the person who has to buy it or not (eg a client in a pitch, or a customer who's viewed an ad). Basically ideas are like jokes or gifts. The recipient either laughs or is pleased – or the idea has failed.

In my working life I have been professionally involved – as well as personally fascinated – by two relatively recent developments in the science – Behavioural Economics, dating from Kahnemann and Tversky's 1979 book ***Prospect Theory***, and Brand Valuation, dating from 1988 and Interbrand's pioneering attempts to put the value of brands on corporate balance sheets. I will cover both subjects – and the parallels with Idea Economics – below.

The Mathematics of Idea Economics

Idea Economics provides us with maths to allow for relevant behaviours during the idea process, for example:

- Being prolific with ideas so there are plenty to select from.
- Sharing ideas to multiply the idea sources and raise the level of those ideas.
- Developing ideas in groups and teams.
- Improving ideas by finessing and tinkering them.
- Not being so judgemental about 'mistakes' to preclude repurposing or recycling.
- Aiming off to avoid unacceptable risk, while recognising that being over-cautious can be a problem too.

In this chapter and the following one we will bring maths

to bear on a number of other behaviours, processes and variables.

The currency of value will sometimes be financial – but often not. The currency will vary according to the type of idea involved. For example –

- Marketing ideas; the currency could be revenue, but also brand share, export markets reached, or brand value.
- Advertising ideas; revenue, accounts won, awards, being bought out.
- Retail ideas; revenue, footfall, share.
- Ecommerce ideas; clicks, revenue, share, being bought out.
- Entertainment ideas; movie deals, broadcast deals, box sets, awards.
- Engineering ideas; revenue, contracts.
- Scientific ideas; revenue, patents/rights, long term income.
- Software ideas; revenue, deals.
- Political ideas; %ages in opinion polls, votes, seats, deals with other parties, negotiations with other nations or blocs.
- Sporting ideas; revenue, points, wins, titles, TV deals etc

This list is far from exhaustive.

Just as Brand Valuation told us that the value and potential of companies depends just as much on what their brands are worth as on P&L and Balance Sheet, so

Idea Economics gives businesses the tools to measure the value and impact of ideas from concept right through to implementation.

In the same way that Behavioural Economics demonstrated that people's behaviour frequently deviates from economic orthodoxy, logic and self-interest, so Idea Economics is a more accurate and useful predictor of success and failure by using ideas, and not money, as the currency.

All of us – not just 'creatives' and 'experts' – have the ability to come up with ideas. Most ideas come from the connections we make between new thoughts and ideas and what we already have stored.

Ideas in the workplace

The idea is a broad church. Ideas should be a vital contributor to success in virtually every field. In Feb 2018 the Daily Telegraph published a list of the "Best 25 jobs in the UK". The list – all what used to be called white collar – was put together by jobs website Glassdoor, and was drawn up using three factors – average annual base salary, the number of job openings and career opportunities, which takes into account chances of promotion. All of the jobs listed were given a ranking out of 5.

The number of job openings per job title represents the total number of jobs posted to Glassdoor in the three months to the end of January.

1. Marketing Manager – Score: 4.5
2. Finance Manager – Score: 4.4
3. Mechanical Engineer – Score: 4.4
4. Sales Manager – Score: 4.3
5. Business Analyst – Score: 4.3
6. IT Manager – Score: 4.2
7. Civil Engineer – Score: 4.2
8. Product Manager – Score: 4.2
9. Lawyer – Score: 4.2
10. Software Engineer – Score: 4.2
11. Human Resources Manager – Score: 4.2
12. Business Development Manager – Score: 4.2
13. Internal Audit Manager – Score: 4.1
14. Solutions Architect – Score: 4.1
15. Network Engineer – Score: 4.1
16. Investment Analyst – Score: 3.9
17. Operations Manager – Score: 3.9
18. Recruiter – Score: 3.9
19. Brand Manager – Score: 3.8
20. Office Manager – Score: 3.8
21. Executive Assistant – Score: 3.6
22. Accountant – Score: 3.6
23. Sales Engineer – Score: 3.5
24. UX (User Experience) Designer – Score: 3.5
25. Trader – Score: 3.5

It's an interesting list, not least for the vast swathe of jobs it omits. That list includes among others advertising, agriculture, architects, armed forces, civil servants, care workers, construction, [most of] the digital industry, diplomats, distribution, doctors, emergency services, the entertainment industry, [most of] financial services, journalists, leisure, local government, management consulting, the manufacturing sector (!), media, medicine, police and law enforcement, politics, property, publishing, retail, sport, teachers, transport, travel and tourism, undertakers, vets.

Please look again at both list A (the Glassdoor 'best 25') and list B (the rest of us). Ask the simple question: 'how important are ideas for people doing this job?' Apply a simple five point scale ranging from:

5 = crucial for everyone
4 = important for at least 50%
3 = important for 25%
2 = you need a few idea people
1 = not important at all

My guess is that the external view would be somewhere between a 3 and a 4, whereas the reality is probably no better than a 2 in the majority of office jobs – largely for the reasons put forward by Crabbe and Coplin, and discussed in Chapter 3.

Given the level of education (at least tertiary) from which the vast majority have benefited, this – if true – is tragic. What is the point of recruiting well educated candidates, and not using their ability to imagine, create or innovate?

Idea Economics is quite like Brand Valuation

Brand Valuation is the process used to calculate the value of brands. Historically, most of a company's value was in tangible assets such as property, stock, machinery or land. This has now changed and the majority of most company's value is in intangible assets, such as their brand name or names.

For Brand Valuation (BV) to be practical, Interbrand and the other pioneers in the late 80's and early 90's had to develop valuation systems. There are three main types of brand valuation methods in use today, and we will need the same flexible approach for Idea Economics.

Brand Valuation works on a value tariff for ideas, based on a basket of criteria and factors. Brand Value is derived from the aggregate of discrete factors, eg:

- Trend
- International potential
- Leadership
- Competitiveness
- Market / sector strength
- Stability
- Protection

In Idea Economics, factors are going to vary far more than in a situation where we are just concerned with brands. Just look at the wide spread of jobs and professions above. But the list above can still provide a reasonable start point. We are going to have to add two points from the VERY! acronym [Valuable, Exciting, Robust, Yes!], Exciting and Yes! (wow/

buzz), as well as, where appropriate, characteristics of successful ideas, in no particular order:

- Development potential
- Originality
- Creativity
- Versatility
- Humanity
- Sustainability
- Cultural impact
- Memorability
- Stretch
- Newsworthiness
- Ease of comprehension and communication

As with Brand Valuation, the value calculation in every situation will be a customised cocktail of criteria rather than a monadic formula (see Chapter 7).

The parallels with Behavioural Economics

Behavioural Economics (**BE**) is the study of psychology as it relates to the economic decision-making processes of individuals and institutions. The two most important questions in this field are:

i. Are economists' assumptions of utility or profit maximisation good approximations of real people's behaviour?
ii. Do individuals maximise subjective expected utility?

BE disrupts classic rational economic rules like price elasticity by instancing apparently irrational human behaviour. The standard economic model of human behaviour includes three unrealistic traits — unbounded rationality, unbounded willpower, and unbounded selfishness — all of which behavioural economics modifies. BE uses psychological experimentation to develop theories about human decision making and has identified a range of biases as a result of the way people think and feel. BE is trying to change the way economists think about people's perceptions of value and expressed preferences.

Idea Economics has paradox in common with BE. It is the paradoxes in BE that convince – the cognitive biases. Thanks to the behavioural revolution, we have become accustomed to familiar examples of Economic Man or Woman deviating from orthodox behaviour, for instance:

- Loss aversion – being more upset about the prospect of losing something than excited about acquiring it.
- The power of now – instant stimulus being more powerful than regular communication.
- Scarcity value – if it's in short supply it must be worth more.
- I'll have what she's having – peer influence.
- The commuting paradox – denying 'normal' behaviour in relation to time and convenience as we post-rationalise where we have decided to live, even if the decision costs a fortune and takes hours out of the day.

- Chunking – greater appeal if something is broken down to its constituent parts.
- Choice architecture – consumers taking decisions according to the way in which choice is presented to them.
- Survivorship bias – being influenced by who or what has come through a selection process.
- Bandwagon effect – being impressed by what others have been impressed by.

...and so on.

There are parallels, but Idea Economics is intrinsically different to Behavioural Economics

- Idea Economics is a method of validating and valuing ideas by head, heart and intuition.
- Idea Economics factors in the requirement for an idea to be desirable, useful and financially attractive to the buyer of that idea, as well as to its creator.
- For an idea to tick all the boxes to a buyer, there almost certainly have to be equivalent perceived advantages for the customer and end user.
- Idea Economics embraces an idea's emotional and social value as well as its rational value.

Idea Economics has its very own counter-intuitive check list

Here are a dozen to start with. There are more!

1. Ideas may be good or bad, big or little, powerful or

weak. But what really matters is how valuable they are. The commercial overrides the subjective. Or to put it another way, the value is more important than the value judgement.

2. Individuals, companies and ad agencies spend a lot of time and money getting their ideas into perfect shape. But the value of an idea does not just depend on what we think of it. Far more important is how it is going to come across to the audience, the buyer, the client, and the customer. Beauty is in the eye of the beholder. Beauty – and therefore value – is in the eye of the beholder, not the artist. A bit like a gift or a joke.

3. We often see quality and quantity as being in conflict. But if we want a really valuable idea – a big winner – it is mathematically far more likely to emerge when we have many options on the table, than if we have narrowed the choice down to one. Rather like the work of many of the great artists, writers, composers and film directors, being prolific pays. They are legends because producing lots of output increased the odds of their coming up with famous work. When an agency distils its recommendation into one route, there'll often be an element of compromise built into it – to maximise its chance of appealing to everyone. So to continue the challenge to conventions, the possibility of discovering excellence in numbers beats the safety of only one option.

4. All ideas come from one person at the outset. Coming

up with ideas is an individual ability. Ideas don't start in meetings.

5. But even the greatest expert in his/her field will struggle to outperform a dynamic duo. 2-5 people will almost always be more effective in creating and developing ideas. Two heads are better than one, however big the one head!

6. It is not true that 6/7+ heads are not going to be better than two, for all the reasons set out in *Mote* – political pressure, frustration through lack of airtime etc. Nor will giving more time make things better. Small, orchestrated meetings (Motes) work best in developing ideas, and too many cooks do spoil the broth.

7. The value of an idea is closely tied to its distinctiveness. Fresh ideas are more valuable than tired ideas. Ideas that are not original can suffer from both inflation and devaluation. Original ideas are far more valuable than safe ideas.

8. Unlike money and things, sharing ideas multiplies the value of those ideas. Creative collaboration is a non-zero game. Active investment in other people's ideas pays off. If I share an idea with you, we both have use of the idea. If we exchange ideas, we each have more ideas to work with.

9. Most creative people are resistant to clients, patrons, and men in suits pushing back on their recommendations. They believe that further creative development (aka tinkering) inevitably blunts the

excellence of their ideas. But mathematically it can be proved that, provided there is creative edge and quality on the table, a certain amount of judicious tinkering (provided not too many people are involved nor for too long) will actually add to the value of the presented idea. Teamwork and collaboration work in the field of idea development, as almost everywhere else. And, yes, clients are welcome participants, because they are paying for it.

10. Ideas are the killer app for Homo Sapiens. There is nothing we produce which is so impressive, so progressive, or so transformational. And it is a skill we all have – both in creating ideas, and working with others to make them better. That is why I have written this book – to convince my readers that they all have built-in idea skills, which inspiration, training and experience can significantly enhance. The theory that skill with ideas is a preserve of the few is just so wrong. Everyone has it in them to be a creative contributor.

11. Specialisation rules in education, the workplace, entertainment, sport etc. But when it comes to idea generation, polymaths excel. People who are good at other things are particularly good at ideas.

12. Procrastination is normally frowned on at work. Time is one of the great imperatives. But great thinkers and artists use procrastination strategically to good effect, eg Martin Luther King's 'I have a dream' speech (finished at the last minute), and Leonardo

who took 16 years to finish 'The Last Supper'. Picasso made over 60 sketches for 'Guernica'. Procrastination works sometimes because of the Zeigarnik Effect (we remember uncompleted tasks), and at others because sitting on the fence is a viable strategy.

Now it is time to look at some of the key characteristics of successful ideas

Starting with originality. We know from experience that an original idea is likely to out-perform a familiar idea or a tired idea that has been seen before. What we don't know is exactly why, or precisely how much better it is likely to do. In *Originals*, Adam Grant says that to be regarded as original an idea has to be relatively unusual within its domain, and with the capacity to improve it.

I asked the Idea Economist how originality affects memory (and where relevant) purchasing, and how and by how much originality decays. How does creativity work on the brain? What is the mathematical difference between the ideas that stick and the ideas that fade away (or don't even get noticed in the first place)? And how come so little sticks?

The Idea Economist on the Originality premium

Various studies have suggested that we are on the receiving end of literally thousands of commercial messages a day. Other studies (or a brief self-examination by the reader) suggests that only a tiny fraction of those ideas stick. What is going on here? Many stimuli may impinge on our short term memory but few ideas (or adverts, or images, or tunes) are good enough to get into the long term memory and become permanent.

Part of the explanation may be to do with decay rates.

Let us say that the most powerful idea possible is one that we think about every day with 100% probability, for ever, and the worst idea is one that doesn't even register day one (nul points, Norvège), then we have a spectrum of ideas with a "memory chance" of 0 to 100%.

The first thing we notice is that **mediocre ideas rapidly get forgotten**. The statistical Mr Average who sits right on the 50% mark has only a 25% chance of still being amongst the apples of our eye on the second day ($0.5 \times 0.5 = 0.25$) and a one in eight chance on the third day. A full week after Mr Average came into our lives there is only a 0.4% chance that we are still thinking about him, a tragic one in 250 chance.

But what is less immediately obvious is that **those ideas that initially seem to be highly memorable also suffer the degradations of time and get forgotten**. So a strapping young buck of an idea with 90% memorability does quite well on the second day (81%) but is becoming quite tiresome and dull by the end of the week (43%).

Given enough time, even pretty good ideas can start to fade in our minds. Mr 90% is down to 21% after two weeks, 10% by three and a washed out 4% by the end of the month.

So what we find is that only a few rare ideas are robust enough to cling on within our careless, fitful brains. A 99%

idea is still doing pretty well after a month at 74 % while the 'one in a thousand' idea that is 99.9%, even after a month is virtually unchanged at 97%.

But, as one economist put it, in the long term we are all dead. And so, using this mathematical model, all ideas that are less than 100% will decay into mediocrity given enough time. As at least some ideas *do* become permanent, perhaps after a certain period of time a select few ideas acquire 'squatters' rights' and – less metaphorically – become a permanent set of neurones firing in a predictable sequence in our minds.

Reading the numbers above, you can see why that won't happen unless the idea is original in the first place. The dividend is the originality premium.

Recognising the downside of ideas that we've seen before

Being original clearly gives the idea a far better chance. Equally an idea that is to a greater or lesser extent an imitation of another idea will fare worse, even if the imitation is unconscious ('kleptomnesia'). Me-too is nothing like as powerful, although we can all understand the attraction of 'well, it worked for them'. The Idea Economist explains the maths.

The Idea Economist on why Imitation doesn't add value

We are talking about inflation and devaluation here, in terms of how the value of ideas can be diminished.

The principle of inflation is that the value of money can decline if the supply of money rises. So my five pound note that used to stand me a round in the 80's will nowadays only just buy me a single pint depending on how close I am to the centre of London.

Devaluation comes into play as the factor that shows how imitation reduces impact for 'me-too' players. But it is worse than that. **It also destroys collective value.** As we saw above, the value of an idea is closely related to its distinctiveness and/or memorability. Over time ideas decay in people's minds, which is mathematically just the same as inflation. A bit like money, ideas just wear out. (Hence, the new £5 note perhaps). The learning point here is that just as a government should not take the easy path of printing more money to fund things, a brand, for example, should not churn out very samey creative work year after year.

Inflation will occur, and the sequential impact of each ad will gradually be less.

The trick is to deliver consistent freshness; build the brand but bring new methods to how you do that on a regular basis. Which is a thing top marketers are good at.

So much for inflation. What about devaluation? Sometimes, external shocks can occur whereby a nation chooses – or is forced to by the markets – to devalue its currency so that it has less international purchasing power (but cheaper and more exportable goods in return).

Now we sometimes talk about the currency of ideas. But

the value of an idea – just like the value of a pound sterling on the continent – is not fixed or absolute. It can become devalued.

Let's take the example of the poster advertising for Apple and its iPhones and Samsung and its Galaxy phones to see how this applies to ideas.

Now Apple created a few years back a highly valuable idea that displayed beautiful images 'shot on an iPhone' on prominent poster sites. There was no mention of Pixels or Megabytes or anything technical. The ads just implied that anyone armed with an iPhone could produce artistry of this nature. For the sake of calibration let's give this idea an economic value of 10.

A few years later Samsung managed to fight off their techies' desire to talk about the amazing number of pixels and rams in their new Galaxy and instead, under the tag line 'unbox your phone', also displayed great photos on prominent billboards.

Now is this idea also a 10? (or maybe a 9 or 8, if you subjectively feel that the photos aren't quite as good)?

No. Idea Economics would predict the value of this approach to be 5 at best.

Because the formula for the value of an idea is a very simple one: the distinctiveness of the idea divided by the number of people using that same idea).

ie $10/2 = 5$

That is because people have already seen this idea (and tend to associate it with iPhones).

The same idea, when repeated by another, will have a dramatically lower effect (whether measured as distinctiveness or memorability).

It gets worse. Because if Apple continue to use their idea, two companies are using the same approach at the same time, and the impact of any ongoing iPhone ad will only be the average of the two singular effects i.e. $(10+5)/2 = 7.5$

Note that if Huawei (or Huever) also use the same approach, then the economic value would be even less: $10/3 = 3.33$. And poor old Apple would be down to around 6 when it was their bold idea in the first place.

In that sense, Samsung have devalued the idea both for themselves and for any other competitors. It was once explained to me that good creativity was about knowing a secret route to the crowded beach. Once everyone else had discovered it, then it is a lot less valuable.

The obvious way this matters is that by being a bit lazy in their creative thinking Samsung have reduced their return on investment by around 50%. Of course there is economic risk in going for something completely new but the downside of their approach is calculable in advance.

This dereliction of creative duty matters at a macro-economic level too. Imitating other people's ideas leads to devaluation, and harms the wealth creation of the entire system.

If Apple and Samsung each have unique (valuable) offers then we collectively have $10+10 = 20$ units of value in our capitalist economy and hence society. When one actor imitates the other too closely then we only get 7.5 + 5 = 12.5 units of value.

Imitating other people's ideas leads to devaluation, and harms the wealth creation of the entire system. As we saw above it is a principle of Idea of Economics that striving to originate and not just imitate doesn't just create value for you it also increases our collective wealth.

Can we apply numbers to the actual business of generating and developing ideas?

In the previous chapter, we looked at the work of James Webb Young, the far-sighted pioneer who invented a five phase idea making system before the Second World War. Now that the Idea Economist has explained the mathematics of originality and imitation, I asked him to apply some maths to the Webb Young formula. He described what he calls 'the ups and downs of creating valuable ideas'.

The Idea Economist on using a pocket calculator to invest in valuable ideas

(With acknowledgements to James Webb Young, the former advertising man who first joined J Walter Thompson in 1912, whose book *A Technique for Producing Ideas* (1939) gave us the classic process stage gates, which we can still use today).

Let's look at a pocket calculator. It uses five symbols, representing the five basic mathematical functions:

$$+$$
$$\div$$
$$\times$$
$$-$$
$$=$$

And an On/Off button.

How can we use these buttons (mathematical signs) in the creative development process?

Remember that the process (see diagram below) will have some strong peaks and troughs. Using 1 as our maximum and ultimate goal, I have inserted possible data points (eg 0.5) at each stage.

I. MAKE FRESH INPUTS. Gather lots of material (+)

This is about striving to add (+) new thoughts, ideas and experiences into your brain. These fresh (+) inputs are not ideas in themselves but are ingredients that your mind may well bake a new cake from in the future. Because if you always have the same ingredients in your brain/cupboard you will only ever find your brain/kitchen serving up the same stale ideas.

As Sainsbury's said, try something new (+) today.

At some point in your gathering phase you will feel that you are getting somewhere, perhaps having some quite decent ideas.

0.5

Trust me, this is a false peak and these ideas will later on look half-baked compared to your final output. 'Sell off' these ideas and keep going.

2. STORE THE INPUTS. Arrange them in your Idea Brain to try to make sense of what the new material is saying to you (÷)

The inputs stored in your brain aren't tidily arranged in jars with clear labels, but rather as millions of ideas and things that we have remembered stored randomly alongside countless others. We use the division sign (÷) to symbolise the divisions in our personal filing system. No idea exists in a vacuum. They are all arranged like a row of hooks. These hooks attach to other hooks that attach to other hooks that all add up to the tangled mass/mess of neurons in your brain.

An idea is only an idea **for you** if it attaches itself to an idea that is already in you. So, the advice here is to have opinions (÷!) in order to make sure the new (+) ideas you experience get reliably stored in your brain. Discuss things with people. Argue, even. With yourself, at the extreme.

But while it's fine to be opinionated, remember it's not about being right. It's about being interesting.

And the benefit of making your brain interesting by helping it store stuff with novel linkages and comparisons (÷) is that when it comes to the next step you are well on the way to having some good ideas. Which means, keep adding to your material, gathering, comparing, making patterns, looking for new angles and insights.

What you will probably start to feel is things getting complicated, loose threads appearing, inconsistencies emerging, irreconcilable anomalies in the data being starkly revealed, confusion all around. In short, things will end up feeling hugely worse than when you started, indeed terrible compared to where you were when it all seemed to make sense a few hours ago. Congratulations you have hit the bottom of the market. Time to buy in.

−0.5

▶ HIT THE OFF BUTTON

REST – literally do nothing. Either sleep on it or do something distracting. Or physical.
When you feel overwhelmed and overloaded just leave it and let your sub-conscious work on the problem. Do nothing for a bit.

0

▶ TURN IT ON AGAIN

3. MAKE CONNECTIONS – COMBINE FRESH INPUTS WITH WHAT YOU HAVE STORED. Ideas will start occurring to you. (X)

When you get going again, ideas will magically start to bubble up to the surface. As you slept and rested your brains, 'automatic traders' will have started buying some real gems based on algorithms even your shrink wouldn't understand.

Things are looking up.

The mathematical opposite of division is multiplication...

The combination of the 'fresh' and the 'stored' can be seen as the genesis of an idea. This combination of ideas is about multiplication and transformation (in their common sense meanings), and thus the creation of more than was there before. It's not about addition it is about x.

Having an idea is special alchemy, and creates some sort of multiplier effect on its base materials. Remember for now, if you have inputted (+) lots of new stuff in your brain and stored it away in interesting ways (÷) then you are increasing your odds of creating (x) the germ of a good idea.

0.9

Now as you gently return to the task – and it started before you returned to the task – great ideas will appear, seemingly out of nowhere; ideas that feel exciting and full of potential. Congratulations, you hung on in there, the boom is on and you have a good stock of gilt edged ideas to look at (and ideas that look twice as good as the initial ones you had the day before).

0.95, 0.99, 0.995, 0.999

4. COMPOSE. Sort through to find the best connections and start the fiddly process of crafting ideas . (−)

Ideas start off a little woolly and unformed – a hunch, an intuition, a sense that something might be occurring to you – and then the brain COMPOSES them into a more structured and clearer thought. This can be seen as the discipline of taking away all the superfluous stuff within the messy bundle of thinking until nothing is left but the core idea itself. This is about a process of subtracting the noise to compose the essential idea. It is like the way painters, sculptors and writers take out material to perfect.

It is about the sign (-).

Now sometimes your brain does this automatically and very fast so that the idea 'appears' to you fully formed. But sometimes it takes a conscious effort for you to figure out (-?) what your idea really is. The mental skill is to keep taking components away until only the essential parts of the idea remain, no more, no less.

0.95, 0.99, 0.995, 0.999

And now a different form of work starts. You are dealing with great assets, but you need to optimise them; to polish them but not knock off the sharp edges too much. Apart from the craft skill of optimisation that varies by field, a universal skill here is to know when to stop. Mathematically you will never reach the perfection of 1.0 (all great creative crafts people I have worked with can still point out the tiny flaws in their masterpieces that are invisible to others) and so at some point you need to 'sell' at what is close enough to the top of the market before you miss your moment. As they say don't let perfect be the enemy of the great.

Well done – you have ridden the wave to deliver the ingredients of a valuable idea.

5. OUTPUT =

Finally what does it all add up to, what have we produced and what remains? In short what do these mental calculations = ?

The ability to express your idea and indeed persuade people that you have something of value (=!) is the final part of the idea generation process.

This OUTPUT process is where the brain turns these internal thoughts into something you can present and sell.

Hopefully it will be a 1/100 idea. Possibly even the elusive 1/1000 idea. What you can be sure of is that this won't just be a good idea. It will be a valuable idea.

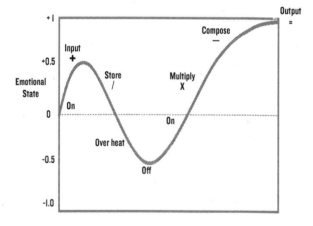

So a principle of Idea Economics is that you need to understand the universal rhythms of the creative process and, much like the economist with the investment cycle, you need ride the ups and down of the creative cycle, conquer your emotions to be able to invest and divest in your ideas appropriately.

Much like profitable investing, creativity takes time – and a few key strokes.

We are told to avoid making mistakes...

...but mistakes are not always disastrous. In fact they can sometimes be beneficial. The creator of Dilbert, Scott Adams, put it this way, 'creativity is allowing yourself to make mistakes. Art is knowing which ones to keep'.

The Idea Economist has the maths.

The Idea Economist on the value of Mistakes

MAKING MISTAKES CAN HELP YOU TO WIN

The late and much lamented theatre critic AA Gill said that you have to witness a lot of mediocrity before you are blown away by one brilliant show. He put the hit rate down as about 1 in 15. So if you go to the theatre once a week then it could take three months to get to that thrilling thespian hit.

This is not good odds and you might ask why didn't he just go to the good shows. Could he not just focus a bit better? He's supposed to be an expert...

The reason is that with first run theatre (and indeed all fresh creativity) you just don't know what you are going to get. As someone whose job it was to see new plays early on, he had to suffer on the critical cross so the rest of us know wherein lies theatrical redemption.

What a saint.

But there are some strong parallels here with generating ideas.

Firstly you have to generate a surprisingly large amount of ideas to be confident that there is a really good one in the stack. A ratio of 15 to one is quite a good estimate.

And the reason we don't just come up with the good one first, and stop making such stupid mistakes, is because much like AA we have to work through the dross to get to the gold.

But, unlike AA, some of the suffering eventually leads to nirvana. All those mistakes are not actually waste, but material we can recycle into future projects.

To model this, let us take the 1 in 15 ratio and say that at any one time we have a 7% (1/15) chance of coming up with a brilliant idea at any one moment. So far so Gill-like.

But on the next project let us say that half of the previous work is wildly inappropriate for the new brief, but 7 of the 'wrong' ideas on the last project are worth considering on the new one. Now we generate our normal 15 ideas, but this time have 22 (15+7) total ideas to consider. Using the Gill ratio of 1 in 15 we now should have around one and a half (22/15) great ideas to present. So we might have two if we get lucky.

And things get better. The next day we are working on a third brief. We generate 15 new ideas, rifle through our mental rubbish bin and dig out the 21 ideas we didn't use yesterday, and even find the 7 rejected ideas from day one under them. We uncrumple our 28 'waste' ideas and consider re-cycling them on our new problem. After a quick check, we bin around half as way off, but that still leaves us with 15+14 on the table.

We should have two great ideas right there (29/15). This job is getting easier!

Of course you can see where the maths is going here. As you work on more and more projects, more and more 'waste' becomes available to be re-cycled into future projects.

Some of the mistakes turn out to be masterpieces later on.

This is very different from the maths of say accountancy or management consultancy. Here mistakes are unwelcome and can't be used on future projects. (Apart from frightening war stories to scare the next generations with).

All this may explain why creative people typically work on multiple projects at the same time. What might be wrong on one project may be right on another. It actually increases productivity to get them working on several projects.

It's not a lack of focus but a way of finding the great ideas.

With that in mind, look again at Francis Bacon's studio. Do you now see a creative mess or a creative machine?

Clue? In 2013 a Francis Bacon triptych sold at auction for $142 million. A record at the time.

For accountants, the economics are clear. All mistakes must be eliminated and all relevant information must be found, so it makes sense to keep people focused on just one project.

But the economics of the ideas trade are different. While just messing around might be unprofessional, working in a messy way on multiple projects isn't just established professional practice.

It can actually be more efficient in terms of creative hit rate.

Ideas become valuable when they are spread

Spreading ideas is essential work in all communications, and of course in Idea Economics. Making ideas valuable is dependent on their reach, and naturally the Idea Economist can give us the numbers to explain how this works in practice, by word of mouth.

The Idea Economist on Cascades

THE VALUE OF CONTAGION

The thing about really good ideas (and these are really rare) is that they spread of their own accord. That's really useful.

This is because people are not just arranged in lines but in networks, to use the mathematical term.

So an idea sometimes doesn't just pass down a wire to a passive recipient's mind (like your average TV advert). On other occasions the recipient will talk to other people about it who may well pass this on themselves etc.

This is a free multiplier effect and is much sort after by

PR people, social media agencies and anyone who thinks they may have a blockbuster on their hands (a retailer with a Xmas tv ad, or a Hollywood film producer, perhaps).

The maths of it can be quite striking. If we assume that a good idea is spotted by an early adopter, who passes it on to around 10 people who then pass it on to five people each who then pass it on (with a similar drop in intensity) to 2.5 people each then we get the following cascade. (The model here assumes that the ripple loses energy the further it moves away from its source. Go and throw pebbles into a still pond if you're not with me here).

So we have 1 person who hears it first and tells 10 people
10 People who tell 5 people each
50 people who tell 2.5 people each
75 people who tell 1.25 people each
92 who tell .6 of a person each
54 who tell .3 of a person each
17 people who tell 0.15 of person each
3 persons who hear it last.
1 original person plus 301 people in the cascade.

AN IDEA THAT IS HALF AS 'CONTAGIOUS' HAS A MUCH SMALLER CASCADE

1 person who hears it first and tells 5 people
5 People who tell 2.5 people each
13 people who tell 1.25 person each
16 people who tell 0.6 of a person each
10 who tell 0.3 of a person
3 people who tell 0.15 of a person

1 person who hears it last (if they are lucky)

1 original person plus 48 people in the cascade

So half the contagion produces around an eighth of the effect.

Going the other way (it will waste too many lines in the book to print it here, but if you get out your own calculator...) you will find that an idea that is just 50% more contagious than the first one reaches 15 on first jump, and then given a decay rate set at 0.75 will reach around 6.5 million people.

This is what people mean by going viral.

Indeed, if your contagion rate is high enough then you will reach virtually the whole population just like a winter virus. A few years back, for example, even if they hadn't bought a copy, almost everyone in the UK had heard of 50 Shades of Grey apart from a few crofters up in the Scottish Islands (who probably didn't catch that cold either).

Different creative agencies try to harness the economics of these cascades in distinct ways.

Those coming from a more traditional advertising back ground will invest lots of money in a very expensive blockbuster ad that they hope many people will share (perhaps because it is so cute e.g. John Lewis). But they also invest even more money in social media in the hope that they can fan the flames and make it catch on fire.

Those coming from a more PR background will put several low-cost ideas into the world of connected media and hope that just one of them takes off. The fact that the others sink without trace doesn't matter if one makes it big. Or as someone put it to me, if the connected world represents a forest fire waiting to happen, then your best strategy is to drop lots of matches. Nice.

So to sum up, both of these strategies make good Idea Economics sense. But in economic terms the former is like putting all your pension in one big blue chip stock and hope they start doing quite well. The dropping matches version is like buying 10 AIM listed investments and hope that one sky-rockets, even if most of the others go bust.

Whether this Word of Mouth phenomenon is any more common in these webbed-up times is hard to prove, but those who work in the Idea Economy are certainly very keen on it, as it does seem to (occasionally) give you something for free. And an economist of any stripe would like that.

Risk

Another fundamental concept in Idea Economics is risk. But as with many aspects of our new science, all is not as it seems. Yes, risk is risky, but sometimes caution can be a risk as well!

Michalko in *Cracking Creativity* described idea generation as being essentially a two stage process: possibility thinking and practicality thinking.

Possibility thinking is raw ideation (coming up with lots of ideas) without applying judgment or evaluation, whereas practicality thinking is about applying the practicality and profitability tests to the most promising. The Idea Economist can explain the principles of possibility thinking. We'll look at the maths of practicality thinking in the next chapter.

The Idea Economist on Risk. Part I: Thinking about Possibilities

THRIVING IN THE CHAOTIC ZONE

I once heard the comedian and actor Eddie Izzard discuss his theory of the 'great wheel of style'. His point was that as you move along the spectrum of fashion – what he called 'fashion grooviness' – and progress from the disastrous, to the merely bad, on through the mediocre to the good, and ever upwards into the genuinely brilliant, things became increasingly risky.

He explained that as you reach the end of the 'brilliant' zone you suddenly discover that the spectrum is actually a circle. Without noticing you will cross the line into 'disastrous' again. Keep pushing it and eventually you will fall off those stacked clogs, Naomi.

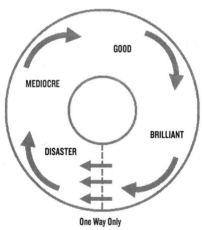

One Way Only

The comic also offered the advice that the membrane at the bottom only allowed movement in one direction: you should not hope that by wilfully lowering your fashion sensibility you will suddenly pop out of the other side of 'disastrous' and achieve fashion grooviness. Geeks and nerds beware (this from a man in red spandex leggings, mind).

Rather than draw this phenomenon as a circle, we can also mathematically plot this as a graph where the smooth rise of fashionability suddenly hits a wild chaotic zone where ideas flip between brilliance and disaster in an alarming and unpredictable manner.

Indeed mathematicians or engineers would recognise this as the maths of 'chaos'. For example, turn a tap on gently and the water will come out smoothly in what is called a 'laminar flow'. Keep increasing the pressure, and suddenly the water starts coming out in a messy, splattery way. This is known as 'chaotic flow'. Keep turning the tap and things will just get messier. Smoothness never returns. Chaos reigns.

Now in the world of fashion, most of us mortals operate in the safe, shallow end: we would rather stick with mediocrity with a small chance of occasionally hitting 'good', than play in the brilliant zone and risk a fashion disaster.

However, some people – presumably most of the fashion industry – are prepared to swim in the choppy waters of the chaotic zone and run the risk of ridicule. But there is method in their madness – they at least have a chance of achieving fashion glory; and the kudos and wealth will be theirs.

The problem here is that us cautious folk never know whether in the real world our fashion purchases will turn out to be good or mediocre (although we do know they are neither brilliant or disastrous). Similarly the fashion leaders never know if they step out of the door looking fab or daft. In the words of William Goldman, the Hollywood film writer, 'no one knows nothing'.

We actually know whether we are playing safe or risky but don't know the precise outcome. In the next Chapter we will look at the practical stage of thinking about ideas, and also at whether tinkering with them works or not.

MYTH #1: Idea Economics is a new notion, and unproven. There are no examples out there.

REALITY: IP, pitches, patents and effectiveness awards are demonstrable proof that Idea Economics is valid and happening around us. The very high value of tech and social media stocks – not just the giants, but the start-ups is further evidence of the validity of the theory.

MYTH #2: It's only executed ideas that have any value. Ideas are easy to come up with, and they are only worth a dime a dozen.

REALITY: This is completely unfair. Ideas are potentially valuable from concept. Frequently the winning idea is chosen from a short list of contenders, and each contender has a value deriving from being under consideration. Only one horse can win, but no horse can win unless they are led into the starting stall.

Chapter 6

THE VITAL ROLE OF THE IDEA ECONOMIST

As we saw earlier, **Idea Economists** are highly numerate idea people with idea brains.

Here is our Idea Economist talking about his own role.

The Idea Economist on the Role of an Idea Economist and where he or she is likely to come from

Perhaps Idea Economists are ideas people who are good at numbers (and vice versa). We play a number of parts: translators, catalysts, persuaders, contributors, analysts, believers, evangelists.

So two key questions:

1. Who might make a good Idea Economist?
2. How common is this sort of mentality?

By my estimate, if you imagine a typical class of 20-30 kids, I would predict that only one or two will grow up with the abilities and interests to be an Idea Economist.

I base this on the personality profiling Myers Briggs system of classifying people. In my experience, we are normally found in the INTJ and INTP boxes. So our numbers are partially limited to roughly 5% the population.

As the chart below shows, these people are typically more interested in 'the possible' over 'the present' and tend to be more logical than personal (or indeed more logical than personable, in my experience). However, in the corner of the chart there are four sub groups:

The Field Marshal
The Inventor
The Mastermind
The Architect

NF Valuing	Possible				NT Visioning
Personal	ENFJ Teacher	INFJ Counselor	INTJ Mastermind	ENTJ Field Marshall	Logical
	ENFP Champion	INFP Healer	INTP Architect	ENTP Inventor	
	ESFP Performer	ISFP Composer	ISTP Operator	ESTP Promoter	
	ESFJ Provider	ISFJ Protector	ISTJ Inspector	ESTJ Supervisor	
SF Relating	Present				ST Directing

Idea Economists tends to be intellectual leaders rather than emotional leaders (aka the ENTJs) who are busy (field) marshalling the troops. And while Idea Economist do have ideas they are just as comfortable working with the ideas of the pure inventor (aka the ENTPs) and figuring out how to make those ideas work.

So by my reckoning it is the INTJs and the INTPs who are most likely to be Idea Economists. Hence, one or two children per classroom.

Incidentally, if you are finding this analysis, coding up and quantification of the human condition weird, disturbing or even distressing, then that is probably because you are (diametrically) opposed to this way of talking about the world! Apologies.

But if you want your buildings, companies and most particularly your ideas to be both robust and brilliant then you are going to need us. We are here living amongst you, (even if we sometimes avoid eye contact).

Several of the people I interviewed would qualify as Idea Economists: most obviously Mark Earls, Rory Sutherland (no reason why you can't be both 'Behavioural' and 'Idea'), Balder Onarheim, Julian Smith, Richard Walker, Nick Kendall and Jim Carroll.

We should study the genre Idea Economist and work out where these abilities are going to be most useful. For instance, there is a big difference between the way briefed and spontaneous ideas work. An Idea Economist has a natural job to do with bespoke ideas.

Bespoke Ideas

If you/your company/your agency/your team are commissioned to come up an idea to solve a problem, develop a campaign, relaunch a brand or whatever, it is not difficult to start putting financial parameters on it.

Both input and output costing come into play. There's probably a fee to negotiate, which will relate to what it costs us to 'make' the idea, and how much it's worth to the client to have an idea they can use.

Then again there's shop window to consider: the better the idea, the more it could enhance the agency's reputation. So not only will the idea be valuable to them as the provider (they earn money from it), but it will also reflect well on them with a view to future earnings – as well as providing the client with something of intrinsic value, launching their brand, solving their problem etc.

With bespoke ideas there are also plenty of ways to gauge value, test efficacy etc:

- Effort
- Time spent
- Number of people involved
- Amount of money invested
- Who came up with it

...which is how agencies charge and clients pay in my industry.

An Idea Economist has a clear mandate where bespoke ideas are being commissioned – specifying, costing, valuing. But almost more crucially in analysing markets, assessing competition, mining insights, researching pre, during and post.

Spontaneous Ideas

The role is less obvious here. It's much more difficult in an environment where spontaneous ideas occur, and vie for love and support.

In the first instance there may be no rational revenue possibility, unless we can find someone to sell it to, or exploit it ourselves. Spontaneous ideas will probably start life as orphans, looking for sponsors – or at least foster-parents. Value would be harder to assess, and testing would be tricky.

Candidate fields for the involvement of Idea Economists

- All the professions
- Health
- Academia
- Education
- Science
- Military
- Central and local government
- Advertising / Communications Planners
- Policy wonks / spin doctors in politics
- News editors and all with the power and influence to blend news and editorial
- Opinion leaders, planners and commissioners in entertainment
- Ditto in sport
- 'Experts' in all disciplines – the kind of individuals

from academia, think tanks, business bodies, who are endlessly interviewed on radio and TV

- In particular experts on dynamic issues with the potential for disaster (eg Climate change, Health and disease, Religious strife, Genocide, Warfare, Refugees, Economic collapse, Natural disasters, Threatened species etc)
- Stars of the blogosphere
- TED, TEDx, and mini-TED speakers

The list could be substantially extended.

Will every company need one or more Idea Economists?

In *Nudge* Thaler and Sunstein contrasted Econs (people who act and make decisions logically) and Humans (the rest of us), who need nudges from choice architects in the spirit of libertarian paternalism. These nudges help the humans make more enlightened – but less orthodox – decisions. In *Rise of the Humans* Coplin uses the same word 'humans', but he is describing people who are fighting back against the 'digital deluge'. Idea Economists are akin to choice architects in one aspect of what they do – encouraging 'humans' not just to be creative and innovative, but to generate and make ideas, as long as they stand a chance of being valuable.

Idea Economics doesn't just create a role for Idea Economists. It also offers great benefits and possibilities to people on the positive side of the idea spectrum.

We are talking here of Idea Positives, as opposed to Idea Negatives.

Idea Actives, rather than Idea Passives

And Idea Receptives, not Idea Resisters.

It would be a waste – given the idea deficit in most companies – if Idea Economist were to become yet another outsourced speciality. Companies need to identify, train and develop their own Idea Economists not just to help tackle the idea deficit, but *pour encourager les autres.*

It goes deeper than that. In **Imagine: The Origins of Creativity** Lehrer covered the interaction aspect, with a famous example:

'Some very notable companies take this principle of cross-pollination so seriously that they have begun to redesign their workspaces around it. For instance, soon after Steve Jobs took over the animation company Pixar in 1986, he designed the building that housed his new project to center around a huge airy atrium. The building was specifically designed in such a way that the workforce would have to pass through the atrium as much as possible (everything important in the building was located in or beside the atrium, from the meeting rooms, to the cafeteria, to the mailboxes, and even the bathrooms). The reasoning behind this design was simple: Jobs wanted his employees to interact with one another as much as possible; he himself stressed that 'everybody has to run into each other'. Ed Catmull, a leading computer scientist with Pixar at the time, and now President of Pixar and Walt Disney Studios, put it this way: 'what's our most important function? It's the interaction of our employees. That's why Steve put a big empty space [at the centre]. He wanted to create an open area for people to always to be talking to each other.'

Sharing

Like all good economists, Idea Economists take pride in simplifying issues and concepts. Sharing is a very important principle of making ideas. In many of the arts individual prowess and pride of authorship is fundamental. We want to believe Shakespeare wrote all those plays and poems. It would be devastating to find out that Haydn only wrote 87 of his 106 symphonies, or that Rodin had help with his statuary. Disputed creation is untidy and unsettling. The value of a painting depends on its provenance. We accept that Giovanni Antonio Canal used minions to knock out all those gondolas and their gondoliers. So strictly speaking not every brushstroke of his masterpieces was in his own hand, but he is still celebrated as Canaletto (an affectionate diminutive, not as some suppose a slightly disrespectful descriptor, 'the canal man'). Canaletto shares with Clarence Birdseye and Forrest Mars the unusual distinction of being born with a brand name.

But idea making, like writing musicals or founding ad agencies is rooted in sharing. Yes, every idea has to start in one person's head, but to fertilise, it has to be shared. Here's the Idea Economist's succinct explanation.

The Idea Economist on Sharing

THE NON-ZERO GAME OF CREATIVE COLLABORATION: INVESTING IN OTHER PEOPLE'S IDEAS

Money (as opposed to wealth) is a zero-sum game. If I give you a ten pound note then I am down £10 and you are up £10.

$$10-10 = 0$$

On the other hand if I give you my ten best ideas, while you are now up ten ideas, I still have my original ideas and so we now are collectively better off. By me giving you my ideas and you being open to these ideas, we now have a collective 'idea wealth' of twenty ideas.

$$10+10 = 20$$

So creative collaboration appears to have the potential to be a non-zero sum game.

Now cynics may argue that we collectively only have 10 ideas as you merely have copies of my original 10 ideas.

But I will raise you your arithmetic negativity and go all in with the power of multiplication.

Because creative collaboration is really about the **exchange** of ideas. So assuming we each bring to the party 10 unique ideas, once we **swap** them we then do seem to end up with 20 ideas each. Each of us is up on the deal.

But actually what we have – at least as a potential maximum – is 120 ideas; your 10, my 10 and the mutant possibilities of crossing each of your ideas with each of my ideas to generate 100 hybrids.

$$10 \times 10 = 100 \ (\text{or even } 120)$$

Now, just as in nature, many of these hybrids will be still born i.e. of no value. But the point is that by daring to expose my pristine intellectual DNA to your exotic but unpredictable cognitive gene pool then we improve our collective chances of creating a vigorous valuable idea.

Which may be why working in advertising used to be described as better than sex.

$$(10+10)^N = ?$$

To put our sensible economic hats back on, the practice of fully investing in other people's ideas may be very similar to being an active investor in a business as opposed to a passive investor.

If you and I both put in 10 units of money (or effort, the maths is the same) then we hope not only to get some cost efficiencies (eg share an office) but to create some commercial synergies (eg invent new products to take to market) between our two sets of capabilities.

Your ten and my ten will grow faster by us investing together in the enterprise. There should be some sort of multiplier effect.

We don't know how much this multiplier will be but we

do know that to make our co-enterprise take off then we need to not just financially invest but emotionally invest too so that:

10 X 10	>	10 + 10	>	10
partnership		co-investment		solo-investment

So another principle of Idea Economics is that you need to not just hear the other person's ideas but emotionally invest in them in order to unlock the maximum value.

Partnerships and behaviour in the Idea Economy can be analysed mathematically

Ideas need a collaborative environment in which to flourish. The dynamics of ideas embrace people who commission ideas, people who create and develop them, people who use and implement them, and people who benefit and profit from them. Long term partnerships offer significant advantages, but not all ideas are hatched in a secure environment. I asked our Idea Economist about the pros, cons and maths of this.

First he told me about 'The Prisoner's Dilemma' a classic counter-intuitive game theory example of why co-operation doesn't always pay.

The Idea Economist on The Prisoner's Dilemma

In this hypothetical situation two men are in jail accused of the same crime. The police are prepared to offer freedom for anyone who will testify against the other guy who will then get a long sentence. But if both stay quiet, then in a few weeks they will probably be released due to lack of evidence.

This creates the Dilemma. There are different ways of scoring the result but let us say that if both stay quiet (i.e. both co-operate) then that is worth 3 points to each of them – it's only a few weeks.

If one of them defects then he walks away with 5 points and the other guy gets nothing.

However, if both defect then they will both get long sentences, perhaps with a little time off for grassing the other guy up, but only worth 1 point each.

These numbers create some interesting dilemmas. The maximum the prisoners can earn as a pair is 3+3 or 6 if they co-operate. But knowing that the other guy knows this, then it is tempting to defect, because while the team earns less, you personally take it all and earn 5.

Knowing that you may be thinking just that, he may then decide to defect at which point the team gets just 2 points (as opposed to the maximum of 6). Anticipating this, both of you may review your options.

So from one very simple choice – whether to co-operate or defect with one partner – a complex situation arises.

The situation becomes more complex if you and your partner commit a series of crimes and keep ending up in jail in the same situation. He knows that last time you co-operated while he defected (and you're still cross about that!). What will he do this time? Try to make it up to you? Defect anyway because he know you're angry with him? Co-operate now to show that in the future he is going to be a good guy? What should you do? Did Shakespeare use this as inspiration for his characters' motivations?

Mathematicians delight in running long simulations called something like 'tit for tat' (I'll do what you did last time) to see what is the best long term strategy.

But we are looking for arguments in favour of co-operation in a more benign environment – let's call it marketing! The Idea Economist talks about longer term partnerships, and why they are likely to be more successful than flirting or one-night stands.

The Idea Economist on Co-operation

In marketing, most commercial organisations (clients) look to work with a creative organisation (an agency) in order to produce the most competitive creative product.

As in the human species, things have also evolved so that it takes the coming together of two different entities – a client and an agency – to produce truly healthy offspring.

The client has a choice of how to behave: does he or she 'mate' with multiple creative partners, or settle in for a long monogamous partner with just one?

With a few assumptions, we can look at the statistical advantages of both strategies.

If we have mathematically shown that long term co-operation between two parties is the most successful way of creating successful, complex entities, then perhaps we also have some insight into why, on the whole, clients and agencies tend to work together for a fair while rather than on a promiscuous basis. (Although there are clients who use agencies in this way).

Perhaps creative ideas take a fair bit of nurturing from two committed parents if they are going to flourish? Does bringing up a brand take the same amount of co-parenting time as bringing up a family? Anecdotally this would appear to be true.

But what is the more intricate maths of these relationships? They both want to stick around for the long term but what else is going on?

The point to observe is that the interests of the agency side people and the client side people are linked but not completely aligned.

While both want a creative idea that sells product (or persuades customers to buy, or boosts the brand's image etc.), there may be other agendas operating.

For example the creative agency (or more precisely the creative people in the agency) may want creative work to be particularly disruptive, or funny or glossy if they think that will help raise their profile in the creative industry. They may believe that their creative colleagues will admire disruptive or funny or glossy creative work independently of whether it does a job for the client or not.

On the other side of the fence, the commercial client may want the creative work to be more cautious or familiar or 'easier to sell internally'. They probably believe this will advance their own careers in their companies. If with a slightly more cautious approach they can raise sales and make their boss think they are a safe pair of hands, then why take the risk of 'edgy' creativity?

At the extreme, it is possible on the one hand for some agencies to have very flashy portfolios of work with not much solid evidence of commercial impact, while on the other, they work with successful corporations with a solid track record of sales growth and a rather dull creative output.

Coming back to our agency-client pair, bonding with their broadly aligned but possibly divergent agendas, when should they co-operate and when should they, if ever, defect? More particularly how should a client behave for their own best interest?

But more on that later. For now we have a way of modelling the client agency relationship. We are defining 'defecting' as pursuing your own career agenda, and 'co-operating' as trying to accommodate your partner's career needs within a solution that also works for you.

To bring a bit of Shakespearean characterisation to this analysis, let's say that the Client can either be Trusting ('Co-operates') or Suspicious ('Defects') of the creative agencies behaviour. Similarly the Agency's actions can be Honest ('Co-operates') or Sneaky ('Defects').

Now when Trusting meets Honest all is well and good (3 points each).

But there is a temptation for the agency to try to Sneak too much of its own agenda in and earn 5 points from a too Trusting client. Similarly, a too Suspicious client can exploit a basically Honest agency and take all 5 points for themselves. In both cases, you could say that greed and envy come into play. One player 'decides' that they aren't earning enough, or the other player is earning too much.

And tragically this can lead to an agency feeling that it might as well be Sneaky if the client is going to be that Suspicious. But it is not a great idea, because that would only net each party 1 point each.

From the client's point of view, trust is a better way forward than suspicion. The Idea Economist explains why.

The Idea Economist on the 'Client's Dilemma'

So just as mathematicians have explored the most successful strategies for playing the Prisoner's Dilemma I can translate the learnings into the best long term strategies for playing a game that we might call the 'Client's Dilemma'.

Two obvious ones are don't be Always Trusting or Always Suspicious whatever the outcomes.

But to cut a lot of mathematical modelling short, a few principles emerge about how clients should treat agencies:

1. Be fundamentally nice. Believe that the other guy is a good guy too, so start nice. And stay nice too. Don't get greedy and don't be envious if they are doing well out of the relationship.
2. Be aware. The world is not full of simple straightforward behaviour. Be prepared to change your behaviour. Watch out for things going wrong as they almost certainly will.

3. Be strict. In the jargon, be prepared to 'retaliate'.
   However, let bygones be bygones and move on. In
   particular, let the other side know that you are ready to
   get back to normal, having made your point. Be seen as
   being firm but fair.
4. Be forgiving. If you do get locked into a bad situation,
   rather than wait for them to apologise, make the first
   move and show some forgiveness.

Rogue clients – and agencies because the maths is
symmetrical – do exist in the simulations and the real world.
And the reason is that clients can always keep jumping
from agency to agency, looking for receptive and honest
behaviour to exploit. Their hit rate may be lower, but as long
as they keep moving they can have enough creative hits
to keep their reputations intact. They may leave a trail of
broken hearts (and brands) in their wake but the population
does host this sort of behaviour.

But on the whole, largely because the other side 'doesn't
allow it', this is not the sort of behaviour most likely to
flourish.

What works for creative work is a real partnership.
Optimistic, collaborative, prepared to be tough when needed
but believing in the integrity of the human spirit.

And with that sort of spirit, it's not surprising that our
creative ingenuity got us out of the stone age, and to where
we are today.

I discussed the partnership issue with Sir Nigel Bogle,

co-founder of BBH, when I interviewed him recently. I described to him the difference I have found between client partners in the pitch environment, and the same people in similar roles working with agencies in ongoing relationships.

He asked me, 'Are you saying that when you were managing the big pitches, there was a huge amount of dynamism and originality? And are you also saying that in recent years when you have been largely monitoring relationships, those relationships have just faded into commodity status?'

I replied that I spent more than 25 years in the back of pitches. It was an extraordinary run when I saw some crazy ideas, but also some amazing people and ideas. The pitch circus is agencies on speed. It's hugely stimulating, particularly if you do a lot of it. I did. Every week, every month, every year. All over the world.

Now our role is long term client/agency relationship monitoring and trying to help people on both sides make it better. We spend a lot of time with senior client people, and a lot with agency heads and senior account people, and also with top planners and creatives.

At worst the contrast is really disappointing. I sometimes think we have moved from idea richness to idea deficit. In pitches there is inquisitiveness and people with transformation on their mind. In run of the mill client/agency interchange, life seems to be incredibly transactional. The lack of inspirational thought is palpable, and that was one reason for writing *Mote*. I think that meetings have a lot to answer for in terms of dulling people, and depriving them of their individuality. I told him that over and above the relationship, the culture in many of these companies isn't what it was. There are some honourable exceptions, but some of the companies I've worked with seem to squeeze the life out of the people that work for them.

I'm really not talking about trying to turn everyone into a creative director, because that would be ridiculous. I'm trying to get people to think more, respect ideas, and strive to generate and develop them. I'm not using technical language. I talk about an idea brain which isn't a CAT scan of the amygdala or anything. It's just my way of talking about the bit of your brain that you use to come up with interesting thoughts, once you have turned off the autopilot

I do believe that there's a real need, and let's say particularly in the client community, for inspiring people to be more thoughtful, to be more idea generating, to be more creative, with a small c.

Nigel made an interesting point in reply, 'When you start an agency, you tend to attract more entrepreneurial clients than when you're running an agency that's mature – people like the great Johnny Mezsaros at Audi, Anthony Simonds-Gooding at Whitbread, and the guys we worked with at Levis. They were all willing to take risks and to understand the power of an idea and what it could do for their business. When you work with more institutionalised clients, and you and the agency are more settled into these big relationships, then there is increasing complexity and an inability to simplify, and to produce briefs that are springboards to excellence, as opposed to buckets full of information that hasn't really been sorted through to get to the key fundamental truths that you want to promote.

And we spend a lot of time trying to simplify complex briefs that need a whole lot of work done to them, if they are going to be a springboard for excellence.

The best brief I ever got, and I still use it in lectures and speeches I give, was the first brief we were issued by Whitbread, when we originally pitched their business.'

Excerpt from brief from Whitbread & Company to pitching agencies in 1982

WHAT ARE WE LOOKING FOR?

- High quality creative work
- Based on sound strategic thinking
- The attention of top level agency management – as the basis of good service
- An agency who are compatible with our own advertising philosophy

WHAT IS OUR PHILOSOPHY?

- We believe the basis of good advertising is accurate strategy
- But we believe that accuracy and clarity are not enough
- Our advertising must have its strategic message distilled into a simple memorable creative idea

- A creative idea that commands attention in the crowded media scene
- And that idea must be executed in a stylish, high quality production approach
- We want exciting accurate advertising which has the capability of becoming famous
- How will we evaluate your agency?
- The creative and strategic quality of your current work
- The people who will be assigned to our business
- Your likely compatibility with the Whitbread team

THE MODE

- Not a speculative pitch
- Tell us why you are right for Whitbread
- Illustrating this through the work for your current clients

THE TIME

- Two and a half hours at the outside
- Please send any additional material one week beforehand
- We will meet in three to four weeks

HOW MANY AGENCIES ARE COMPETING?

- Three/Four

HOW SOON WILL WE GIVE A DECISION?

- Within one week

HOW WILL WE PAY YOU?

- Please ask our current agency if they think we pay fair fees
- As there is no speculative work, we would not propose to pay a fee for the pitch

Nigel's comment on the brief

'It's beautifully simple, and one of the reasons it's simple is that was the style of the chap who wrote it – Gerald Wright, who had moved from Birds Eye, to work for Anthony Symonds-Gooding at Whitbread.

He used very short sentences. He just drilled the way he wrote down to very punchy short sentences, and it was a very inspiring brief to read, because of what it said. It was a very easy brief to read. And even though it's now 35 years old, I still think it's probably one of the finest single briefs that I've ever been given.

Working with the big clients now, you spend a lot of time in rooms full of people with the power to say no, but not the power to say yes. You should have the decision maker in the first meeting, which often doesn't happen. There's a sort of fear culture in a lot of organisations, therefore everything has to be checked and double checked. There's a recent possibly true, possibly untrue story about a marketing director at a big client, who got quite excited about some work presented to her, and said, I'm going to stick my neck out on this one. Let's go straight to research!'

Particularly in some sectors, like packaged goods, the quality of the people you're dealing with has definitely gone down.

There are other things. I think procurement is part of this. It puts a lot of pressure on the relationship, because clients are constantly wanting to know every single penny that accounts for their fee, and how much people earn and so on. It's not a great starting point for a relationship. And I notice how marketing people try to avoid being in the procurement meetings. Because they're going to be tough and not very nice.

Great clients are, by definition, brave. If an agency believes in the power of difference, you've got to work out what are the things in this category from a communication point of view that you absolutely must have and respect, and what can you change?

There's a great story about Emma Cookson, when she was our planner on Lynx in America. The business came into the agency from McCann. The client came in to brief us, and said, we want you to work on this now, and we're going to give you the business. We want to be clear that there are four or five things that are essential in any deodorant/body spray commercial. They went through all these inputs they were certain that you had to have, like a beefy guy, and a girl admiring the guy etc.

Emma Cookson famously said, 'Look, why don't you tell me the four or five outputs you want from this advertising, and what you want the advertising to do. I'll come back to you in a couple of weeks and tell you what I think the inputs should be.

Please don't tell us what the inputs should be. Tell us what the outputs are.'

One of the most important – and slightly surprising – facets of Idea Economics is the finding that beyond reasonable doubt the route to quality is through quantity. In my interview with Balder Onarheim recounted in Chapter 1 he told me that the most successful idea makers are prolific (consistent makers of lots of ideas), and many of them are also polymaths – good at a number of different things.

In his excellent book *Cracking Creativity* Michael Michalko put it like this, 'a distinguishing characteristic of genius is immense productivity. Thomas Edison held 1,093 patents, still the record. He guaranteed productivity by giving himself and his assistants idea quotas. His own personal quota was one minor invention every ten days and a major invention every six months. Bach wrote a cantata every week, even when he was sick or exhausted. Mozart produced more than six hundred pieces of music. Einstein is best known for his paper on relativity, but he published 248 other papers. T. S. Eliot's numerous drafts of *The Waste Land* constitute a jumble of good and bad passages that eventually was turned into a masterpiece. Nature creates many possibilities and then lets the process of natural selection decide which species survive. Most do not survive; in fact, 95 percent of new species fail and die in a short period of time. In a study of 2,036 scientists throughout history, Dean Keith Simonton found that the most respected produced not only more great works, but also more 'bad' ones. Out of their massive quantity of work came quality. Geniuses produce. Period.'

I asked the Idea Economist if he could give us some numbers on this.

The Idea Economist on the Mathematics (and Desirability) of being Prolific

If we are to believe the social scientists and assume that (in round numbers) we are on the receiving end of about 1000 ideas a day, does that mean that every day a real charmer starts worming its way into our mind and takes up permanent residence?

Probably not, due to another piece of maths known as the normal distribution or the bell curve. This theory suggests that most biological populations arrange themselves with a lot of people around the middle and increasingly less numbers toward the edges. So if the average man is 5'10" tall then there are loads of men who are 5'8" or 6', quite a lot (but not so many) who are 5'6" or 6'2" but not many at all at 5'0" or 6'8". And when we get to 4'6" and 7'2" then these are rare flowers indeed.

And this is the case too with creative artefacts which are, after all, just a product of the biological phenomenon that is mental innovation. Many more ideas are in the 40% to 60% range than in the 80-100% range. And so encountering an idea that has 99.9% memorability power is not a one in a thousand (or daily) event but something much rarer than that.

Creative people are not so arrogant to think that all their ideas will be at that level, so they instinctively generate far more ideas than they will ever need. This may seem wasteful for those who don't create ideas for a living. Why not just think of the good ideas first? Unfortunately, much like extracting gold from low grade ore, you need to churn through a lot of stuff to find the value.

This is arguably the core challenge for the creative industries. If 'natural' creativity is clustered around the 50% mark then it will decay rapidly, as we saw in the previous chapter to something like 0.4% within week, and not be memorable or useful. Even 90% creativity isn't that much better. So the job of the creative professional and indeed the creative organisation is to deliver creativity that is way up in the high nineties, for only then will it have real commercial power.

Now as discussed above, if we are looking for ideas that will stick, then we need to get out to the 99% or even 99.9% mark.

As an aside, they will often re-cycle some of this 'waste' into other projects. (In the trade it is known as the 'bottom drawer').This is why the creative process can take a bit of time. If you need to generate 1000 ideas to find one great one (as Thomas Edison is alleged to have done with his light bulb), then even the hardest task master will agree that you need to be cut some slack (one and a half years in Edison's case).

Now that we can see how creativity works mathematically, what can we as individuals do about it?

As a starter, the obvious thing to do is not agonise for ages about searching for the perfect solution. Much better to generate a lot of creative ideas; dozens, hundreds even. The explanation for this (although this is not how they would put it) is just basic probability theory.

If you have one idea, then on average, it will be...er... average. As above let's call it 50%. If you have three ideas, then one of them will probably be bit above average (say 66%), and one a bit dodgy (33%).

If you keep adding in ideas then they will tend to spread out into a 'normal' distribution much like human heights do, or as if you were dropping grains of sand on the same spot.

In the previous chapter, the Idea Economist explained how the principles of Michalko's 'Possibility Thinking' work. I asked him to take us forward into 'Practicality Thinking' with some numbers.

Risk Part 2: The Idea Economist on the maths of thinking about Practicalities

THE ETERNAL DILEMMA. BE SAFE? OR BOLD?

By observation, in the world of fashion you make money (and margin) if you can persuade people to try something new. Furthermore, as you turn up the 'creative' knob the designs become more novel, stylish and valuable. But if you turn the knob too far the outfit become ridiculous and no one buys it at all. But actually it's more subtle than that. By displaying bonkers designs that no one is ever going to wear and thus seemingly making a loss, the designer is actually maintaining his/her edgy credentials in the industry and so is making an astute investment.

There is a cliff awaiting at the top of the slope up the foggy, fashion mountain. While the follies of high end fashion are just part of life's rich tapestry for most of us, the strategic choice of which end of the creative spectrum to explore is a matter of commercial effectiveness for all companies.

For example, should a conservative corporation play safe and produce its advertising in house knowing that their ads will rarely embarrass, but rarely will they shine? Or should they hire one of those scary advertising agencies and trade off the risk of a creative howler with the greater possibility of putting a blockbuster on air?

Given that most corporations don't produce their ads in-house but employ somewhat chaotic agencies, there must be some statistical advantage in working with companies who are good at playing in the chaotic zone. Can we model how this works?

Let's divide the creative spectrum into four zones so we can get some numbers going:

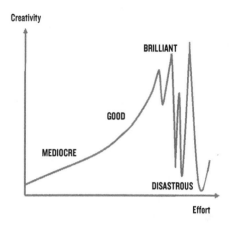

And let us assume that creative artefacts (an ad, a new product, some new packaging) when they fight it out in the market place with other ideas, do so in a 'rock, scissors, stone' sort of way. Thus Good beats Mediocre, Brilliant beats all, but notably Disastrous loses to all, including humble Mediocre.

SAFECORP

Let's then imagine two competing companies. One, a conservative company, SafeCorp – makes its own ads. It has a culture whereby 80% of its ideas are at the safe end of the spectrum and 20% at the scary end. Now, as no one quite knows how an ad will play out in the real world, half the safe ideas will be 'mediocre' and half will be 'good'. Similarly with the scary ideas. They don't know until they put them out there that half of them are stunners and half are stinkers.

Thus, if SafeCorp enters the 'rock, scissors, stone' marketing game 100 times – these might be new adverts, new promotions, new packaging, new product variants – in any given period it will arrive with the following stance:

Mediocre	Good	Brilliant	Disastrous
40	40	10	10

BOLDCORP

But matched up against SafeCorp is BoldCorp who employs an advertising agency and hence operates with 80% of its ideas up at the scary end of the spectrum. In mirror formation to its rival it comes to the contest with the following stance:

Mediocre	Good	Brilliant	Disastrous
10	10	40	40

So who wins? Well to model this mathematically, we can imagine a world where the two sets of ideas fight it out in the market place.

I will spare you the spreadsheets but totting up the scores and splitting the points for any ties, we discover that it's a bit of 'game of two halves' score draw: BoldCorp's brilliant inventiveness scores plenty of points but SafeCorp's slow and steady approach picks up points when BoldCorp gets carried away by their creative enthusiasm.

So if there is no advantage in being BoldCorp then how come 'creative' agencies are so frequently employed by corporations? It barely seems worth risking a heart bypass operation being the manager of Team Bold. Why not make life easy on yourself and sit in mid table mediocrity with Team Safe?

The answer comes from deliberately shifting yourself along the creative spectrum, in particular what happens when you push risky ideas back towards the safe zone.

Tinkering is a dirty word in creative circles, but maybe it deserves better. No artist relishes his/her work being micro-managed, pored over, and 'improved'. But in all branches of commercial creativity there are creatives who create and suits who decide – largely, it has to be said, because the suits are also the commissioners and paymasters of the work.

I asked the Idea Economist about tinkering, and his response was interesting. Apparently it CAN work well. But it's not straightforward.

Risk Part 3: The Idea Economist on the maths of the 'Creative Development Process'

Here's where the Tinkering starts!

Now a lot of creative people don't like it when others tinker with their ideas because it can turn good ideas into mediocre ideas and knock the edges off brilliant ideas to make them simply 'good'. This must be very frustrating.

However, mature creative people also know that 'tinkering' can take a high risk, scary, even disastrous idea, and turn it into a brilliant one.

This process is known as 'creative development'. It is a common phenomenon in the creative industries. And it seems to be the thing that gives the statistical edge to those corporations prepared to work hard at the creative end of the spectrum.

So rather than let their ideas appear into the market in the pattern above, let us say that with a bit of creative development – from we might call BoldDevelopCorp – the ideas appear in a new pattern.

Let us assume that after a bit of tinkering an idea still exists in its original box, but also in the box one to the left. So 'brilliant' ideas get diluted to 'good' but critically, 'disastrous' ideas suddenly become 'brilliant'! Let's also say that when you tinker with a mediocre idea it just evaporates (cries of 'if only!' from the creative dept).

Working it through, we find that after one round of tinkering we have the following distribution of ideas:

	Mediocre	Good	Brilliant	Disastrous
Start	10%	10%	40%	40%
One tinker	11%	26%	42%	21%

Now let's not pre-judge things but it is interesting to note a bulge of good/brilliant ideas starting to appear in the middle of the spectrum. This bulge becomes even more pronounced after another round of developmental tinkering in the creative laboratory:

Two tinkers	19%	36%	33%	11%

It is interesting to note some tensions here. With two rounds of developmental tinkering, the amount of good/brilliant 'quality' in the middle has risen from 50% of the mix to 69%. But while the chance of a disaster has been quartered, the possibility of mediocrity has doubled. It is perhaps this tension between disaster-fearing accountants and medioc-rity-fearing creatives – both very understandable positions – that makes managing creative businesses such a challenging task.

But of course, it is not just the creatively adventurous companies who can carry out developmental work. A more developmentally minded version of SafeCorp, namely SafeDevelopCorp can also do the same trick and achieve the following output:

	Mediocre	Good	Brilliant	Disastrous
Start	40%	40%	10%	10%
Tinker one	50%	31%	13%	6%
Tinker two	54%	29%	13%	4%

Again we see a drop in the potential for disaster matched by only a modest rise in mediocrity (this is why they are doing the research/tinkering of course). But it is in the middle of the spectrum that we find things have gone a bit stodgy for SafeDevelopmentCorp, with the good/brilliant section of the spectrum having been diluted from 50% of the mix (the same as BoldCorp incidentally) down to 42%.

But the only way to see who has the overall best strategy – no one knows nothing! – is to pitch the two approaches against each other.

	Mediocre	Good	Brilliant	Disastrous
BoldDevelopCorp	19%	36%	33%	11%
SafeDevelopmentCorp	54%	29%	13%	4%

Even by eye BoldDevelopCorp would seem to have the

advantage and running a simulation we find that it wins 63.5% of the time compared to SafeDevelopCorp on 36.5%. While Bold does let in a few howlers, its 'class is permanent, form is temporary' midfield bosses the opposition, whose determination to park the bus with a 54% zone of mediocrity proves to be a bad tactic.

So what the maths reveals is that, as the very first match up showed, if you are just going to punt your first creative thoughts out there, then there is no statistical advantage to being /bold or cautious.

But if you can create an environment where creative ideas – and in particular scary, potentially disastrous creative ideas – can be tolerated and nurtured, then with a bit of time you can face the market with a better mix of ideas than just playing in the safe zone. To spell it out, scary ideas are statistically advantageous if handled in the right way.

Just to check this conclusion we might wonder if these companies who develop their ideas are fitter beasts in the corporate jungle than their 'stick your first ideas out there' ancestors.

Intriguingly, BoldDevelopmentCorp beats simple old BoldCorp 57% of the time. But SafeDevelopmentCorp achieves what we should take as a statistical draw with SafeCorp: 49 to 51.

Working all through, the only one of the four strategies that is better than any of the others is that of BoldDevelop-mentCorp and it beats all the other three. The other three are all equal in terms of competitiveness.

So the ability to handle 'hot' ideas is both a personal skill but also an organisational capability.

There are clearly some people who seem more comfortable working with creative ideas.

And with training and experience it is possible to walk the creative high wire with a smile on your face, even if your heart is still racing.

So maybe if you haven't got this skill, acquire it or stay out of the way.

But perhaps more importantly, it reveals the statistical advantage gained by corporations who nurture productive relationships with creative people whether within their own ranks or in agencies.

It is this ability to create a developmental capability between rational, process driven corporations and scary but brilliant, creative individuals that gives these companies a competitive edge.

And that is the maths behind how companies thrive in the chaotic zone, and why tinkering – if done intelligently – pays.

But you can have too much of a good thing – including Tinkering. In the example above, Bold companies with development programmes beat similarly Bold companies without. But it does not follow that the more development the better. In fact this model suggests that too much development doesn't start to deliver diminishing returns but negative returns.

Risk Part 4: The Idea Economist on why you shouldn't tinker endlessly

Coming back to our BoldDevelopmentCorp (or BDC for short) we can create variants of it depending on how many rounds of research they partake in. These variants we can put into battle against each other (and indeed variants of SafeDevelomentCorp) until our mum drags us away from the computer and tells us to go and play in the garden with some real people.

The finding is that research helps you win, but too much research means you lose. I will spare you the tabulations but the results conform to what less mathematical practitioners would say: the optimum process is to do some pre-testing/ developmental work but not too much.

Out in the real world, knowing when it is time to go to market (because the research has to stop) is a valuable skill. And, as yet, I can offer no exact formula for that skill. It's a zone you just need to land in.

But what the maths does tell us is that the ideal set of competencies needed to 'thrive in the creative zone' are:

1. Being able to generate a preponderance of gems in the risky zone.
2. Being able to develop them sufficiently to knock off the rough edges.
3. Knowing when to stop developing before you grind them to dust.

#3 is really important. Knowing when to stop is the crucial

skill. This capability is hard to deliver, and it probably explains why the creative industries can be high margin businesses with highly paid staff.

It's not easy. But it is statistically advantageous.

MYTH: Idea Economist is an invention too new to take seriously.

REALITY: We have had Idea Economists among us for years – clever people who know how valuable ideas are, and capable of demonstrating it regularly. Not just communication planners and spin doctors. There are Idea Economists in every kind of media, in every new organisation, and across the lucrative areas of entertainment and sport.

Footnote

There is a parallel here with the investment industry – the construction and risk management of investment portfolios. People who use creative ideas for commercial ends know that you cannot and should not attempt to completely eliminate probable duds from the system. On these numbers, the winning organisation entered the market knowing that 10% of their portfolio of ideas were bound to the strong to emerge, the long-shot crazies had to be invested in too. Ultimately, if managed professionally, this would get better returns in the market than a cautious portfolio.

Advertising and fund management. As we saw earlier, maybe they're not that different really.

Chapter 7

HOW WE VALUE IDEAS

Idea Valuation in the context of Idea Economics

Idea Economics is a significant new branch of economics that works synergistically alongside Financial Economics, Market Economics and Organisational Economics, without seeking to take their place. Ideas need capital investment – the finance that can amplify a thought and turn it into a success. Ideas cannot become strong unless they have been forged in a competitive market environment. Ideas can't flourish unless they are managed in a well-organised business or organisational structure. Equally ideas will not become valuable unless they are rooted in the human reality of behavioural economics.

Above all no economic system can deliver growth and progress without creativity, and the original and innovative thinking which we call an idea. Idea Economics will emerge as the organising ecosystem of mathematics and creativity that quantifies both the inputs and outcomes of ideas

But who – then or now – is going to be charged with doing the valuation? Will the creative trust the accountant to do it? Equally pertinently, will the accountant be sympathetic to the creative's viewpoint?

Creatives and Accountants

The Idea Economist and I discussed this tension between creative people and accountants. He prepared a piece explaining what he calls the 'hard sums of commercial creativity'.

The Idea Economist on Accountants, Creatives and the Law of Diminishing Returns.

'Guttenberg vs Spielberg', or More Bangs, Less Bucks

As men have found of women, so Accountants have found of Creative People: can't live with 'em, can't live without 'em.

Businesses know they will suffer from competitive imitation and that their advantages, margins and profits will tend to zero (and below) if they do nothing. So they need to innovate or add value to keep in profit. They need to create.

But as both Lord Leverhulme and John Wanamaker are reputed to have said, 'I know that half of my advertising budget is wasted, I just don't know which half'.

Accountants know how cost cutting works. If I reduce my costs by £1,000 then, all other things being equal, my profits will go up by £1,000 (at least in the short term). Unfortunately, when I invest £1,000 in a creative product my profits might go up £1,000, or £10,000 (or any figure you like to choose) but also they could go down a £1000, £10,000 or any figure you choose.

Accountants would love to pin down creativity (and creative people) but this may just not be possible. There may just be some aspects of human behaviour where numbers don't fit. There seems to be a big cultural divide between the creative and accountancy cultures. Accountants see things in terms of A being 10% better than B, or x scoring 6.7 on a ten point scale.

Creative people are more binary than that. An idea is either a 1 or a 0 (or as they tend to put it, given they don't use numbers that often, it's either 'shit' or 'brilliant'). So if, in mathematical terms, one bunch of people are asking 'is this idea adding 10% or taking away 10%?' and the other people are asking 'is this idea a 100%-er or a 0%-er?' then they may find it hard to work together.

To take a real life example, when the new script for 'Police Academy 6' was served up, was this a 'good idea'? From a creative angle the answer surely would be a resounding 'no'.

But to fill in the back story here, the original Police Academy had been a minor hit in 1984. It had ranked No6 in box office takings that year (Ghostbusters, Beverley Hills Cop and Indiana Jones had been the big smashes) and to this day is given a credible score of 6.2 out of 10 by the IMDb community. (By comparison, Footloose, the film it just beat at the box office, scores 5.9). And its lead Steve Guttenberg has found paid work ever since.

The producers then decided to churn out one Police Academy film per year for the next five years. Again taking the IMDb ratings as a sign of creative quality they scored as follows:

Police Academy 1	6.2
Police Academy 2	4.9
Police Academy 3	4.3
Police Academy 4	3.9
Police Academy 5	3.3

Pretty easy therefore to predict that Police Academy 6 was going to be a stinker. And sure enough it scored 3.2.

However, the accountants were watching another set of numbers, the box office takings.

Police Academy 1	$81 million
Police Academy 2	$56
Police Academy 3	$44
Police Academy 4	$28
Police Academy 5	$19

Now this data supports the creative people's belief that the idea had well and truly been squeezed dry. But the accountants didn't look at it that way. They saw another pattern.

Police Academy 1	$81 million	
Police Academy 2	$56	−28%
Police Academy 3	$44	−21%
Police Academy 4	$28	−38%
Police Academy 5	$19	−30%

So, the question they asked themselves was not 'is it a good idea', but could they make Police Academy 6 cheaply enough that it would still be in profit assuming it takes 30 to 40% less (allowing for a little margin for error) than Police Academy 5 i.e. about $11.5 million?

They found some people who could.

And when it did indeed take $12 million dollars they (at least) were happy. It was a good idea!

(There is a sorry end to this tale. Five years later, they tried to make Police Academy 7, presumably thinking that it would gross around $8million. It didn't even make $1m! Perhaps the decay rate wasn't 30% per film but 30% per year).

So even if making Police Academy 6 may be a creative exercise, to an accountant it is not a risky one. For the accountant the real risk is in making Police Academy 1. However, and this is where it gets interesting, the accountant knows (remember Episode 7), at some point he will need to walk out onto the suspension bridge of disbelief with this scary creative visionary, and genuinely innovate if he is going to stay in the film business.

Creative people look at the same thing rather differently. On the one hand making episode 2, 3 or whatever is quite good fun and certainly pays the bills. However they know they will never get the same rush from doing this as shooting an original hit.

Steven Spielberg has made a few sequels in his time and he seems to be incapable of resisting the laws of creative gravity as anyone else, whether in the Jurassic Park franchise or the Indiana Jones series. However, what is striking about Steven Spielberg is that he seems to strongly favour making completely new films rather than churn out a franchise.

He is happy to try his hand at thrillers, historical dramas, romantic dramas, sci-fi mysteries, action adventure.

As a man who has created vast amounts of money for his backers perhaps he has earned the right to be such a creative adventurer. But it is one hell of a ride for the accountants. The one thing he doesn't do is give you 'approximately minus 30%'.

If there is a pattern to his films then a big hit seems to be followed by a big flop with a drop in box office of around –80% (compared to the churning out the franchise decay rate of –30%). But then he seems to return to form again.

Once, he broke out of this pattern and had two big hits in a row (Raiders of the Lost Ark followed by ET). Then, (instead of doing what the accountants suggested and making "ET – the Return", perhaps) he made the Color Purple (–80%) followed by Empire of the Sun (down 80% even on the Color Purple!). Perhaps he was creatively exhausted by the two big hits?

If you try to work out what genres he reliably delivers on then your forensic accounting skills may not work either. Think he's good at Family Favourites then surely a film based on Peter Pan and Pirate must be a safe bet? But no, you get Hook (only 9% on the Jawsometer). Sci-fi themes looks good with Close Encounters and ET but then he gives you Artificial Intelligence (also 9%).

But give up on him on sci-fi and he will come back with War of the Worlds, his biggest hit of the 00's. And if you think he's always been rubbish at World War II movies

(Empire of the Sun) then he may well confound you with Schindler's List, and then follow it up with Saving Private Ryan.

All we know is that Spielberg is a creative genius. But when his genius will strike is anybody's guess.

Ultimately there is a tension here. Accountants would prefer to keep making more of the same as long as it is 'only' 30% worse. Creative people would like to keep making truly original things even if 'only' a few of them are hits.

But both need each other. The accountants need the breakthrough innovation, the creatives need the venture capital. The key thing that makes the difference is whether they can work together or not...

Valuable Ideas

Of course, not all ideas are valuable. Sadly many lack the potential to deliver at all. Others are promising, but not strong enough when executed. It is the **valuable ideas** that we need to achieve change and growth.

We have the means to value ideas, but seldom get beyond using value judgements. We frequently describe ideas as good, big, powerful, exciting, brilliant etc. To use Idea Economics we need to apply the appropriate mathematics. In short we need numbers to quantify how much an idea is worth. We also need the formulae, criteria, weightings and and structured analysis to get to those numbers. Not all these influencing factors will be positive. Risk and jeopardy also have to be taken into consideration in the valuation process.

The concept is not unfamiliar. For instance, arithmetic is regularly applied to every branch of sport and all the arts.

The book is populated with plenty of mathematical formulae to help value complete ideas and to apply a weighting to the constituents and characteristics of them (eg original, unique, difficult to imitate, versatile, long-lasting etc).

Implicit in the whole exercise is the principle of comparability. The value of anything is relative to the value of things to which it can be compared. Nearly all ideas, whether they are the result of innovation, imagination, making creative connections, or some combination of the three, emerge from a competitive process.

Idea generation and development are fundamentally important, but idea selection is crucial. And to select a winner, there have to have other potential winners to choose from. This naturally applies whether we are selecting ideas internally, or if other people – a client, a potential partner, buyers, consumers – are making the selection. In both cases, selection may be subject to research or some kind of scientific enquiry.

Effectiveness Awards have formalised Idea Valuation in the marketing world

In the marketing and advertising field where I work, Effectiveness Awards have recognised marketplace success since 1968, initially in the US, but now in all major markets. In recent years, papers have been accompanied with detailed econometric supporting evidence – so quantifying just how valuable the garlanded ideas have been. My 'day job' for many years has centred on the advertising pitch – a process which firmly established the principle that ideas are not just the tie-breaker for choosing a winning agency. In the majority of cases, the client goes to pitch in pursuit of an idea that will hopefully be valuable for their business.

A classic success story – 'Try Something New Today'

A particularly successful idea was Sainsbury's famous 'Try Something New Today' campaign, featuring celebrity chef, Jamie Oliver, launched in 2004. Econometrics showed that it actually achieved £2.5bn in incremental revenue over three years, an increase of around 5%. What is truly remarkable is that Sainsbury's ad agency AMV BBDO had actually been tasked with achieving that very sales lift: £2.5bn. So this was an idea that was pre-valued, commissioned and implemented extremely successfully.

At the time, customer satisfaction was low, sales were dropping and Sainsbury's competitors were gaining market share. Instead of pursuing an acquisition strategy – aiming to win customers from other supermarkets (Tesco, Asda etc) Sainsbury's, the team at AMV BBDO looked at what this £2.5 billion sales target would mean for a single basket of groceries.

How much would each existing customer need to spend additionally in order to achieve the £2.5 billion in sales? The calculation revealed that each Sainsbury's grocery shopper would need to spend an additional £1.14 each time they visited the store.

Research revealed that a significant percentage of Sainsbury's customers habitually shopped on autopilot. The agency described it as 'sleep shopping'. Over the course of a month on their various visits to store, they basically bought the same basket of groceries. Customers weren't thinking laterally. They weren't looking for new ingredients for new recipes. The communications challenge was to change the mindset in order to bring about the behavioural change needed to deliver the incremental average £1.14 spend.

The agency's 'valuable idea' was to get Jamie Oliver – as a trusted food authority and established Sainsbury's spokesperson – to talk about sleep shopping. 'There are a million meals to choose from, so why eat the same thing over and over again? Why not try something new?'

The 'Try Something New Today' campaign was launched with a 40-second TVC, followed by shorter spots, and also advertising in magazines, on the radio, in newspapers, and before & after drama series on TV. The strategy wasn't to recommend exotic ingredients or haute cuisine. Oliver was just suggesting that customers should think beyond their normal shopping list – a different sauce, a different sandwich filling. In the first spot of the 'Try Something New Today' campaign, Oliver showed how you could bring Spaghetti Bolognese to life, just by adding a little nutmeg. The next week, sales of nutmeg went up from 1400 jars of nutmeg to 6,000.

Over 200 million recipes were distributed to customers

in-store. Sales of the ingredients in Oliver's recipes increased, but sales of many other items increased as well, and as well as bringing about behavioural change among existing customers, the campaign attracted new customers.

The 'Try Something New Today' campaign was simple but smart and it had a massive impact for Sainsbury's. And deservedly won the IPA Gold Effectiveness Award for integration in 2008

Idea Valuation – the recommended approach

The Sainsbury case history was written up and awarded ten years ago, but we are some way away from having a recognised Idea Valuator system, despite the fact that many people in worlds as diverse as of brands, entertainment and politics, devote much of their time striving to calculate the value of strategies, scripts, slogans, concepts etc.

To introduce money into the methodologies for evaluating ideas suggested by the idea Economist, we need an approach to valuation which tells us what an idea is worth now, and what the future earning potential of that idea might be. Having a viable Idea Valuator system is a crucial aspect of Idea Economics. So how might we do this? Here are some of the people trying to perform the function of Idea Valuation:

(in alphabetical order)
Advertising agencies
Brand valuation businesses

Business plan writers
Case study writers
Commissioning editors
Corporate strategy departments
Data analytic businesses
Econometricians
Historians
Hollywood producers
Journalists
Manifesto writers
Market research companies
Marketing directors
Party leaders
Political strategists
Procurement departments
Professional critics
Strategy consultants

Some of these offer only qualitative assessments (It's a big idea. It's a guaranteed hit. It's a winning message). Others offer more numerical assessments (It delivered £10m in incremental sales. It will go on to take $200 million at the box office. Or it gave us a 3% swing in key marginals).

Can all these people see the whole wood here, or just the individual valuation tree that they are barking up? Indeed, to pick up on the 'comparability' issue, can we find some broad patterns or even a formula to show how to calculate the value of *any* idea in *any* category?

Idea Valuation in action

Do we have ways and means to calculate and compare the value of any tree in any wood?

In terms of cutting through the tangled undergrowth of the valuation forests a good place to start is to understand that there are four stages where the value of an idea might be professionally discussed:

1. Targeted value. What is our objective here? What do we need the idea to be worth for it to be worth commissioning? With Idea Economics we can calculate in advance the value we need, as well as measuring the actual and potential value of delivered ideas. Targeted value will need to take account of **cost** (what will it cost us to develop/implement the idea against the anticipated returns?), **market** (what's out there now?) and **income** (how much is the idea going to make us over time?)

2. When we are looking at contending ideas......Judged value. What do we think (estimate? guess?) that this particular idea is worth? When we compare ideas, which one do we judge to be the most valuable?

3. Anticipated value. Before we press Go (or as it is first appearing in market) how much value do we think this idea is going to end up having?

4. Achieved value. Totting it all up, after the event (and trying to separate out all the other contributory factors in the sales) how much was the idea worth to us?

For example, in an advertising pitch:

1. The **targeted** figure (let's say £23m) might be the master benchmark, calculated as the aggregate of incremental profitable sales and increased brand value over three years.

2. In terms of **judged** value, is the winning idea (now we've chosen it, and can properly evaluate it) as potentially valuable as we hoped for (the £23m)?

3. Now that it's been executed and ready to roll, is its **anticipated** value worth more, less or about the same?

4. Three years into the campaign, what is the **achieved** value? How are the sales figures and brand value looking? Did we achieve our goal?

Using this framework there would appear to be major industries – and indeed skilled practitioners with refined craft methods – trying to get precise answers to these questions all along the Value Path*. For example, in the marketing trade:

1. Calculating **targeted** value: strategy consultants, business plan writers, corporate strategy departments, market planners, brand strategists.

2. Calculating **judged** value: advertising agencies, marketing directors, procurement departments.

---

the sheer number and ferocity of the perils along this path, not to mention the jostling of so many idea-rivals along it, may explain that with Ideas, many need to be called so that a few are chosen. It's a dense, dark jungle out there, not a leafy, sunny forest. Almost all ideas that are born will die before they get to see the light of day. It's nature's way.

3. Calculating **anticipated** value. Market research companies, analytic businesses, professional critics.
4. Calculating **achieved** value. Econometricians, brand valuation businesses, case study writers, historians.

We need to establish an idea valuation structure on the lines of the various brand valuation formulae, but on a much less complicated basis.

The formula must be flexible to embrace ideas for a variety of applications – brand ideas, comms ideas, innovation ideas, corporate ideas and so forth. Criteria will vary according to application, but they will be based on the value determinants listed in Chapter 5.

Now we can start the valuation process.

We can put a value on each idea we are looking for – on the principle of 'the idea we are looking for will be worth around £23m'.

We then establish a five point scale of value from, say, A = the one in a hundred idea that could be worth £50m, to E = a run of the mill idea that is probably not worth pursuing.

And a 10-1 scale of being ready to roll from 10 = implement tomorrow to 1 = interesting, but half-formed.

Which enables us to value ideas from concept to execution in terms of say a progression from A1 x £50m through to a pretty satisfactory B10 x £20m.

Key principles are:

- Brief the idea precisely.
- Or devise a post hoc brief for a spontaneous idea.

HOW WE VALUE IDEAS

- Calculate in advance what the idea we want needs to be worth.
- Value the idea throughout its development (the four stage process).

Outside exposure is critical. As we have seen earlier, ideas are similar to jokes and gifts. Whatever we think about our idea (or joke or gift), it is of extremely little value if it fails to excite and delight whoever it has been designed to receive or buy it. On any project, it is important that we come up with working definitions and ready reckoners of:

- Impact
- Excitement
- Originality
- Durability ('legs')

The M&C Saatchi Initiative

In 2015 M&C Saatchi pulled off a spectacular coup de theatre to celebrate the agency's 20th birthday. They threw a magnificent party for 500 or so guests in the Victoria and Albert Museum, with speeches about the art. Then half way through proceedings they persuaded all their guests to walk across the way to the Science Museum. Even more guests. Even more champagne. More speeches – this time about the tension between art and science. Even more amazing – they transported the cloakroom, and not a coat or briefcase was lost!

Apart from the considerable feat of sustaining the most

dramatic agency breakaway for two decades, why did they go to all this effort? Here's what Margareta Pagano of *The Independent* wrote at the time, 'M&C Saatchi has created a new formula and think-tank, the Saatchi Institute, to help resolve the war between the Maths Men and the Mad Men of advertising'.

David Kershaw, chief executive of M&C Saatchi, said: 'There's a war raging between the artists and the scientists in advertising today – the Maths Men versus the Mad Men; between so-called fluffy, arty creatives and the highly-targeted precision data scientists. We want to show both are important but, without the message, marketing is nothing.'

He added: 'Working with the London Business School, we have devised a new formula... which has been tested with many of the world's biggest brands and will be as important to advertising as E = mc2 was to the world of physics.'

The formula:

$$y = ae^{k\frac{\lambda}{\xi}}$$

Was the brainchild of Tim Duffy, group chairman, M&C Saatchi UK. He said, 'The creativity for which Charles Saatchi and Jeremy Sinclair are famous has always been a mystery to me. There is no equation for measuring it. What can be measured is the relationship between creativity and science in a way that allows marketing directors to minimise waste. This is not about trying to create the perfect ad but getting the right combination between art and science. One without the other doesn't work.'

Essentially I believe M&C Saatchi were looking, like me, for a 'Valuator' to put a value on ideas, and chose the tension between art and science as their start point.

Tim and I have discussed the initiative at length, because the creative development process, how it is working, and how each side contributes to it is the key issue on which we advise, armed with the evidence. Our most interesting and challenging assignments are when a client asks us to help them achieve significantly enhanced creativity. I also believe, based on our extensive experience of working with global and UK clients, that this kind of determination will yield positive results, once internal mind-sets change, and quality agencies have been identified and engaged. It is also a far better idea than simply bullying six agencies to come up with spec creative – which I won't do any more, unless the client is prepared to pay for it.

I wrote as follows to Tim, 'Is this quest for 'breakthrough creativity' somehow old-fashioned in this digital era? In his introductory speech at the event Lord Saatchi said, 'advertising is not about seducing people, it's about being there'. But is he right? It's about both isn't it? Take political advertising, about which you guys know a thing or two. Would it have been enough in April [the 2015 General Election] to stick up lots of 48 sheets saying Vote Conservative? That would have fulfilled the 'being there' part of the deal. But of course that wouldn't have been enough. Just as *Labour isn't working* helped to bring Thatcher to power, Miliband in Salmond's top pocket was the visualisation of a creative insight that seduced floating voters and helped achieve the unachievable – a Conservative majority.

Is Art vs Science really the debate? Is a single formula enough? I'm convinced most clients will react by asking how the application of the formula can bring THEM better ads and better ROI. I suppose I am still searching for a script for an elevator conversation that starts with the client saying, 'What's this Holy Grail that M&C have come up with? That's your challenge, I believe. But it's also a challenge for us introducers and recommenders. Perhaps the best way to explain your Holy Grail is to give examples of unholy messes created by getting that balance between Art and Science horribly wrong.'

There's one thing I have learned from writing business books which I wish I'd known years ago. It's that the best way to explain a new idea, a new campaign, or a new way of doing something is often to demonstrate how old ideas, previous campaigns or default settings don't work any more – or at least as well.

At this point I asked the Idea Economist what he thought about formulae.

The Idea Economist on the problem with complicated formulae

It seems counterproductive to combine all available measures into one uber-equation. For example, the world of physics summarises how light waves 'work' thus:

$$
\begin{aligned}
I &\equiv \frac{1}{c^2}\frac{\partial^2}{\partial t^2}\int_{-\infty}^{\infty} e_\mu \varepsilon_{\mu\alpha}(\omega) E_\alpha(\mathbf{r},\omega)\exp(-i\omega t)\,d\omega \\
&= -\int_{-\infty}^{\infty}\frac{\omega^2 n^2(\omega)}{c^2}\underbrace{\frac{1}{2}\sum_{\omega_\sigma\geq 0}[\mathbf{E}_{\omega_\sigma}(\mathbf{r},\omega-\omega_\sigma)+\mathbf{E}^*_{\omega_\sigma}(\mathbf{r},-\omega-\omega_\sigma)]}_{\text{quasimonochromatic form of } \mathbf{E}(\mathbf{r},\omega)}\exp(-i\omega t)\,d\omega \\
&= \{\text{denote } \omega^2\varepsilon(\omega)/c^2 \equiv \omega^2 n_0^2(\omega)/c^2 \equiv k^2(\omega)\} \\
&= -\frac{1}{2}\sum_{\omega_\sigma\geq 0}\int_{-\infty}^{\infty} k^2(\omega)[\mathbf{E}_{\omega_\sigma}(\mathbf{r},\omega-\omega_\sigma)+\mathbf{E}^*_{\omega_\sigma}(\mathbf{r},-\omega-\omega_\sigma)]\exp(-i\omega t)\,d\omega. \\
&= -\frac{1}{2}\sum_{\omega_\sigma\geq 0}\int_{-\infty}^{\infty} k^2(\omega)\mathbf{E}_{\omega_\sigma}(\mathbf{r},\omega-\omega_\sigma)\exp(-i\omega t)\,d\omega + \text{c.c.}
\end{aligned}
$$

I hope that helped.

But before you snigger at the opacity of physicists explaining light, here is an economist showing how Marxism "works":

$$
\frac{dp}{dt}=\frac{(1+j)\left(\frac{dx}{dt}\right)-x\left(\frac{d}{dt}\right)(1+j)}{(1+j)^2} \qquad =\frac{(1+j)\left(\frac{dx}{dt}\right)-x\left(\frac{dj}{dt}\right)}{(1+j)^2}
$$

As $p=\dfrac{x}{1+j}$, solving it for x we get $x=p(1+j)$ and putting it in place of x.

$$
\begin{aligned}
\frac{dp}{dt} &=\frac{(1+j)\left(\frac{dx}{dt}\right)-p(1+j)\left(\frac{dj}{dt}\right)}{(1+j)^2} \qquad =\frac{1+j\left(\frac{dx}{dt}\right)}{(1+j)^2}-\frac{p(1+j)\left(\frac{dj}{dt}\right)}{(1+j)^2} \\
&=\frac{1}{(1+j)}\left(\frac{dx}{dt}\right)-\frac{1}{(1+j)}(p)\left(\frac{dj}{dt}\right)=\frac{1}{1+j}\left[\frac{dx}{dt}-p\left(\frac{dj}{dt}\right)\right]
\end{aligned}
$$

Good luck with explaining that to the proletariat, comrade.

But this Chapter is about the value of ideas and how we go about the calculations, so I persuaded the Idea Economist to come out from behind his equations.

The Idea Economist on valuing ideas

If we are going to write a formula that explains how ideas 'work' (i.e. create value) then maybe we need to set ourselves a more user-friendly standard.

So how about $E=MC^2$ from Albert Einstein, mentioned by David Kershaw of M&C Saatchi?

This simple equation shows how nuclear bombs work. They convert a small mass into a huge amount of energy because – as we all know – light is very fast, and because we also know that the square of a large number must be huge. Genius.

Can we combine just three factors to determine how much of a big bang an **idea** makes?

Here is our first stab. If we consider just:

1. How many people were reached (the raw head count)
2. How much effect per head (the average value of each sale, if you like)
3. How long the effect lasts (the repeat purchase rate, if you like)

Then all we need to know about an idea is how many, how much and how long. The combination of these three effects is the total effect.

So let us use # for how many reached, £ for the average sale value and T for how long the effect lasts, then multiply them to get V for the value of the idea:

$V = \# \times £ \times T$

(or $V = \# \times € \times T$ if you are in the Euro zone).

After Albert, it's clearly the done thing to take out all the multiply signs:

$$V = \#£T$$

Or HET for short.

This sounds like a memorable valuation formula in the making, so I asked the Idea Economist to develop it.

The Idea Economist on HET

So ... HET. And indeed, as they say in the North of England 'how het up are we about this, pet?'. Or 'how heated up are we,' to translate. Which in our world is often put more simply as how 'hot' is this idea? Or, paradoxically, 'how cool is this!?'.

The maths within HET claims that the Value of an(y) idea can be calculated by considering how many people, to what average effect and over what time. This defines its #£Tness.

This is a bold claim: the value of any idea in any category can theoretically be calculated and compared to any other idea if you can measure just those three quantities.

For example in his exhaustive and exhausting* history book **Ideas: from Fire to Freud,** Peter Watson selects his three most important ideas:

- The idea of the soul
- The idea of Europe
- The idea of the scientific experiment

HOW MANY PEOPLE?

DISTINCTIVENESS. SHAREABILITY. UNIVERSALITY. INTERNATIONALNESS. VERSATILITY. NEWS-WORTHINESS.

£ HOW MUCH EFFECT PER HEAD?

EXCITEMENT. IMPACT. MEANINGFULNESS. RESONANCE. USEFULNESS. BUZZ. ACTION TRIGGERING. COMPETIVENESS.

Now he is talking about 'important ideas', not 'ideas with the highest commercial value'. But the way he tells the tale, each of these ideas were encountered by many people (#) who were greatly affected (£), leading to profound and lasting (T) changes across the entire world. Each had massive #£Tness and hence each was of huge value to the world.

If you were prepared to attach a value to the #,£ and T for each, you could calculate which was the biggest idea ever. Difficult but not impossible, to a scientist. And if the very

---

* *Exhausting? For example, when he indexes the thousand or so ideas in his book, there are 77 entries beginning with A and even 4 beginning with Z: Zealots, zero, zoology and Zoroastrianism.*

idea of bringing objective Science to subjective History offends those in the Arts faculty, as someone who was taught the History of Science at University, you guys started it...

Coming back to the 21st Century, if we examine the concepts that idea valuers use in their specialised fields we find that they seem to fall into the three buckets of the #£T equation.

T HOW LONG WILL THE EFFECT LAST?

MEMORABILITY. UNIQUENESS. STICKINESS. DEVELOPMENT POTENTIAL. SUSTAINABILITY. CULTURAL RESONANCE.

Now, in offering our universal valuation formula of V=#£T we are not suggesting that any particular way of estimating, predicting or tallying up the value of an idea is the right one. Any might be good ways of getting to an estimate or even the actuals of the higher order effects of #,£ and T.

Rather, our goals are to create 'proof of value' and idea-to-idea 'comparability'. These are our big ambitions.

To achieve this we must come back to the daily task of working with ideas and describing their value to each other and especially to our market-, financial- and organisationally-oriented economic cousins.

Here the formula helps us de-compose 'Big ideas', 'Guaranteed hits' and all the chutzpah of our trade into three components of value that we know are the components of how ideas work. And critically, we now have a non-complex formula that makes sense to all-comers.

So for example:

- 'Try Something New Today' gets **all** Sainsburys customers, to buy a little **extra**, as a new **habit**. H#T= V. It's a big idea.
- The 'Star Wars' re-boot with a young female protagonist is about a **universal** hero who gets people **back in** the multiplexes and establishes a new **franchise** for them to follow. H#T= V. It's a hit.

Our claim is that ideas, are not soft and elusive, but have a definable economic value that, with sufficient effort, can be quantified. Ideas have economic value that is created in a structured way. This can be demanded by commissioners, judged, anticipated and indeed **calculated** by experts.

Markets, money and organisations may have hard, measurable, economic edges. But so too do the seemingly ephemeral Ideas that sit in the fourth cylinder of the growth engine.

Furthermore, as we have argued throughout this book, we believe it is the ideas that create the big bangs that fuel the other three cylinders.

$$E = MC^2 \qquad V_I = \#£T$$

The Derek Sivers version

American entrepreneur Derek Sivers (the founder of CD Baby and author of *Anything You Want*) has this on his website:

'Ideas are just a multiplier of execution.'

It's so funny when I hear people being so protective of ideas. People who want me to sign an NDA to tell me the simplest idea.

To me, ideas are worth nothing unless executed. They are just a multiplier. Execution is worth millions.

Explanation:

AWFUL IDEA	= -1
WEAK IDEA	= 1
SO-SO IDEA	= 5
GOOD IDEA	= 10
GREAT IDEA	= 15
BRILLIANT IDEA	= 20

NO EXECUTION	= $1
WEAK EXECUTION	= $1000
SO-SO EXECUTION	= $10,000
GOOD EXECUTION	= $100,000
GREAT EXECUTION	= $1,000,000
BRILLIANT EXECUTION	= $10,000,000

To make a business, you need to multiply the two.

The most brilliant idea, with no execution, is worth $20.

The most brilliant idea takes great execution to be worth $20,000,000.

That's why I don't want to hear people's ideas.

I'm not interested until I see their execution.

It's a bit extreme – and I certainly don't buy his main point about ideas in development being worthless. But he is surely right about the huge gap in value between great ideas and the rest.

MYTH: There are no valid mechanisms for valuing ideas in execution – let alone at the briefing, concept or development stages. 'Ideas are a dime a dozen', people say, and 'The real value lies in executing an idea'.

REALITY: Once we accept that ideas are potentially and actually valuable, there is no reason why a valuation system in parallel with brand valuation cannot be developed and accepted. Given a robust set of criteria for determining the value of ideas, the potential value of an idea can be calculated.

Chapter 8

USING YOUR IDEA BRAIN TO THE FULL

Tips and Tools to help us use our Idea Brain and become Creative Contributors

One of my ambitions for this book is to take readers who are probably over-modest about their creative skills, and give them the confidence to use a precious gift we are all born with, which I call *The Idea Brain.* In the book there are numerous tips and exercises explaining how to turn your Idea Brain on and off. Also when, where and how to use it. The Idea Brain is wonderfully versatile. It can import new inputs, retrieve stuff that is already stored there, analyse, connect and process, and of course output. What it cannot cope with is multi-tasking. Scientists say that we can manage sequentially, but not literally simultaneously!

So attempts to force-feed too much information are destined to fail. As is asking people to import, retrieve and output all at the same time. In the end the Idea Brain simply ignores new inputs and shuts down. But used with skill and good technique, the Idea Brain is a very powerful tool.

But it helps to know some tips and tricks of the trade as well. My job for 30 years has involved managing advertising pitches – one of the most highly charged examples of

Idea Economics in action. Before writing the book I also extensively researched idea generation techniques across innovation and commercial creativity, and interviewed highly successful idea people. *The Very Idea* is peppered with invaluable tips. They are just a selection. There are no right and wrong ways. Some will work for us better than others. We can also work out for ourselves new and improved methods of firing up our Idea Brain and getting the most out of it. As Oscar Wilde said, 'you can't use up creativity. The more you use, the more you have'.

Here are suggestions from both experts I interviewed and authors of relevant books. Further on, I will aggregate some of these ideas with ones of my own. I have asked Tim Cordell to illustrate some of the key tips.

DAVID OGILVY (LEGENDARY ADMAN)

- If at first you don't succeed, don't try exactly the same thing again

BALDER ONARHEIM (PROFESSOR OF NEURO-CREATIVITY)

- Ideas take up a lot of working memory. Write them down immediately in the parking lot. Don't let the brain be overloaded
- Intense physicality can stimulate creativity
- Use sleep as a structured method
- Use daydreaming as a technique
- Analyse your dreams
- Breathe deeply

- Take down your normal filtering system

TONY CRABBE (AUTHOR OF BUSY)

- Turn off the autopilot before you do anything else
- Strategic snoozing
- Defocus and get the obvious out of your head
- Turn off the autopilot

HEATHER ANDREWS OF NEURO-INSIGHT

- Looking out of the window and day-dreaming is a good way to change focus, but beware of walking through a doorway. It can have a short-term on the memory

DAVE BUONAGUIDI (CREATIVE DIRECTOR)

- The brain is a creative muscle, and it doesn't get flexed enough

DAVID DROGA (CREATIVE DIRECTOR

- Allow ideas to creep up on you
- Use a sheet of A3 with boxes to capture up to 100 ideas

SIDSE BORDEL (DESIGNER)

- Introduce constraints. Then take them away
- Reframe problems

DANIEL ROSENFELD (MUSICIAN & MAGICIAN)

- Calm down your brain with an activity (he practices juggling!)
- Interrupt yourself
- See the funny side. Introduce some humour

LUCAS PEON (CREATIVE DIRECTOR)

- Leave your prejudices at the door
- Trust your instincts
- Distil
- If you're stuck, go back to the beginning
- Don't criticise or dismiss ideas or work when they are still warm
- Take risks
- It's OK to get distracted
- Further into the tunnel you go, the better the ideas get

MARK EARLS (PSYCHOLOGIST)

- Borrow. Steal (he quotes Grayson Perry, 'originality is someone's short memory')
- Divergent thinking model: start from the inside
- Have I seen this before?
- Creative disruption
- Schumpeter: 'value lies not in the idea, but in doing something with it'
- Small interventions make a big difference
- You don't have to get it all right NOW
- Social media is like the Nile – don't drink straight out of it
- Smart doesn't equal creative

GRAHAM KERR (CREATIVE DIRECTOR)

- Ideas come from people watching
- Ideas don't come at your desk
- Get in the zone and you can think very fast

- Creating an idea and judging are two different things – don't try and judge while you are creating

JIM STENGEL

- Get into the habit of taking strenuous exercise regularly (he plays competitive tennis)
- And using it as a break from ideation
- Your brain will be much livelier afterwards

MARTIN RILEY (MARKETING DIRECTOR)

- Idea starts as a flash – sleep on it, wake up with it, deepen it
- Don't let the noise of other people's opinions drown your own
- Make sure you have lots of ideas every day
- Ideas need to be mad (quoting Einstein)

50 tips for unlocking your Idea Brain, and using it

MEET YOUR IDEA BRAIN

We all have the ability to come up with ideas. Our brain can be seen to have five distinct functions:

- **Inputting new things**. (Could be a proper brief. Could be new data or numbers. Could be an insight. Could be just an unconscious stimulus, ie something we've seen, heard or experienced). This is the vital + button, from the calculator metaphor in chapter 5.
- **Storage** – incredible capacity, but not always beautifully filed (the ÷ button)

- **Making connections** – combining stored things with stored things, and new things with stored things (the x go forth and multiply button)
- **Composing** – analysing and using the connections – the activity we most closely and consciously control in this process (the crafting, editing – button)
- **Outputting** – in this case, ideas (what it results in when we press =)

Tips for using your Idea Brain

I. UNDERSTAND YOUR AUTOPILOT SETTING

- Never forget how much of the time you are on autopilot or cruise control. It could be 80% of your waking hours
- Recognise that it is your default behaviour
- Work out how you use autopilot + when it helps, and when it stops you doing important things like thinking

2. DISENGAGE AUTOPILOT BEFORE YOU WANT TO COME UP WITH IDEAS

- Make a conscious effort to snap into action, disengage autopilot, and take over the controls
- Many people find that taking a deep breath acts as an effective physical mnemonic for this and other important setting changes
- Or consciously change your breathing pattern

3. AND REMEMBER IDEAS DON'T NORMALLY COME AT YOUR DESK

- Be as geographically neutral as you can
- If necessary, be prepared to move around

4. SWITCH ON THE IDEA BRAIN

- Shut your eyes. Imagine you are waking from sleep. Then open them again
- Breathe deeply
- Feel that you're opening your Idea Brain as well
- Concentrate
- Get in the zone as fast as possible
- But don't try too hard to get it all right NOW

5. FOCUS ON THE PROBLEM

- Focus on the problem or challenge
- Make sure you have understood it exactly right
- Allow thoughts to come into your head
- Get used to doing it, and make it a routine
- Don't try and concentrate for too long. Get used to short, sharp, intense shifts

6. SWITCH OFF THE IDEA BRAIN WHEN YOU NEED TO

- Have confidence in the 'on and off switch'
- Defocus – it's a mistake to spend too much time in full focus
- Answer a question
- Take a call
- Look away
- Take a walk. Go to the loo. Get a tea or coffee
- If you are looking at a screen, turn instead to pencil and paper. Or vice versa
- Watch sport on TV, listen to music, eat, work out, hot tennis, walk

- Have lunch
- Take the occasional day off
- Relax for a while, **but don't default to autopilot** if you are going to need your Idea Brain again soon
- But sometimes you may need to empty your brain – prior to a fresh start

7. THEN SWITCH IT ON AGAIN

- As above
- Blink. Breathe deeply
- Open the Idea Brain
- Concentrate
- Remind yourself of the exact challenge
- Renew the inputs, if necessary
- THEN give yourself a limited time (one hour max) to unlock your brain and see what's in there!

8. HAVE A CONVERSATION WITH YOURSELF

What do I think about that?

- Don't feel that you're behaving oddly!
- Literally talk to yourself, ask yourself questions, and if necessary have a debate
- It's a rehearsal for sharing ideas further down the line
- Use these conversations to make sure you have understood the challenge, the complexities of the problem, and mastered the brief
- Try to leave your prejudices behind – and get the obvious out of your head
- Trust your instincts

9. ON CAR JOURNEYS, TURN OFF THE RADIO / MUSIC AND REHEARSE IDEAS, ARGUMENTS, SPEECHES ETC

- One of my favourite thought starting ploys
- Not just talking to yourself, trying out ideas aloud

10. IF YOU'RE NOT MAKING PROGRESS, STAND UP, RELAX, SHAKE ARMS AND HANDS VIGOROUSLY

11. STRETCH TILL IT HURTS OR TAKE STRENUOUS EXERCISE

- And return to idea-making afterwards

12. SHUT YOUR EYES, AND OPEN THEM

- Not just a blink
- A conscious device to stimulate brain activity

13. DON'T CONFINE YOURELF TO WORDS ON PAPER. OPEN YOURSELF TO THE MOST POTENT STIMULI

- Some you seek actively
- Others come to you
- Think deeply
- Remember the power of synaesthesia
    - More impact the more senses are involved
    - Don't just read words
    - And if you're briefing, remember how it works much better with visuals, sound, smell, touch etc – and that video beats a still

14. LOOK OUT OF THE WINDOW

- Start by opening the curtains/blinds
- Look out. Listen
- Let the sights, sounds, smells come in
- It's quite OK to get distracted
- You will refocus soon enough

15. STEP THROUGH A DOOR

- Walk outside
- Take it all in
- Go where your imagination takes you
- BUT remember that it will take a while to refocus

16. THE IDEA BRAIN IS A MUSCLE. EXERCISE IT. TRAIN IT. BUILD IT UP. SEE HOW MUCH YOU CAN GET OUT OF IT

- **Stretch yourself**
- To use the Idea Brain well, we follow the same pattern as with any other learned skill
- The brain benefits from being exercised and flexed
- Understand its capability, and be ambitious to practice new drills and improve
- The brain is like the technology we buy (cars, smartphones, cameras). We only use a fraction of the functionality
- We need to devise exercises to train the idea brain and use more of its capability

17. USE GUT FEEL. IT IS AS IMPORTANT AS LOGIC

- **Think AND Feel**
- Your Idea Brain doesn't work in a linear way
- It does the connecting itself – that's the beauty of it!

18. WRITE DOWN AS MUCH AS POSSIBLE

- Some ideas come – and go! – so fast you need to capture them immediately
- Write everything down to clear the working memory. See it as a parking lot. Don't over-analyse
- Record valuable ideas before they disappear
- Clear the working memory
- Make room for more ideas
- Keep producing more and more ideas.
- Sift. Sort. Eliminate. Re-evaluate
- Updating your 'to do' list often works as a way to bring a smaller problem into play
- Use a Mote Pad

19. SWITCH FROM PROBLEM TO PROBLEM FOR BEST EFFECT

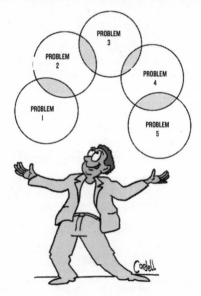

- Tackle several problems at once – and switch at will.
- It won't reduce the effectiveness of your generating ideas and solutions. Quite the reverse
- Make big or baby steps, but make notes before switching.

20. BUT BE PREPARED TO FLATLINE IF NECESSARY

- Concentrate 100% on an idea or problem for a given time – probably one hour maximum
- Full on
- Software like Ommwriter can make it easier to avoid distractions

21. IF YOU ARE STUCK, UNPACK THE BRIEF

- Breaking down a brief, a challenge or a question into its component elements

- Look to develop ideas to fit each important element

22. OR TRY REFRAMING THE PROBLEM...

- Have another conversation with yourself
- Am I asking the right question(s)?
- Is the problem I'm trying to solve EXACTLY the correct one?
- Should I look at it another way
- Reframe as often as you need to

23. GO FOR SOMETHING DIFFERENT

eg
- Pick up the ball instead of kicking it
- Don't eat all the food now; plant some seeds
- Repurpose – remember that sea travel was A to B until someone invented cruises
- Laugh. Smile. Use the humour weapon

24. LOOK FOR OPPORTUNITIES, INSTEAD OF IMMEDIATELY AT SOLUTIONS TO THE PROBLEM

- Always be prepared to use the other end of the telescope
- Is this just about problem solving, or can you see an opportunity?

25. TURN OFF YOUR FILTERING SYSTEM

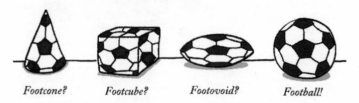

Footcone?   *Footcube?*   *Footovoid?*   *Football!*

- Don't allow the filtering system to slow down inputs
- Or just do less filtering
- When you're accessing the brain's storage system AND trying to make connections, the last thing you need are filters saying 'don't go there'

26. TRAIN YOURSELF TO BE RESTLESS

- Don't be complacent
- Don't be too satisfied by your first thoughts
- It's all right to be distracted
- Revisit. Revisit. Revisit

27. THINK THE OPPOSITE

- Often idea generation is competitive (as in a pitch)
- You may not win if you just follow the obvious routes
- Don't be afraid of being radical

28. DON'T BE WORRIED ABOUT BORROWING OR STEALING IDEAS

- It's a useful technique
- And there's plenty of time to edit and adapt later
- 'Have I seen this before?' is a great question. But 'yes' isn't a good reason for not pursuing it

29. TAKE RISKS

- You know from the Idea Economist that playing it safe can be as risky as taking risks

30. REASSEMBLE THE BUILDING BLOCKS IN YOUR CONSCIOUSNESS

- Remember how storage in the brain is affected by the order in which items have been inputted

- Don't hesitate to repeat the inputting. It might help you to make a fresh connection
- Shuffle the moving parts. It may make it easier to make a breakthrough

31. LIVE OFF ADRENALINE IF YOU'RE UNDER TIME PRESSURE

- Push yourself hard
- Give yourself tight deadlines
- Reward yourself – drink, food, exercise, relax, fun, bath, sex

32. FEAR IS A POTENT DRIVER THAT YOU CAN USE CREATIVELY

- Understand the significance of 'misattributed arousal'
- Fear can make you far more receptive and observant

33. REMEMBER THAT EVERY IDEA STARTS WITH ONE PERSON

- No significant idea first saw the light of day in a room full of people
- Ideas come initially from one brain
- In this instance – YOURS!
- You become an idea person by searching for ideas
- They won't be fully formed and ready to roll. But that doesn't matter
- You need people to develop the idea – but not to have it in the first place

34. AND THAT THE MOST EFFECTIVE HUMAN UNIT IS TWO PEOPLE – THE DYNAMIC DUO

- Share – but only when you are ready
- Cultivate special friends, collaborators, partners, family members, colleagues to be the other half of your dynamic duo
- Share problems
- Be indiscreet
- Encourage these oppos to work alongside you as ideas people, creators, problem solvers, opportunity identifiers

35. MEETINGS ARE VITAL FOR DEVELOPING IDEAS

- (Especially when the meeting is a Mote)
- Take ideas into meetings
- Use meetings to develop ideas
- Take ideas out of meetings

36. DON'T FALL FOR THE 'LOTS OF PEOPLE AROUND A TABLE' MYTH

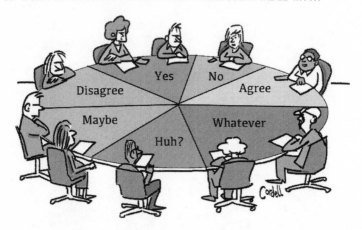

- This isn't about democracy. Don't confuse processes for idea generation, problem solving, decision making with democracy
- Just because it's a big project, you don't have to have a big meeting
- Add expertise selectively using 'Stepladder'

37. USE THE MOTE SYSTEM TO FORM A LEAN AGILE TEAM

- Get inputs from people, keep people informed, get advice from specialists and experts
- Recruit Leader, Navigator and Moters

- Stepladder to bring new people on board, and allow those who have contributed to leave

38. DECIDE ON THE ROLE THAT'S MOST APPROPRIATE FOR YOU

- ...and for each member of the team
- Are you a Driver, Extrovert, Amiable or Analyst?
- In project work, do you take the initiative?
- Or tend to follow?
- Are you more of a generator?
- Or more of a developer?
- Are you good at spotting other people's gems?
- Or helping to mould rough ideas into the finished article?

39. TRY SOME ROLE REVERSAL

- If you get stuck, a swap might work
- For you and for other members of the team

40. WORK TO A BRIEF AND A LIST OF CRITERIA

- Whether this is your project or someone else's, you need clear goals and selection criteria
- Use the criteria throughout

41. GET AWAY FROM THE NOTION THAT YOU ARE ONLY LOOKING FOR ONE IDEA

- If you are looking for a 1/1000 idea, or a 1/100 idea, it's most unlikely that the one that comes first off the production line is going to be the big one
- You need as many ideas as possible to choose from

- Choosing the winner is as important as coming up with ideas in the first place

42. KEEP PRODUCING LOTS OF IDEAS

- Aim to produce plenty of ideas
- Great ideas come from lots of ideas
- You'll run out of energy before you run out of inspiration
- Sift. Sort. Eliminate. Re-evaluate

43. NOT EVERY IDEA ARRIVES IN A EUREKA MOMENT

- Deduction can be as effective as inspiration

44. GROUP THE IDEAS IN CLUSTERS

- Make it easier to choose a winner by assembling a coherent list of candidates
- Always keep your criteria in mind

45. DON'T RANK THE IDEAS IN ORDER OF EXCELLENCE. ELIMINATE THE WEAKEST IF YOU WANT TO REDUCE THE CONTENDERS

- You need to be able to choose
- Even more importantly, when you present your ideas to your boss, your client, consumers in market research, or whatever, you need THEM to have options to choose from
- It's like recruitment or party invitations – you want a short list, not a winner, at this stage

46. HALF AN IDEA CAN BE WELL WORTH PURSUING

- Don't dismiss an idea just because it isn't fully formed
- Particularly when it is 'still warm'
- Developing it might produce a winner

47. TRY TO SLEEP IN A STRUCTURED WAY

- Plan sleep as well
- Use resting time at night as well as daytime , but don't be too intense
- It's a different discipline when you're in bed:
  - Not being led by your eyes and hands
  - No page or screen to watch
  - No keyboard or pen
- So use other levers: stretch, curl up, change position

48. GO TO SLEEP FAST, WAKE UP SLOWLY

Go to sleep   ...fast.

Wake up   ...slowly.

- This is a critical technique
- We are all busy, and most of us worry a lot
- So we tend to collapse into bed exhausted and then

fail to sleep because we are still agonising over all the unresolved issues of the day

- And after a fitful night, we jump out of bed – still tired – as soon as the alarm goes
- This makes no sense!
- Much better to clear the brain (as in #3 above). Get to sleep as quickly as possible. Breathing deeply also works well if you are having trouble falling asleep
- Your idea brain will have been processing through the night
- And in the morning, give yourself time to review the analysis your clever brain will have conducted on all those vexatious issues, before making a gentle start to what should be a terrific day
- Don't be surprised if you wake up to excellent solutions and ideas. But do write down the key points as soon As you can!

49. PRIME YOUR DREAMS AND LEARN HOW TO USE THEM

- Dreams are some of our most creative productions
- They mostly occur during the REM (rapid eye movement) cycle, which occurs every 90 minutes. This is when the brain is particularly active, and we are quite close to being awake
- Learn both to stimulate dreams and to interpret them
- Dream activity is important in understanding and also controlling our idea capacity
- Find the system for recoding dreams that works best for you

- Use daydreaming as a deliberate technique – 'strategic snoozing'

50. DON'T JUDGE WHILE YOU ARE CREATING

- It will confuse you
- And slow you down
- Plenty of time for editing in the idea-making process

MYTH no.1: We all understand that inventors, innovators and creatives are uniquely gifted humans. 'Normal' people can't aspire to become expert ideas people. (See Mark Wnek article)

REALITY: There are far more potentially creative people around us than has ever been acknowledged. The experts have shared stories and techniques with us. We can all learn from that. And even people who find it difficult to come up with valuable ideas in the first instance, are perfectly capable of becoming creative contributors who help develop and implement other people's ideas.

MYTH no.2: The Idea Brain is not a scientifically valid explanation of how we come up with ideas.

REALITY: That's true. But it is a useful way of helping people use tried and tested techniques and tips for problem solution, idea generation and creativity.

Chapter 9

TEAMWORK – DEVELOPING IDEAS TOGETHER

Quoting Lehrer again (from *Imagine: How Creativity Works*):

'Creative ideas rarely come in finished form. Perfecting these ideas requires deep persistence and hard work. The attention to detail and focus that this process requires. Nothing good is easy.

At times, and indeed more and more nowadays, difficult problems require the creative efforts of more than just one person: they require a collective effort. However, getting groups to be creative is not an easy task, as it requires the right mix of people, and the right approach. For instance, the most creative and productive groups tend to be those where the members are mostly well-acquainted with one another, and have worked together before, but who are also joined by a healthy measure of new and unfamiliar talent. In addition, the best approach for groups to have seems to be one where the members practice a kind of constructive criticism, and collective responsibility.'

We have to believe in our own ability – but two heads are better than one

Every idea starts life in the head of one person. Never in a meeting. But ideas are a journey, and we need process and a team (meeting specialists, not just random attendees) to keep up the momentum, and avoid loss of focus. The Dynamic Duo – two people – are the ideal core team. Idea development and implementation will need additional players, but teams should be kept lean and balanced by using the Stepladder Principle (the process of adding only one person at a time, and letting people go when they have made their contribution). The Mote System is perfect for developing ideas – with trained Leaders, Navigators, and team members.

But to develop ideas we do need meetings. I have been so convinced of the need to do business meetings in a radically different way that in 2015 I published *MOTE: The Super Meeting*.

Mote is a better way of doing meetings

There is an enormous cost of wasteful, inefficient meetings to both companies and the executives condemned to suffer in them. It is astonishing that the cost of wasted meeting time in the UK is an £50bn, if experts are right. Almost certainly the same degree of wasted time and money is to be found all over the world.

But the problem with meetings is not just time and

money. Bad meetings contribute to stress and poor health. They also have a significant effect on life/work balance, by eating into work time and obliging executives to work longer hours, travel more, and see less of their families.

We have seen what causes this waste: basically far too many meetings that last too long, too many people in the room, and a widespread lack of professional meeting managers. But poor behaviour and meeting etiquette, which is endemic in many organisations, is equally to blame. Confrontational and aggressive attitudes have invaded conference rooms all over the world.

What does a Mote look like?

A Mote is diamond-shaped, or more accurately like a pyramid on top of an inverted pyramid.

The shape symbolises both the balance between the initial, middle and final stages – and the likely number of players. The Mote starts small with the Leader and Navigator, and as the decision comes to be finalised a small group will again work best. During the exploration of options, the reward/ risk analysis, and discussion of possible solutions, more expertise will be brought to bear.

We already have our goal, because we set it in advance – expressing what the Mote is designed to achieve. This effectively defines the agenda – there is no room for other items, any other business etc.

The English word agenda comes from the Latin – what has to be done. But we use Motion in a Mote, to stress the degree of focus that is needed.

A Mote is driven by what has to be achieved – often a decision. You don't need the minutes of the last meeting. You don't need a shopping list of 12-20 items that have to be discussed. You need a simple Motion that focuses precisely on why everyone is there, and what they have to decide upon.

Almost certainly a Mote will consist of more than one session, because Decision Making, Change Management and Problem Solving are all journeys. Individual sessions are likely to have different participants – with, as we have seen, few players at the beginning and end of the process, and more in the middle.

Motes can take place anywhere, but it can help underline the importance of a Mote if it does take place somewhere special. This might involve going to a particularly appropriate city or country, where geographical, political or cultural influences might add to the impact. The venue itself must be comfortable, well-appointed, and equipped with all necessary technology, including facilities for importing contributions from remote participants (Remoters).

How does the Mote help us produce a decision? Our

main job is to look at the options we identified at Pre-Mote stage. To qualify, each of the options has to be a valid way forward. We start by looking at the upsides and downsides of each option – and in particular the most attractive upside, and the most worrying downside in each case.

Levitin in **The Organized Mind** advocates what he calls 'Planning for Failure' – thinking about anything that can possibly go wrong to ensure that every downside has been anticipated, with a ready-made course of action in hand.

Then we do a reward/risk analysis in each case. The most attractive option is almost certainly going to be the one with the most positive upside, consistent with not having potentially disastrous consequences.

But that is not necessarily going to be the Decision we are going to make? All the evidence from the neuroscientists tells us that our emotions and instincts are as important as our rationality. We need to feel comfortable with our Decision, as well be able to justify it logically. Traditional methods like sleeping on it are as valid as ever. Then we need to do something that sounds painfully obvious (but you'd be amazed how often it is not done properly), writing the Decision down. Precisely. Accurately. That is the job of the Navigator. It can't be delegated, although obviously Moters can be asked to help.

Mote gives us the chance to escape from the crazy busy vortex

We can do meetings differently – and better. It will help us maintain focus and attempt less manic and pointless multitasking. With less stakeholders in the room, meeting will be less internally driven. There will be a chance to listen to experts and study case studies and evidence from **outside** the company.

Mote gives us a break from constant problem-solving. We can look at identifying and realising opportunities.

Mote is the answer for dynamic meetings

Here is a summary of what makes it special – and effective: I think I have found a solution in my Mote idea, and I am really heartened by the positive indications from early trials. I am grateful to all our trial partners for having enough belief to want to make Mote work in practice.

Mote has been designed for 'dynamic meetings' –change management, big projects, and decision making. I believe it will work because it is a head and heart solution. It is a system to manage however many meetings it takes to make a decision, manage a change, or turbocharge a project. But it is also an emotional and people solution to the meeting nightmare.

So a Mote is essentially a turbocharged meeting dedicated to driving a project or making a decision. I term these meetings 'dynamic'. Henceforward we will give change management and decision making the importance they deserve by holding Motes, and leaving the word 'meeting' to refer to other kinds of meeting.

The Mote will be effective, I think, because it will help

people co-operate more readily, and work together better in all types of meetings and in business in general. If I was allowed one sentence to sum up Mote, it would be; 'the moment we understand that a meeting can be compact, cast, produced, and perfected, we will never willingly go back to big meetings, where people behave badly, and seldom achieve a great deal'.

Mote is an ancient word, that will hopefully soon return to general usage. It certainly was not designed as an acronym. But lovers of mnemonics might care to remember Mote like this:

- Method (Game Plan. Leader and Navigator. Stepladder)
- Outcome (A meeting entirely geared to outcomes and deliverables – not people, inputs and discussion)
- Time (Designed to save time and cost)
- Empathy (Built around collaborative behaviour)

I asked the Idea Economist about teamwork, and rather than developing a mathematical formula, he took me through an anthropological explanation of how our pack skills have developed.

The Idea Economist on Teams

As one of the many animals fighting for survival on the African savannah, Homo Sapiens looked like a sure-bet loser: no claws, blunt teeth, not very fast (although good at running away), fragile hide, a weak sense of sight/smell/ hearing. What a dud.

It seems unlikely that our physicality was our strong suit in the evolutionary battle. Rather, the two things that got us through these tough qualifying rounds was our cognitive abilities – compared to other animals we don't just use our instincts, we have the creativity to solve idiosyncratic problems – and secondly, our ability to work as a pack.

Humans are very social animals and since the dawn of time have worked collaboratively in small groups to solve problems, whether trapping a fast moving animal or packaging a fast moving consumer good. Not only can humans come up with novel ideas/strategies to solve tricky problems but they can also combine their ideas with other people's ideas for even greater effect.

So what we lack in physicality we make up for in cognitive and social skills.

Most of us are not on the savannah now, but looking at sports we see all sorts of sized teams being deployed in the hunt for victory:

Tennis	2/4
Polo	4
Netball	7
Rowing	2/4/8
Football	11
Cricket	11
Rugby	13 or 15
Dragon Boats	c.50
Grid Iron	>50

Now while being creative is often done best in a playful spirit it isn't actually a game. But nonetheless an optimum team size seems to have evolved and to some extent been coded into the rules of the creative game.

And this number is much closer to a Polo sized team than a Football team (excluding the horses, except in some very posh agencies).

So what is the maths behind this ideal number? And what happens to creativity when a meeting of rugby scrum proportions takes place; do good ideas get squeezed out or trampled into the mud?

One obvious social behaviour of creative people of all sorts is they seek each other out to work in pairs. Bouncing ideas off another brain seems to be something that works for us.

So in creative agencies the term 'creative team' almost invariably refers to a pair who work together all the time (classically, in their own office) and are so closely linked that they get hired (and fired) as an indivisible pair.

However, it isn't quite as simple as that. Creative pairs will regularly meet up with a Creative Director for a creative review, where as a trio they work on the problem. Or they might have meetings with Account Handlers or a Strategist or Media Planners to discuss the problem as part of a 4–5 person Project Team.

Larger groups may be put together in a later part of the overall creative process (such as the production phase), but certainly when an agency is in the generative phase, rarely more than 4 or 5 people are present in the room.

Indeed one agency in Canada christened itself 'Taxi' to signal that it thought that the ideal problem solving unit would fit into a taxi (and nothing bigger). So three or four was ideal, and maybe – at a squeeze – five (but only if they all knew each other really well).

Similarly, the smallest unit in most modern armies is the fire team of 3 or 4 soldiers that operates as a tight, indivisible, intimate unit. Years of combat have found this size to be the best way of organising the clever yet collaborative survival-machine that is mankind.

You can see this pattern in the names of most advertising agencies that thrived in the UK in the 70's, 80's and 90s. Whereas management consultancies often bear the name of their legendary founding partner (McKinsey, Bain, Arthur Andersen), these agencies typically ended up being known by the initials of a team of 3 or 4 founders: AMV, BBH, WCRS, HHCL etc.

Now this naming etiquette isn't entirely about fragile egos. There is an explicit belief that the best creative unit is formed of 3 or 4 people.

Small, agile teams are as dynamic and effective in creative development as everywhere else.

Meredith Belbin – was a true pioneer of team theory

No analysis of the dynamics of successful teams would be complete without acknowledging the huge contribution of Cambridge academic Meredith Belbin. Now 92, Belbin carried out seminal research at what was then called the Administrative Staff College at Henley-on-Thames during the 60s and 70s into what contrasting and complementary skills are needed to form a successful team.

In the post-war period, with most leading business people, civil servants and academics being military veterans, command and control was the order of the day. Teams were either vertically integrated or formed on an organogram resembling the family tree of John of Gaunt. Hierarchy ruled (to coin a phrase). The boss basically issued instructions, and his (always a he in those days) direct reports did the same to their minions, and so on.

Belbin's genius during a week long class was to be able to pick a team with different abilities and styles, which could always defeat any assemblage of drivers and power figures selected by his fellow lecturers. It's choosing a playground football team all over again. You do need a goalkeeper, some defenders and playmakers as well as strikers.

He identified nine typologies (originally seven):

- Chairman/Co-ordinator (leader)
- Shaper (creative strategist)
- Plant (problem solver)
- Resource Investigator (networker)
- Monitor-Evaluator (devil's advocate)
- Team Worker (HR)
- Implementer (workable solutions)
- Completer Finisher (king of detail)
- Specialist (expert)

Critics have questioned whether nine is a magic number for a successful team, and whether or not certain roles couldn't be combined in the same individual. But Belbin's insight about the need for a balanced make-up has been crucial in the search for effective problem solving and decision making. We owe him a great deal.

The core principles of Mote

There are five:

- GAME PLAN
- SMALL AGILE TEAM
- STEPLADDER
- PERFORMANCE
- SPIRIT OF MOTE

Game Plan (the first principle of Mote)

First is the **Game Plan** – a hand-picked Leader and Navigator managing a series of meetings to achieve a specific and usually ambitious goal. Each session to be meticulously planned. The Leader is the driver of growth and change. Fortunately Leader candidates are easy to identify by role and personality, although they need training to maximise the effectiveness of the Mote . The Leader is not a Chairman – because a Mote is not an Assembly Meeting. The Leader should also be in charge of the Spirit of Mote.

The Navigator role is crucial – both a Monitor Evaluator and Resource Investigator. This is the key innovation – and

Navigators also need specialist training. Navigators are likely to come from planning or ops. It is vital to recruit people particularly suited to being meeting specialists. Navigator represents a career development opportunity for graduates.

How to manage a Mote and run the best meeting ever with a Small, Agile Team (Mote principle #2)

Preparation of the Mote is indeed crucial. But you only get one chance to run a Mote brilliantly, and that is in real time.

Motes need Leader, Navigator, Moters and Remoters to drive progress. But it all starts with two people – Leader and Navigator (the 'Dynamic Duo').

TWO CAN DO (ALMOST) ANYTHING

If he can say as you can
Guinness is good for you
How grand to be a Toucan
Just think what Toucan do

This legendary campaign by SH Benson for Guinness first saw the light of day in the late 1920's, with none other than Dorothy L Sayers as the copywriter.

'Just think what Toucan do' was a great slogan for Guinness, but in these politically correct days, it would have suffered the same fate (for encouraging too much consumption) as the even more famous 'Guinness is good for you', which it probably isn't, and which was banned by the truth police!

I like the slogan because I worked out a long time ago that a dynamic duo is by far mankind's most efficient grouping. Better balanced than even the most outstanding individual (few old sayings are as true as 'two heads are better than one'). More agile and higher performing than conference rooms full of clever people. Faux democracy has much to answer for when meetings of all the 'right people' fail to deliver.

The moment you see lots of chairs around a table in a meeting room, take time to reflect that the meeting problem has already started. All those egos. All those agendas. The attraction of speaking over listening. The influence of the loudest. The marginalisation of the quieter ones. Whereas a determined twosome can make dramatic progress – in moving a project forward, or towards a decision.

Capitalise on the Power of One (Leader) to produce strong ideas and the ability of a Dynamic Duo (Leader and Navigator) to take an idea forward at pace. Leaving the two to conquer the world.

The Navigator's job is to keep the Mote on plan, and tightly in line with the Motion. Also to support the Leader – and encourage all the Moters to use their skills, knowledge and energy to contribute to outstanding team performance and behaviour.

The second principle is that the Mote is essentially a **Small Agile Team**, quite unlike the big meetings packed with mavericks pursuing their own agenda that bedevil the process in many companies. First and foremost it is a team of hand-picked Moters, with balanced personalities and roles, tasked to *think together*, and then *work together*. It is a similar situation to sport, the theatre or music. Before Moter, there wasn't a specific word for someone who attends a meeting? Not everyone will be a good Moter, but we want:

- Serious meeting professionals for what they can contribute, not their status or job title
- Dedicated to high levels of meeting performance...
- ...and to helping colleagues do well also

THE IDEA ECONOMIST ON THE MATHS OF THE DYNAMIC DUO

The bonus effect of a creative/thinking partner.

Observing Lennon and McCartney*, Dolce and Gabbana, Saatchi and Saatchi, Rodgers and Hammerstein, a regular

*Analysing their collaboration is hard to do as some songs were written 'nose to nose', some were originated by one partner with the other adding and tweaking, and some, while completely attributed to Lennon or McCartney are very much Beatles songs. What the stats do tell us is that as solo artists Lennon and McCartney created 17 No.1s either side of the Atlantic. Working as a team they created 46. Were they three times more potent together?

feature of the creative world is the creative duo. And even us lesser talents often find it easier to work with a good partner when trying to crack a brief. What's the maths behind working with a partner?

As mentioned in Chapter 6, when we share 10 ideas, unlike with a 10 pound note we are both better off.

But another thing that is going on here is the phenomenon of 'creative tension'. If two people are committed to working together then it doesn't matter if the initial reaction is negative. Here's how that works:

- Creative one: here's my idea +2
- Creative two: I don't like XYZ about that idea +2 X −2 = −4
- Creative one: you're wrong about that because of ABC −4 X −2 = +8
- Creative two: I love what you did there because now I can see PQR +8 X +2 = +16
- Creative one: we've cracked it!
  (note the 'we')

Now all of this is not to encourage people to be routinely negative about ideas. The phenomenon of creative tension is best seen in high trust, highly committed partnerships where honesty is helpful and is delivered with 'positive intent'.

The Vulnerability of Ideas

The second aspect of a successful creative partnership is working with someone who is good at nurturing your creative ideas.

Ideas are incredibly vulnerable entities when they first appear. Like premature babies, if not rapidly incubated, they will expire. However, if they can survive those first critical minutes then even the oddest, ugliest, scrawniest idea can grow up to be a Nobel Prize winner.

Similarly, in the middle of World War One, young officers had extremely high mortality rates when serving in the front line. But rather than there being a steady attrition rate for all front-line officers, it was the newest arrivals that tended to get killed. Indeed, if you could survive the critical first few days and learn your trench warfare survival skills (which could not be taught at Sandhurst) then you had a fair chance of surviving your tour of duty.

And so it is with your creative ideas, as they stagger out into the hostile landscape of other people's opinions. What they really need is a friendly NCO who can stop them getting blown up in those first, most deadly moments.

In creative terms you need a partner who is sufficiently positive and 'gets what you really mean', as your naïve, fresh-faced ideas present themselves at the front line. Perhaps as a rule of thumb, you need someone who can talk about any of your ideas for five minutes without you losing your nerve and killing the idea yourself.

Now no one has a 100% confidence in their ideas so let's say you send one of your ideas over the top with 90% confidence that it's a contender for greatness.

If you have a good partner who can talk about this idea with the same degree of support as you, then it will have a survival rating of .9 × .9 or 81% after the first minute. But even if this continues with the same degree of positivity and empathy, its survival chances will drop as it crosses this dangerous conversational no man's land until after 5 minutes it has a 53% (0.90^5) chance of still being alive.

At this point, we don't know if the idea is going to be a great one (this will only be revealed in the long term), but it still being above the 50:50 line after five minutes can be taken as it being more alive than dead and so it lives to fight another day.

But, contrast this with working with a partner who, while very positive perhaps they don't quite 'get' you. Let's say they are just 10% less good at nurturing your ideas. Tragically, with Sergeant 80% your ideas are a lot less likely to survive: after one minute the idea is 72% alive but after five minutes it is not looking good with only a 29% chance of being home by Xmas.

Using the 50% survival line notion, in the third minute the idea is fatally wounded: you've lost confidence in it and so has your partner. You might spend two more minutes thrashing about in the mud but it's a goner.

All of this is about believing in ideas. Indeed, I once worked with a Creative Director who had three responses

to creative work 'yeah', 'yeah, yeah!' and 'yeah, yeah, yeah!!!'.
He kept many young whipper snapper of an idea alive in the
bloody warfare of 90's advertising.

You, if no one else, needs to believe that your (crazy?)
idea might just work. Even better is to have a creative
partner who can suspend their disbelief for long enough to
walk along beside you and see where your new idea goes.

In cartoons, characters can walk off the edge of a cliff and
defy gravity AS LONG AS THEY DON'T LOOK DOWN.
If you (or your partner) start doubting an idea and 'look
down' then it will fall out of the sky and die a lonely death
in a corner of a field that is forever England. What you need
is a partner who will take a few steps with you across the
'Suspension Bridge of Disbelief' because if you take enough
steps you may just find that you have got to the other side of
the chasm.

Good creative partners are those who can look into the
distance ('share your creative vision') with you and help you
skip gleefully towards it, ignoring the insanity of what you
are both doing. It's a magical feeling when it happens and
as such, when you look back, you can't quite remember how
you did it.'

You just know that 'we' did.

Three More Principles of Mote

The third principle – also designed to keep Motes lean and
fit – is **Stepladder**, the process of adding only one Moter at
a time (or Remoters dialling in) and letting people go when

they have made their contribution. It is vital to include talent who can't be physically present – without disrupting those who are. Stepladder was a problem-solving technique, now largely forgotten, from many years ago. I think it has a big future in the world of Mote.

The fourth principle is **Performance** – as in driving projects, managing change, and making decisions. Motes are dedicated to outputs and outcomes. We use short and focused Motions – not long agendas. The inflection point is critical, where we move from inputs to outputs, accelerating the project, bringing change that bit nearer, and making the decision. It is crucial to keep stakeholders informed and involved by excellent communications, reporting progress regularly, and letting everyone know how far we have travelled towards our goal. This ensures that the Mote is efficient and productive. Finally we wrap up this Mote, and start planning the next one.

Finally the fifth principle is **Spirit of Mote**, the philosophy which bakes in empathy and overtly collaborative behaviour to avoid debate becoming adversarial and counter-productive. Emotional intelligence is very important for good meetings. The Spirit of Mote is a team ethic. Meetings should be where we play with each other – not against each other! I explain in the next chapter how Spirit of Mote can be very effective in **all** meetings (not just Motes), and in the workplace at large.

Let's return immediately to the fourth principle, Performance, to see how it is impacted by Spirit of Mote.

Performance in a Mote is delivered in three modes: Thinking together, Working together, and Succeeding or Winning together. Thinking together is critical.

Thinking Together

Bright people love meeting other clever people. It's one of the main reasons university is such fun. A great dinner party, a good lunch, even a drink after work with an old friend can have the same effect. Dialogue between two or more intelligent men and women generally produces interesting ideas, exciting opportunities, and if there's a need, answers to problems.

But did I say 'or more'? How many more? How many clever people do we want in any one room before more becomes less, there is a fight to be heard, and the meeting becomes counter-productive?

Having studied the meeting phenomenon, and what can go wrong when there are too many people around the table, I would recommend starting with two, adding maybe one or two more, and stopping there – at least for the first session of what may turn into a series of several. Meetings are the way we have settled on working together. Meetings are not basically for talking, or listening, or even debating. The purpose of strategic and dynamic meetings is to get things done – to make a decision, to turbo-charge a project, to solve a big problem, or realise a juicy opportunity.

What is the key dynamic in a dynamic meeting? Working together – yes. But even more important, *thinking* together.

I believe it is by thinking together that we maximise mutual brainpower. When we talk enthusiastically about two heads being better than one, thinking together is what we are talking about. Encouraging children to think together is one of the pillars of the education system, and yet we easily forget how powerful this joint activity can be, and lapse instead into wall to wall words. The lust for communicating in public has a lot to answer for.

The next time you call an important meeting – one where a goal has to be achieved, and a result is imperative – let me suggest this approach.

'Can you, Rachel and I find time to meet this week. Ideally for 90 minutes, but an hour might do it. The Pure Ptarmigan campaign clearly isn't working. I know it won us the pitch, and the Link results were extraordinary. But no one is buying the stuff, and it seems to be a disaster in the on-trade. 'Pure Ptarmigan' is a useless bar call, because the bloody bird starts with a 'T', not a 'P'. Far from quaking on its moor, Famous Grouse is laughing at us. We need to get together and think together about what we should do. I absolutely don't want to fill a conference room with a dozen people who will tell us they knew it wouldn't work, although they said nothing at the time. Nor will we learn anything from a couple more focus groups and a bit of quant. It will just confirm it isn't working – and that we already know. Please just bring your brains. We will huddle. We will share our thoughts. We will think our way through this.'

Thinking together is the innovation, compared to an ordinary meeting. We tend to regard thinking as a solitary activity and working as something which is very often collaborative. It is not like that in a Mote. Empathy and collaborative behaviour, mean that Moters are empowered to literally and figuratively put their heads together to think, strategise, analyse, solve problems and identify opportunities.

Working together is not necessarily the start point. Moters don't tend to start working together until the inflection point has been reached – the moment when the group feels ready to move from gathering and assimilating inputs to generating outputs.

Succeeding or Winning together is the process of preparing to take the achievement of the meeting out of the conference room into the outside world.

Let's look now – with help from the Idea Economist – at how teams work in developing ideas. These are the vital numbers behind Mote.

The Idea Economist on Groups

IDEAS DON'T MULTIPLY ON THEIR OWN

Most creative work – and in the context of business, pretty much all creative work – is done in a group context and the hard truth is that it takes a lot of effort to get an idea to be adopted by the group.

As a physical reality an idea starts as a singular experience in a singular brain: every idea starts in a single brain as a set of connected neurones firing together.

However, how a singular idea spreads across groups creates a more interesting pattern than 1 person, 2 people, 3 people, 4 people etc. This is important because if an idea is to have any value it needs to spread through the population. But it's journey follows a predictable – if non-simple – path as it travels.

So if the obvious pattern of how an idea spreads would be
1 2 3 4 5 6 7 etc.
a more interesting one would be
1 2 4 8 16 32.

This is a geometric growth pattern and is certainly tempting to imagine that each person who hears your brilliant idea then tells two other people who are so captivated by it they each tell two more until the whole world is talking about your idea. This would be lovely, but is not how it usually happens (the rare exception being ideas that 'go viral' as modelled in Chapter 5).

A better fit of the progression is
0 1 1 2 3 5 8 13 21 34 55
(If you can't see the pattern, each number is the sum of the two before it.)

This is the Fibonacci series, named after the medieval mathematician who popularised it in the West. It is found in many biological settings such as the branching of trees, pineapple seeds and artichoke petals to name but a few.

Modern biologists rather charmingly point out that the family trees of male bees also fit this pattern. So your average male bee has 1 parent, 2 grandparents, 3 great-grandparents, 5 great-great-grandparents and so on. This must make bee birthdays and bee Xmas slightly less enjoyable to my mind but that is the maths.

So in my experience an idea flows with a strange bee-like dance through the people in the organisation. Its early progress is slow, but if things go well, eventually the whole hive is buzzing with energy. I will use an advertising agency making a TV commercial as an example and give you a first person view of the creative hive.

0 – I have nothing. And the dead line is approaching. F@@K!

1 – thank God. That might be an idea! Yes. It might just work. I'll sleep on it.

1 – (next morning). What was that idea again? Oh yes! I still like it. Time to share.

2 – Oh good. My thinking partner likes it too. Its 'our' idea now. Let's take it to the boss.

3 – We're on. Time to tell the client service rep and their sidekick about it.

5 – OK. We all agree as a team that this could be a winner. In fact, they love it. Let's present it to the client.

8 – Brilliant. After some debate all 3 clients are on board and we need to start making it.

13 – well that was a big meeting but you need a lot of people

to make a good ad – a director, their assistant, the location manager, the casting director, the producer and me and the client turned up mob handed too. There were a few tricky discussions due to the tight budget but I think we can really deliver this idea now.

21 – I can see why it costs so much money to make an ad with all the specialist roles. Another 8 or so people were involved along the way there. I'm still not sure what the Key Grip does. But I got what I wanted out of the team – it was a good shoot.

34 – Blimey. An all agencies briefing meeting. We had two from the media agency, four from the social media agency, a PR bod, the procurement person from the client popped in again, and there were a few other odds and sods doing stuff I don't really understand to be honest. Still they all seemed to like the idea when I presented it to them.

55. Well I'm on to the next job but I here that there are lots of teams in lots of agencies working on making this idea spread. And to think it all just started in my head...

What this means is that unlike with the simplistic model that an idea just naturally gathers supporters one at a time (or more optimistically, spreads like geometric wild fire) it is actually hard work recruiting people to your idea, persuading them that it is of value and acting as its guardian as more and more people crowd around it. But that is the nature of As a practitioner it means that you need to be good – albeit in diverse ways – at several types of 'meetings'. From the intimate talks with your most trusted collaborator, to those taxi sized meetings where you shape and develop the idea with a close knit team, through to those big set pieces where you have to carry the room (see next Chapter). All these take skill.

But all these skills are necessary if an idea is going to get to 'Yes'.

Mote will deliver beyond making meetings better, because it is a philosophy, not just a system

Mote is a system to manage however many meetings it takes to make a decision, manage a change, or turbocharge a project. It is also an emotional and people solution to the meeting nightmare.

It is a head and heart solution. It will help people co-operate more readily, and work together better in all types of meetings and in business in general. Every time I expose Mote to people, they can see that it is far more than just a better approach to managing meetings.

It is a *philosophy*. It is a way of behaving. A differentiating way of doing business. A more civilised and constructive way. The core reason that Mote works in meetings is because it allows clever, dynamic people to be positive, creative and inventive – as opposed to egotistical and point-scoring. Mote allows everyone – especially the brightest people – to flourish, because they don't have to wrestle with everything that slows meetings down, or waste time scoring points.

Look at the distinctive characteristics of Mote in the meeting context:

- Positive behaviour and language
- Emphasis on etiquette – only one person speaking at a time, and avoiding the use of devices except to look things up or take notes
- Fewer meetings
- Smaller meetings
- More productive meetings
- Agenda driven by individual ideas
- The Leader role
- The Navigator role
- The Recorder role
- The 'dynamic duo' factor
- Always starting small not big
- Concentrating on the people there, not the 'remoters' dialling in
- Planned, not largely spontaneous

Mote may be an old word for meeting and meeting place. But it is also a new word to signify a new streamlined meeting system, with the promise of liberating business from the broken, atrophied world of meetings with which we are so familiar.

How many people can a meeting cope with?

I developed the Mote system before Jon Leach officially became an Idea Economist, so I didn't have the benefit of mathematical proof that too many people around the conference room table looking for ideas was...well, too many. Here are the numbers the Idea Economist has put together for me.

The Idea Economist on Group Creativity and Numbers of People Present

Mathematical proof – if any were needed – that group creativity doesn't work unless you limit the number of people present.

I am indebted to an ex-Chemical Engineer and Innovation expert by the name of Doug Hall for this section. Hall has published several books, including the *Jump Start...* series. He worked at Procter & Gamble as 'Master Marketing Inventor' (his real title). He started the Eureka! Ranch, and claims to have invented, written and tested more ideas than anyone alive today.

He has presented some data for 'how creative' people are feeling they are being when working on their own, in pairs or larger groupings.

The data does not cover large groups but supports the ideas that 4 or 5 is the optimal number. Looking at the shape of the curve, the suspicion is that adding more people to the group will decrease creativity, which is the received wisdom from agencies.

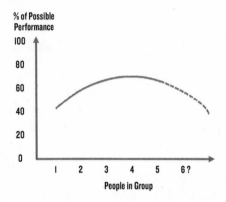

The explanation for this 'first it rises, then it peaks, then it declines' shape is perhaps that there are two forces at work, pushing in opposite directions.

The upwards force is probably the extra creative stimulation that you get from hearing other people's ideas, (or even better hearing what they think of your idea). This social ability to build on another's ideas is part of what makes us such effective hunters/problem solvers.

However there may be a price to pay for working with another partner, a social cost. At its crudest you are going to have to share 'kill' with them, and negotiate tricky issues such as who tried hardest, who needs it most, whose idea was it in the first place etc.

In softer terms you are going to have to attend to the relationship and put some mental energy into checking what the other person is thinking, assessing the likely impact of your words on them before you voice them, trying to detect any hidden meaning behind their words, not to mention what their body language means etc. etc.

And much like for a computer's CPU, all these complicated social calculations take processing power away from the core task of solving the problem.

Now for people who know each other well (such as the typical creative team) the social cost may be negligible (although I suspect not zero). But on average, and Doug Hall's data is just that, the social cost of collaborative creativity will take away a notable chunk of the stimulating benefits.

If, as Doug claims, the base line is 40% and we assume that the 2nd person should give us another 40% to make 80%, given that the output is only 60% then the social cost must be 20%.

Using this way of calculating things we then find a puzzle in the data: with three participants and a theoretical maximum of 120% (as in 'the lads gave 120%' perhaps) the actual performance is 70%. The third participant seems to be bringing in a social cost of -30%. That's -20% for just turning up but there seems to be an extra -10% on top.

The reason for this (and why larger and larger groups diminish creativity) is that 'social costs' can spiral out of control.

It is true that the human brain has evolved to be able to track and respond to a large number of social relationships. In a group I can track what several people are thinking (about me), I can even track what one person is thinking about another and what that means for me. And I can sense the subtle shifting relationships of pairs and triples, minorities and majorities within social groups.

But, and here is the crunch, all that social geometry takes cognitive processing power. And while some people may be able to 'read the meeting well' or be 'good at politics', this is not what creative meetings are about.

Put another way, if you are having to divert large parts of your brain/CPU to thinking about the politics of the meeting you are not in the relaxed, creative flow-state you really need to be.

So, to come back to Doug Hall's data, putting another brain into the meeting probably does put another 40 percentage points of creative stimulus into the room.

However each foreign brain our brain has to deal with takes away about 20 percentage points. Not only that but when we have to deal with, in the trio situation, a pair of brains (conspiring together?) then that somewhat trickier social tracking costs us an additional 30 percentage points on top.

So each extra person, not only brings the previous social challenges but also ones of a whole new order. A fourth party leaves us trying to track, three individuals, three pairs and a trio. It's amazing we have time to think for ourselves at all!

At some point, even if our brain is taking short cuts, the 40 point bonus is outweighed by the social cost. With one set of numbers, it looks like this...

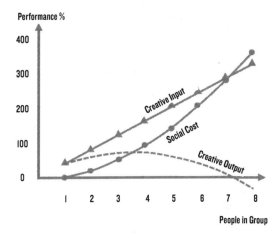

This set of numbers predicts a big drop in performance when the sixth person arrives and a horribly uncreative meeting when there are seven of you sitting there. The eight person meeting is hardly worth imagining.

It's not just about how many people there are in a meeting, the creative energy, and the social cost. Other important factors are in play as well, as the Idea Economist explains.

The problem with this approach is that if you don't generate multiple solutions, you can easily miss several dimensions of the problem, and fail to find new and better angles than your first instinctive response. Equally, if you arrogantly decide what the answer is ('mine!') too soon, you can't use the available time to work collaboratively with other problem solvers who could probably multiply your own creativity. On many of 'his' best ideas, the genius that was Steve Jobs worked on multiple variants with Jonny Ive, by getting multiple prototypes made up for them to review together.

The Idea Economist on Diversity, Stimulation and Fear – the key dynamics of successful meetings

...and the ones that don't turn out so well

Do your creative meetings have a multiplier effect? Or are they divisive?

Once, having just spent 13 hours being hosed down by PowerPoint while floating along on the soothing corporate speak of a Management Consultant-led brand workshop, I was inspired to bring some maths to the eternal question of why are some meetings such 'poorly leveraged interventions' in consultant speak.

Actually this one wasn't that bad, it was a good, productive sharing of information and initial opinions. But it was not very creative. And to be scrupulously fair, maybe at this point in the 'Process' it wasn't meant to be.

Aside from his success in explaining the maths of small meetings, Doug Hall also had a formula for the creative output of any meeting (whether workshop, brainstorm, board meeting, tetchy conversation with spouse etc.) is as follows:

$$C = (D \times S)/F$$

Where:

C = quality of creative output (note 'quality', not 'quantity')

D = diversity of people in the meeting

S = amount of stimulation experienced by people in the meeting

F = fear level of people in the meeting

Now my particular beef is not the normal agency whinge that management consultants don't understand creativity (darling), but more a worry that they don't seem to know how to push for high levels of creativity in meetings. For them a meeting is a meeting and is run like all meetings. I think creative agencies could teach them a trick or two.

But now is not the time to go all creative and fluffy, but to illustrate my point with some hard numbers.

To simplify things, let's say that each of Doug's variables of Diversity, Stimulation and Fear can have three settings low, average or good. And let's quantify that on a three point scale of 1, 2 and 3. Now, with those numbers, a superficial understanding of the creative dynamic might say that a good meeting is just 50% (3/2) more productive than an average meeting.

But applying Doug's formula, the meeting I experienced was creatively 'average' in three distinct ways and, as I shall mathematically show in a moment, fell well short of its creative potential.

On the diversity front, we had people from 7 different markets, some management consultants, some HQ marketing types, a couple of guys from the agencies (including me). But really it was 'a bunch of beer guys in blue shirts'. Not a lot of functional or cultural variety. Just a normal meeting. I'll give it 2 for Diversity.

Similarly, they all brought in good informative presentations about their markets, the consultants shared some interesting stuff from other markets. But again nothing from the broader world; nothing about (say) the political and cultural journey of South Africa; nothing about the mass-affluent consumer in the States. Again, normal beer stuff. So, again, 2 for stimulation.

On fear, the meeting was reasonably well run, the senior people 'behaved'. But we sat around a ghastly oval shape 20 person board room table. Actually it was the board room of the plc. The top person sat in the dominant position all the time. And with the exception of a one hour break-out session, all conversations were done in the full glare of the whole group. Normal business practice perhaps, but again I couldn't give it a 3 for getting the fear levels right down. So it is a 2.

Running the numbers, Doug's formula says that the meeting rates (creatively) as follows:

$$C = 2 \times 2 / 2 = 2$$

Now this is 6 times better than the worst possible meeting...

$$C = 1 \times 1 / 3 = 0.33$$

... but if we had been bolder about the diversity of the group, more imaginative with the stimulation provided and more active in reducing fear levels we might have achieved the following:

$$C = 3 \times 3 / 1 = 9$$

So the formula suggests that a well-run creative meeting is not just 50% more productive than an average meeting but 350% or 4.5 times more productive. This is something the

Management Consultants might point to as a 'capability' of creative organisations.

But this could just be the maths talking.

What kind of a project most needs the discipline and dynamism of Mote?

Change management is probably the greatest challenge for leaders. We know from the research carried out by the Gyro agency in the UK that 79% of the leaders surveyed had experienced significant change in the organisations in the previous three months. It would not be an exaggeration to say that nearly all leaders are dealing with virtually continuous change.

There are three basic types of change:

- **Developmental** – doing what we do now, but doing it better. The frame of reference stays the same, but we concentrate on improvements.
- **Transitional** – having a specific goal in sight, and moving from where we are to where we want to be. The destination has been decided in advance. This is a journey where we use familiar skill sets and actions – eg innovation, M&A, hiring new people.
- **Transformational** – major change is needed, but this time we don't know exactly where we are going. We are going to have to get there by trial and error. A linear approach on a pre-determined schedule is unlikely to work. The change process will have to be developed

in real time. Because the destination is going to be radically different from where we started out, new mind sets and behaviours will be needed to drive the necessary changes in people and culture. Envisioning the future is a challenge in itself. Finding it is a bigger challenge. Making it work – an even more serious challenge.

Transformational Change is obviously the blue riband event. Meanwhile let us look at how planning a Mote differs from planning an ordinary meeting.

The hard yards in Mote pay off, given collaborative behaviour

Conventional meetings are normally free-flow. Motes have to be planned in advance as we have seen above, and carefully orchestrated once under way. The Leader has to take the initiative and start things off with a dynamic opener, and also rise to the challenge at the end with a dynamic close.

The Navigator has to work hard throughout keeping the Mote on track.

Let's go back to the three change management scenarios:

For Developmental Change moters can move straight into working together. The objective is to change from an unsatisfactory or merely adequate way of doing something in the organisation to an improved process or system. Both the goal and the nature of the journey have been established. There are some 'who?', 'when?', 'what?', 'where?' questions to be posed and answered, but delivering the project efficiently within the Mote process should be reasonably straightforward. The group will be outputting from the outset.

For Transitional Change a destination will have already been identified at the planning stage, but the journey is less obvious, and moters need to start by thinking together, gathering new inputs, analysing and strategising. This is more complicated than Developmental change. But given good Leadership and Navigation and judicious use of Stepladder to make sure the right people are in the room, it should not be long before the inflection point, and the transition to working together.

Transformational Change represents a different scale of challenge. Neither destination nor journey are clear. The title of Goldsmith's book *What got you here won't get you there* sums up the situation perfectly. Almost everything may need to change: culture, people, systems, process, scale. Even fundamental markers like purpose and mission may need to be recast. There are quite likely to be big financial issues, also HR implications, and negotiations with government, regulators and unions. This is the kind of task and challenge for which Mote was invented. Goldsmith didn't know about Mote, but he is very mindful of the need for leaders to involve stakeholders, managers, suppliers, customers etc, and to be empathic and collaborative, rather than dictatorial.

He conducted a massive survey of 11,000 leaders in eight multinational on four continents and discovered that taking people with you is far more likely to be successful than refusing to dialogue, but largely for Spirit of Mote reasons. 95% of the leaders who dialogued with stakeholders measurably improved their interpersonal behaviour and chances of success. The leaders who walked alone, unsurprisingly carried on behaving badly, and their chances of achieving successful outcomes were barely above random.

The Idea Economist on Creative Process

HOW CREATIVE PEOPLE CREATE GOOD IDEAS

Linear and non-linear processes

[Credit to strategist Fred Pelard for generating the original framework]

It would be nice if making creative ideas was a bit like making flat pack furniture. Keep calmly following the steps one by one and low cost Swedish chic will be yours.

Rather, being in the ideas trade feels more like making a cake – get inspired by the ingredients, get a bit messy as you mix them up, stare anxiously in the oven door, trim off accidentally burnt bits, ice the top with a flourish (filling in the gaps), serve with a confident smile (while your heart is beating as fast as your whisking machine).

But just because it gets a bit messy and emotional that does not mean that it is chaos.

It follows a predictable, almost mathematical path even if it is not a straight line: in a 10 day project it is not that 10% of the idea is created each day so that by the first Friday we are half way there and the night before the big reveal we are at 90%. Things are non-linear.

But this non-linearity does not mean that the creative process is chaotic. In fact a good creative process is quite predictable and hence robust.

A diagram may help...

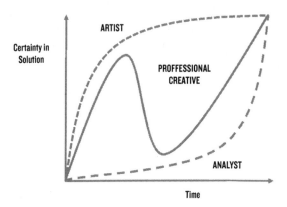

On the vertical access we have the degree of certainty that we have got the best possible idea, and time is along the bottom.

Let's plot the approaches of three people.

The 'analyst' who believes that you should gather and analyse all the possible material until the idea (magically) pops out at the end.

The problem with this approach is that by NOT speculating what the answer might be – albeit on limited information – there is a danger that you leave the 'creative bit' so late you might only get to mediocre.

The 'artist' who believes that their first brilliant thought will magically gather support and evidence if we just wait for everyone to (magically) catch up.

The problem with this approach is that by a) not generating multiple solutions and b) being a bit arrogant you can't use the available time for a) exploring several dimensions of the problem and b) it's hard to work collaboratively with other problem solvers if you decide what the answer is too soon, on your own.

The third path is taken by the (professional) creative mind who believes that you should generate some attractive options early on but then robustly challenge and explore these options to generate a final option (which may be none of the early options).

This is the most complex of the curves but seems to be the most effective path to take. As it is more complex than the others it takes some skill to navigate:

- You need to be prepared to speculate early on (even if that risks looking like a fool).
- You need to include other people's ideas in your thinking, and the need to emotionally invest in other's ideas (you need options to hedge for the uncertainty).
- You need to be tough on your ideas and diligent in your analysis (even if that means that your early favourites wither on the vine).
- Your need to make decisions and choose which one to go with (even if you want to use all your ideas).
- You need to build to a crescendo and make sure the idea stays strong to the end.

These activities are not what analysts (in a 'building spreadsheets' sense) do but nor is it what artists (in a 'who cares what others think' sense) do. But it is what professional creative organisations do.

So another principle of Idea Economics is that the processes are non-linear, non-chaotic, complex but robust.

We can't be brilliant every time

Don't beat yourself up if you have an off day. We are surprised when we fail to hit the heights at something we are normally good at. We didn't make the sale. I didn't get the job. We lost the match.

We shouldn't be surprised. We are humans not robots. There are days when it doesn't work out – sometimes because we've goofed, but often because of competitive pressure or outside factors. Remember when we used to get excited about biorhythms? Perhaps I was having a triple critical last Thursday.

Why have I gone all philosophical this month? Partly because of my commitment to Mote, and reminding everyone that meetings should be a team game, where we compensate for individual weaknesses by picking balanced teams to maximise the chances of success. But partly because – after many decades – I think I have finally come to terms with the fact that I play bad golf as often (or more so) as good golf. I was starting to dread playing in case I had a bad day. Now I'm telling myself just to enjoy the exercise, the company and just being out there swishing in the fresh air!

After all kids learn to walk, not by standing up, but by falling over. We learn more from mistakes than when we get it right. Winning feels good, but we don't always know why we have won. If we lose, it is useful – as well as therapeutic – to find out why. I've always offered agencies post mortem sessions to try and explain why they didn't win the pitch. They might well have missed out because of poor chemistry or creative that the client didn't like. Very often on the other hand they haven't won because another agency performed better. Blaming the timing, the venue, or the unfair client can be a natural reaction. But it's not helpful – any more than having a go at the referee or umpire.

What is a problem is losing the war, not the battle. There's a difference between a poor press conference and a failed launch. Losing a sale is a not as bad as losing a customer. A bad meeting is bearable – being fired by a client less so. And this is where failing and not beating yourself up pays off. You can learn – and live to fight another day.

Kipling was write about treating the twin impostors – Triumph and Disaster – exactly the same. I'd just add that being a bit less excited about triumph, and a lot less depressed about disaster could be really helpful. Why do I know this? Because I have always been the worst offender.

MYTH: The business workplace is not an appropriate theatre to encourage individuals to come up with ideas. And the 'dynamic duo' (advising people to work in twos) would waste potentially more time. Getting all the stakeholders around a table is the democratic and efficient way of developing ideas. If you need ideas, brainstorm from time to time.

REALITY: Untrue on all counts. Brainstorming is scientifically unsound. ALL ideas start in the brain of one person. And two people for humans is the ideal team for early and fast idea development. My book *MOTE* explains in detail how to plan, manage and expedite lean, agile, effective creative development meetings to develop ideas on a team basis. Team work is crucial.

Chapter 10

FINDING THE VERY! IDEA AND BECOMING AN IDEA HERO

Innovation is everything

In 2010 Steven Johnson wrote an insightful book on innovation, **Where Good Ideas Come From.** He picked up on a
phrase first coined by biologist Stuart Kauffman – The Adjacent Possible. What might we be able to do in the future?

Epiphanies and eureka moments tend to come about
when you are good and ready – and also when the moment's
right.

Let's enjoy Johnson's own poetic language. 'The strange
and beautiful truth about the adjacent possible is that its
boundaries grow as you explore those boundaries......Think
of it as a house that magically expands...You begin in a room
with four doors, each leading to a new room that you haven't
visited yet. These four rooms are the adjacent possible. But
once you open one of those doors and stroll into that room,
three new doors appear, each leading to a brand-new room
that you couldn't have reached from your original starting
point. Keep opening new doors and eventually you'll have
built a palace.'

Thirty years ago one of my favourite groups was The Beautiful South (famous for *Rotterdam* and the lyrically ambiguous *Don't marry her, fuck me*). They also wrote a song about what we would now call a sex worker, in which she sang a line that has always intrigued and haunted me, *'Imagine a mirror bigger than the room it was placed in'.*

She was dreaming of escape, and the process of coming up with ideas and innovations has much in common with that. Commercial creativity can be frustrating for creatives, who deep down want to paint, write TV drama or make art house films. But a craft area like the ad industry where I have spent my working life offers many compensations – and not all material ones. The pitch world is incredibly stimulating because it is pressured (ie highly competitive). It is also driven by innovation – you can't win a big pitch by serving up the same old material. The buzz, I believe, comes principally from those wonderful moments when the connection is made, the magic mirror is hypnotising you, and we can visualise the adjacent possible.

The Idea Economist (reprise) on The Engine of Growth and the crucial importance of ideas

As we outlined earlier, Mother Nature and civilisation need variety, selection, amplification and codification to create growth. In the case of economic and societal growth this means that we need new ideas, markets to test them, financiers to invest in them and organisations to organise them.

In Chapter 2 we showed in a simple equation that when an economy, society or company malfunctions in any of these four areas then it will have markedly less growth.

But even more than this if any of the dials on our growth machine ends up reading zero then the whole system stops completely because $0 \times 1 \times 1 \times 1 = 0$. The engine jams.

It doesn't matter how well you have engineered and refined your market, financial and organisational economics, if you have left out the idea economics bit then you are going to get no growth at all, because inspiration, innovation and connections are essential to generate the valuable ideas you need.

Idea Heroes are always looking for the Very! Idea

Value – and in particular added value – is what we need our ideas to deliver. Idea Economics is primarily about the value of ideas, and the difference valuable ideas can make.

There is no point in ideas being 'good', 'big' or 'powerful' if we and (if relevant) the organisation don't benefit from them. And ideally we need to be able to quantify that benefit, both in the early stages when one idea is vying with others, and particularly later on when we are developing and shaping the idea.

Let's go back to my mnemonic for Very!

V stands for Value. What we think the idea is worth, and why we are enthusiastic about investing in it.

E is for Excitement. Not ours – the excitement potential among the people we are trying to convince or sell to.

Originality and competitiveness are important factors here.

R represents Robustness. This is partly a Reward / Risk assessment (as in the 'Smart Decisions' formula from **DECIDE**). But it also relates to all the detailed checking needed to ensure the idea stands up, checks out, and is generally bomb-proof.

Y is for YES! Has the idea got the wow factor? Does it stand out? Will it pass the social media test for buzz? Is it hashtag-ready?

Ideas are the dynamic of change management. And change comes in different ways and at different levels.

Some Very! Ideas are 'big' in a significant sense – important, over-arching, very influential. Brexit (love or detest it) is a big idea. Buying a major competitor is a big idea. Building a factory in the US (or Vietnam) is a big idea. Focusing online rather than the High Street is a big idea. Moving the family to Brazil is a big idea. These are ideas that spawn many other ideas, which are required to deliver, and make the big idea happen. They tend to be transformational ideas – where the ultimate outcome can't be fully understood when the decision is made. Like Brexit!

They can also be transitional ideas, where we know where we are going – but just need to work out how to get there.

However big ideas are seldom needed for what we might call routine change – rearranging the deck chairs (as the cliché goes) – whether or not the ship sinks.

The first Very! Idea in my career

Zal Pinefresh Dustbin Powder was one of the cleverest new product ideas I ever came across. Manufactured in 'Death Valley' between Sheffield and Barnsley from a derivative of coal tar, it was packaged in one of those tall cardboard containers with a tin closure (like Vim). The housewife paid two shillings (10p) or whatever, took the package home, removed the lid, and tipped the contents in the dustbin. Simple as that. And the bin smelled like roses. Well, better, anyway. What commercial genius.

It was my first ever job in advertising in April 1968 to brief the creatives to make an ad for this. We didn't have much budget, so it was going to have to be a press ad. But I was reckoning without John Webster and Brian Mindel – the creative team. (How did I luck in to starting my agency life at Pritchard Wood & Partners, working with a legend like Webster?) They were doing some work at the time with a famous American stills photographer called Lester Bookbinder, who, as it turned out, was ambitious to make a name in TV commercials. Between them they came up with a low budget / high impact 15" TV spot that opened on an extreme close-up of a beautiful little boy. Only problem, he has a bluebottle on his cheek.

Except that he hasn't. The bluebottle has alighted on a glossy pic of the boy, and we pull back to see that the photo is in a dustbin, into which an unseen hand pours Zal Dustbin Powder. This does three things: sanitises the dustbin, sells a shedload of dustbin powder, and wins a sheaf of creative awards. A Very! Idea indeed. Did it make the tyro account man who persuaded the client to stretch the budget to go on TV, an overnight Idea Hero? Sadly not, but it gave me a taste for cracking and unexpected ideas.

Now that we have sharpened up the use of our Idea Brain, and used the *Mote* system to facilitate the creative development process, it's time – taking advice from the Idea Economist – to look for valuable ideas, and in particular for that one in a hundred Very! Idea (like the dustbin powder spot) that ticks all the boxes. Of course we are not confined in the marketing and innovation world of 2018 to conventional 'old world' media. There is digital. There is online. There is social media. There is the possibility of coming up with an idea that people actively want to be part of – and that doesn't have to rely on storytelling.

The digital era has changed the world of ideas in two massive respects. First, the internet has delivered uber-encyclopaedic knowledge for research and referencing at a mouse-click. Secondly social media has made broadcasters and pundits of us all. But of itself instant access to limitless data and information doesn't make us better at ideas. Nor does our ability to reach bigger audiences more rapidly. To be valuable, the idea still has to be well made to make a big impact. Technology has not diminished the importance of valuable ideas. It is a tool, not a substitute for thinking. Idea Heroes – the stars of the Idea Economy – will rely just as much on creative thinking and understanding the numbers that tell us which approaches (and which ideas) are most likely to deliver.

Where are Very! Ideas going to come from?

Sir Ken Robinson, the guru and celebrated TED speaker, describes creativity as 'the process of having original ideas that have value'. All right as far as it goes, but it begs the question of how we can know which ideas are valuable, and which not. This is heartland Idea Economics territory, and hopefully this book helps guide readers on both optimum process and effective selection.

In her book *In your Creative Element: The Formula for Creative Success in Business*, Claire Bridges quotes Vicki Maguire, now Chairman of Grey London on what makes a great creative idea. Maguire says, 'it's a mix of experience and gut feeling. If it answers the brief perfectly. If you can see it having a role in culture. If you can see people talking about it, writing about it in the press. If that idea's time is right, it's a good idea. Ideas have energy that's infectious. If the team are excited and there's a buzz around it, then it's a good idea.'

I would add....provided people react positively to it. The Yes! In VERY! relies on output not input.

Claire herself talks about 'unlearning what you know', and advocates taking people out of their workplaces to stimulate ideation.

In *Cracking Creativity* Michalko provided probably the most useful framework. He sees the way forward as knowing HOW to think, instead of WHAT to think.

He sees geniuses – and indeed all creatives, thinkers and ideators as being in constant competitive strife with rivals.

Michalko defined the two basic competitive techniques as:

1. **Seeing What No One Else Is Seeing** – which incorporates two strategies: 'Knowing How to See' and 'Making Your Thought Visible'. This is about adopting radical perspectives and, wherever possible, using graphics, pictures, diagrams etc to explain things visually, and not just in words

2. **Thinking What No One Else Is Thinking:**
   a. Producing lots of ideas, to cover the waterfront
   b. Novel combinations and connecting what other people haven't connected
   c. Looking at things from the other side
   d. Analogies and metaphors
   e. Finding what you're not looking for

How can WE find Very! Ideas?

In his interventions in the previous chapters, the Idea Economist has guided us with some pretty heavy hints. In descending order of importance, here are the key ingredients:

- Chapter 5: Using the Idea Brain. **The pocket calculator analogy is the very best mnemonic for making the connections that all expert creators use to fire up ideas.**

+ MAKE FRESH INPUTS. Gather lots of material. Plus sign because we are adding new stuff.

÷ STORE THE INPUTS. Arrange them in our Idea Brain to try to make sense of what the new material is saying to us. Division sign to symbolise the way our Idea Brain is divided into files and folders.

Off button. Do nothing – wait for the connections to emerge.

On button. Start up the Idea Brain again.

x CONNECT. Make connections between new inputs and what is already stored. The combination of the 'fresh' and the 'stored' will be the genesis of an idea. This combination of ideas is about multiplication and transformation, and the creation of more than was there before. Multiply sign because it's not about + it is about **X**.

– COMPOSE. Sort through to find the best connections and start the process of crafting ideas. Minus sign because composing is mainly about deleting the bits we don't need (like sculpting).

= OUTPUT. The point at which the brain turns these internal thoughts into something we can present and sell. Equal sign because the idea is the outcome of all our efforts.

- Chapter 6: Being Prolific. **The more ideas we come up with, the better the odds of one being really valuable.**

Once we have bought into the logic of this, the maths are pretty straightforward. Choosing a winner from a list of promising candidates, which will almost certainly (always in a pitch situation) is a far better bet than settling for the first one to show promise and polishing it. If we have the resource to choose from 30 ideas rather than 3, the odds are a lot better.

- Chapter 5: Originality vs Imitation. **Use uniqueness – or at the very least fresh thinking – to trump your rival.** The acid test of value is not the impact our ideas have on us, it is the effect they have on the intended target. Because original ideas stay in the mind longer, ideas that haven't been seen before are going to work better – and have more value.

- Chapter 6: Sharing. **An idea shared is an idea which has another great chance to win through.** We instinctively share ideas that we are pleased with. And that's not just because 'Dynamic Duo' (Chapter 9) is the development process most of us instinctively use. It's because we also know that anyone we trust enough to share our precious idea will tell us if they think it won't fly, and will make helpful comments to make the idea better.

- Chapter 6: Working Together. **Collaboration makes us more competitive.** The maths are different, but the sharing truth applies here too.

- Chapter 9: Teams. **Small agile teams are essential for

making winning ideas. The maths are unmissable: the more people in the team, the more frustrated everyone becomes, and the more potentially negative inter-reactions will get in the way of constructive creative development.

- Chapter 6: Tinkering. **Developing ideas pays.** Tinker away as long as the gemstone shines more brightly.

- Chapter 7: Diminishing Returns. **But too much tinkering can lead to diminishing returns.** Know when to stop!

- Chapter 7: Valuation. **Learn how to calculate the potential value of your ideas, so you can choose the one with the highest market potential.** We are most unlikely to maximise the value of our special idea unless we target a value from the outset (based on realistic criteria), and continue to monitor value throughout. Also, if it's a competitive situation, it is about out-thinking the enemy, and only settling for a seriously valuable idea that can help us win the day. Not only do we have the principles of how to make valuable ideas and succeed in a competitive environment, we also have the maths to guide us.

Developing ideas is surprisingly straightforward

Chapter 8 is all about learning to use our Idea Brain to its full potential, and Chapter 9 is about teaming up with others to develop the idea we have come up with. There's no

FINDING THE VERY! IDEA AND BECOMING AN IDEA HERO

expensive technology required. We need very few people. We can move fast.

The 50 Idea Brain tips in Chapter 8 embrace both solo and joint activity. Here are the top 5 in each category:

WHEN YOU ARE THINKING OF IDEAS ON YOUR OWN

- Turn off your autopilot and switch on your Idea Brain
- Focus on the problem
- Have a conversation with yourself – every idea comes from one person, but you might need a little debate!
- Turn off your filtering system, and be prepared to take some risks and make mistakes
- Keep producing lots of ideas – you want a 1/100 idea, not the first cab off the rank

IF YOU GET STUCK:

- Switch the Idea Brain off – and then on again
- Look out of the window
- Juggle this big challenge with any others you are wrestling with – and switch between them
- Make sure you go to sleep fast (without agonising any further), and wake up slowly, by which time you may already have made the connection
- Unpack the brief and reframe if necessary

WHEN YOU ARE WORKING WITH OTHERS (CHAPTER 9):

- DON'T start by getting all the stakeholders round the table
- Select a trusted friend/colleague to form a dynamic duo

- Trust the Mote system (it's ideal for creative development). Pick a lean, agile team on the Stepladder principle
- Keep looking at ideas (from any source) for as long as possible. Don't judge while you are creating, nor rank the candidate ideas too early. Group them in clusters
- Pick a 'winner', and keep valuing the idea as it develops

The Elephant in the Room

In this book I have focused on coming up with ideas and developing them, largely because a lot of the people I've worked with really don't think they've got an idea in them. They are self-deprecating about it and in the client community especially, a great deal is automatically deferred to creatives. They are over-modest about their ability to think and come up with and articulate ideas. I think that that has a great deal to do with spending half their time, in meetings.

As a world, and as a country, we face some fairly severe problems, and I'm convinced that unless ordinary people believe they can think their way through them for themselves, it's a pretty poor outlook. Because if you have to trust just creative directors or politicians, it could be very difficult. So it's a call to the colours to be more confident about your ability to have ideas.

I've interviewed a lot of people. I've got some great tips. The first part of the book is encouraging people to believe that ideas are actually the most important thing in the world and, therefore, instead of being driven by money, we should really be driven by ideas. It's about the knowledge economy being succeeded by the idea economy and by what I call idea economics, which is celebrating the value of ideas. Not the value judgement on them – not that they're big or good or whatever – but that they're really, really valuable. The second part of the book is urging people to use their idea brain more, and becoming better at it. It is thinking that's going to solve problems; not money or thermonuclear weapons or digital technology. It's going to be solved by people thinking and making ideas.

But great ideas cannot work unless they are listened to and appreciated. The elephant in the room is lack of receptivity to ideas. However strong an idea is, however valuable, it cannot flourish and grow without encouragement and support.

It's not what we say, it's what *they* feel

We know all about presentations in marketing and advertising. Even if we aren't too hot at French, and haven't learned to code, we are all pretty fluent in PowerPoint. Yes, I know everyone says they hate PowerPoint, but we use it all the time, and how else can you do credentials or show the new strategy?

At AAI I have 30 years' experience of watching agencies present their credentials and pitch for new business. What insights and understanding has it given me? The main problem, as I see it, is that agencies (and it's true of virtually everyone who presents to sell in business) only tend to concentrate on one aspect of the presentation – the input bit. All efforts are directed at the impactful opening, assembling the meat in the middle, crafting the segues, and finishing on a high note. So what is there to go wrong?

Even if the whole 58 MB has been meticulously prepared and punctuated with standout video and motion graphics, it is sadly not want you put into the presentation that matters. It's what the audience takes out of it. This is another of those input/output/outcome challenges – like advertising or mass entertainment. We can say something telling, and say it brilliantly, but the success (or otherwise) of the presentation depends squarely on the people across the table.

It's like food. You can chuck in all the fancy ingredients, and follow the preparation and cooking instructions to the letter, but either the dish has appetite appeal, or it doesn't. And the chef is not the final arbiter of that. The customer is.

At Harvard University these days, the hottest ticket is Michael Puett, Walter C. Klein Professor of Chinese History in the Department of East Asian Languages and Civilizations. How so? His lectures are sold out, and attended by students of many other disciplines, because Puett is spreading the teachings of Confucius and other Chinese philosophers from 2500 years ago about how even our smallest gestures and habits can mould our destiny, and influence others. Better still, he shows his students how they can change their behaviours (facial expressions, mannerisms, actions and words) to be more likable and therefore more successful. He advocates trying new things and new ways, as opposed to the traditional advice to 'stick with what you're good at'. He's a big enthusiast for smiling, and not defaulting to looking serious or severe. He urges people to be far more self-aware about those of our habits, expressions, and phrases that irritate or grate on even our nearest and dearest. In the West, we are taught to be clever, skilled, and full of rationality and knowledge. Puett promises to change his students' lives by persuading them to concentrate instead on what they might think are the secondary and trivial signals they send.

Take these insights from distant millennia into the world of pitch and present, and what is the learning? For a start it gives new ammunition to the emotional intelligence movement. Beldoch and Goleman and their followers have been criticised by some of their fellow psychologists, but the early Chinese behavioural gurus provide convincing evidence for EI and EQ.

More specifically Puett's teaching suggests that just as we know the importance of personality profiling (our own, our colleagues and those we seek to influence or sell to), we should also submit to merciless appraisal of how we come across in action. Pitch doctors need to get up close and personal. Team mates should agree to be both frank and less sensitive with each other. Winning behaviour needs to be encouraged. Annoying habits have to be acknowledged and, if possible, cured.

It's not just what the audience feel about the presentation. It's very much about what they feel about the team and individuals who are delivering it. We've always known about chemistry and gut feel. Professor Puett is telling us why we should take them very seriously indeed.

Presentation skills

As must be obvious, I don't buy the famous Theodore Levitt adage about an idea not being worth anything till it's implemented. The core principle of Idea Economics, and the valuation system in Chapter 7, is that promising ideas can and should be valued at every stage for their potential value. One extremely important variable in the idea value chain is presentation, because value of our idea is going to be established vicariously (ie by the people we need to convince), not by ourselves. And these outsiders vitally include gatekeepers as well as end users. How can we influence gatekeepers? Usually by presenting to them.

From the school debating society, through to my brief political career, for three years as a Nielsen presenter, 20 as an adman, 30 as a consultant / adviser, and as an author, campaigner and speaker, presentation has been my bag of tricks. Also I have had so many talented exponents of the art to learn from. Not just in the business environment for all those years, but by watching politicians and opinion leaders live and on TV.

Idea Heroes aren't just the highly creative people who come up with them in the first place. Developing them, honing them, using the Idea Brain to work as a team, knowing where to look, and knowing when you've struck oil – these skills can make an Idea Hero too.

But it doesn't end there. All ideas need to be sold. And selling ideas is another task for an Idea Hero. Equipment and software help, but presenting is really just another ultra-competitive sport where winning comes from performing a learned skill (often based on natural ability) that bit better than your competitor. Presenting ideas – like developing ideas – is not an area where money, technology and data are the crucial factors.

Remember the advice from Oren Klaff (*Pitch Anything*)

'There is a fundamental disconnect between the way we pitch anything and the way it is received by our audience. As a result, at the crucial moment, when it is most important to be convincing, nine out of ten times we are not. Our most important messages have a surprisingly low chance of getting through.'

Klaff's killer point is that excitement resides in the eye and ear and consciousness of the beholder. If we want someone to buy our idea, THEY have to be excited by it. It matters not a jot whether we and our friends and colleagues love the idea to bits. If the pitcher's presentation doesn't excite the pitchee, too bad. That's why we put the magic 'E' in VERY! That's the message of the 'Elephant in the Room' earlier in this Chapter.

Klaff talks about the 'crocodile brain'. That's his description of the pitchee's trash bin:

- If it's not dangerous, ignore it

- If it's not new and exciting, ignore it
- If it is new, summarise it as quickly as possible – and forget about the details
- Do not send it up to the neocortex for problem solving

Klaff tells us that at those pivotal life or death moments when we are pitching for our life, we effectively have less than five minutes to sell our company, ourselves, and our idea.

It's a brutal insight into the reality of selling competitively. The idea better be good.

Lessons from my experience as a presenter, and watching others perform

I led a lot of pitches in my 20 years on the agency side, and I have made scores of platform appearances in numerous countries in recent years. But for the last 30 years I have played what the behaviouralists call the 'choice architect' role. In the pitch context, while admiring the tricks of professional presenters (see below), I have always tried to remember that the name of the game is picking an agency, not buying an idea. But despite the fact that in recent years I have counselled agencies not to give their best ideas away to other agency's clients, and tried to restrain clients from demanding free speculative creative work, old habits die hard. Clients often pitch to trawl for game-changing (or brand-saving) ideas, and many agency people have the enthusiasm for spec creative that steeplechasers have for fences (even if they have unseated their jockey!).

KNOW WHO YOU ARE TALKING TO

Of all the skills I have been taught over the years Personality Profiling is undoubtedly the most useful. I wrote about it extensively in Chapter 6 of my first book *Decide*. We have established the importance of making sure our idea makes a big impact on the audience – whether that is the ultimate decision maker, or an intermediary. It has to make total sense to find out as much as possible about the personality of that person. Fortunately there are all sorts of techniques available for profiling people without getting them to fill in a questionnaire! I use the 'Headline' system adapted by Stuart Sanders of Sanders Consulting from William Moulton Marston's DISC approach.

IF YOU CAN CONTROL YOUR ENVIRONMENT YOU HAVE A BIG ADVANTAGE

Presenting on home territory is most people's preference. On home ground, there is no excuse for technology or climatic snafus. You just feel more confident, and help will be at hand if anything starts to go wrong. But no one can have home advantage for all their matches. Having sight of a venue in advance helps. Making friends with the local receptionist, EA, technicians can make all the difference. With their help, it may be possible to dress the room (new corporate colours on display in the boardroom of a financial conglomerate) and even add 'smellorama' (for a rum brand).

There are also geographic and locational considerations. As a pitch organiser I tried to pick inspiring locations for really important meetings. For example I persuaded Cadbury to hold final pitches for their global account in Niagara-on-the-Lake, as Canada was at that time the home of the richest, creamiest Cadbury's chocolate. Automotive plants in Gothenburg, Wolfsburg and Gaydon made the perfect setting for pitches to Volvo, VW and Jaguar respectively. The Cape Town atmosphere added a lot more to pitches for Guinness Africa than holding them in London would have done. One of the most successful final pitch sessions I ever ran was for Chiquita Bananas in a Brazilian restaurant in Antwerp's old ghetto. All four agencies excelled themselves, and the environment was a big factor. Perhaps the most striking example was a 'no pitch pitch' briefing for which we flew a new pan-European agency team to Havana for a week. The 'two room' technique beloved of BBH and copied by other agencies, including McCann, was also very effective. Setting up the problem in one room, and solving it in another, where the idea was revealed, worked well, as any psychologist could have predicted.

It can also go the other way. Having a client team of 40 in meetings in New York City that lasted four hours each, was a mistake. So was holding pitches one after another in a room next to the office of the MD of an electrical retailer. He left the meetings constantly to take phone calls. Condemning agencies to present their ideas at airports very seldom works out. Airports are transitory by their very nature, and somehow the ideas become a bit the same.

THE MOST IMPORTANT PRESENTATION IN A PITCH PROCESS IS THE BRIEF FROM A GOOD CLIENT

If a brand owner wants valuable ideas, making an inspiring, spell-binding, motivating presentation is a great start.

MORE IS LESS, AND LESS IS MORE

Very long presentations don't make an idea more appealing. Klaff is right, often there is very little time to get across your own personality, your company's reputation and the idea itself. Just as digging into your audience's time doesn't go down well, so giving them back half an hour in their day can often be a winning card. I am personally a serial offender on the 'more is less' front. I can never resist heaping Pelion on Ossa in my eagerness to leave no argument out.

BLAMING THE INCUMBENT ISN'T A SMART MOVE

Being disrespectful about the previous or current agency can rebound on you. After all, if the client team have been around for a while, one or more of them will have approved the previous campaign!

IT ISN'T A REHEARSAL

Always field your best presenter(s). But if the object of the exercise is putting forward a team, give each of the key players a speaking part.

BUT REHEARSE, REHEARSE THE PRESENTATION

And if you have the time, rehearse it again. Use someone you trust to watch and play devil's advocate. Rehearsal should cover the way the team interacts, not just one speech after another.

ARE THERE TRULY OUTSTANDING PRESENTERS OUT THERE?

Absolutely there are. We see them on TV. Stephen Fry, David Attenborough, Len Goodman, Fiona Bruce are good examples, in my opinion. Confidence, knowledge, articulateness and likeability help in roughly equal proportions. We see politicians who have 'got it'. And many who haven't. We see sports personalities, show business stars, and business leaders and gurus with these gifts, and the reverse.

During my AAI years on the pitch circuit, I have watched very gifted performers in action – creatives, suits, planners, agency and corporate heads, and also charismatic clients. Unfortunately agencies sometimes suffer from the apparent difference in presentation skill between Mr/Ms Charisma and the rest of the team. But rather than giving you a roll of honour – and risk losing the friendship of the giants I have left out – I will confine myself to two examples. HHCL was the agency of the 1990's decade – an accolade it fully deserved. This made it all the sadder that the agency scarcely made it into the new century. They had a presentation technique, mainly using an account man called Robin Aziz, who was very funny and a brilliant mimic, to act out their usually humorous TV scripts. Hilarious – and effective. In my line of work, new business professionals are the super sales people.

They can make a big difference too, especially if they bracket stand-out persuasive oratory with the preparatory and softening up skills that new business directors are famous for. I would have to name the anglophile American Kevin Allen (late of McCann. Lowe and M&C Saatchi) as an outstanding performer. His book *The Hidden Agenda* is a masterclass in doing research on the client you are trying to win over.

Listen to Chris Anderson. He knows about presenting!

I would rate my presenting handicap as considerably lower (ie better!) than my golf handicap. But there is one acknowledged expert, who I think is quite the best on this subject. I am talking about Chris Anderson, the owner of the TED organisation. His book *TED Talks. The Official TED Guide to Public Speaking* is a fund of great suggestions, not just on how to wow an audience at a TED or TEDx event in a maximum of 18 minutes, but in general for presenting yourself and your ideas as effectively as possible.

And this certainly applies to the passage from making a VERY! Idea to becoming the Idea Hero who sells, develops and implements it.

Here are 10 priceless Anderson suggestions

1. Many people massively underestimate the value of their work, and their learning, and their insights. More likely, **you have far more in you worth sharing than you're even aware of.**

In any case, there's one thing you have that no one else in the world has: Your own first-person experience of life. **People love stories and everyone can learn to tell a good story.**

2. OK, you have something meaningful to say, and your goal is to re-create your core idea inside your audience's minds. How do you do that? Humans have developed a technology that makes it possible to re-create things in a group of strangers' minds. It's called language and it makes your brain do incredible things. You can only use the tools that your audience has access to. **If you start with only YOUR language, YOUR concepts and YOUR assumptions, you will fail. So start with theirs.**

3. Take something that matters deeply to you and rebuild it inside of the minds of your listeners. An idea is anything that can change how people see the world. It can be a simple how-to. Or a human insist illustrated with the power of a story. A beautiful image. Or an event you wish might happen in the future. **Even just a reminder of what matters most in life.**

4. You're nervous right? But, with the right mindset, you can use your fear as an incredible asset. It can be the driver that will persuade you to prepare for a talk properly. No matter how little confidence you might have today in your ability to speak in public, there are things you can do to turn that around. Your goal is not

to be Winston Churchill or Nelson Mandela. It's to be you. If you're an artist, be an artist; don't try to be an academic. Just be you. You don't have to raise a crowd to its feet with a thunderous oration. **Conversational sharing can work just as well.**

5. Presentation literacy isn't an option extra for the few. It's a core skill for the twenty-first century. If you can commit to being the authentic you, I am certain that you will be capable of tapping into the ancient art that is wired inside us. You simply have to pluck up the courage to try. Your number one mission as a speaker is to take something that matters deeply to you and to rebuild it inside of the minds of your listeners. **We'll call that something an idea. A mental construct that they can hold on to, walk away with, value, and in some sense be changed by.**

6. **Throughline – the connecting theme that ties together each narrative element.** The point of a talk is to say something meaningful. But it's amazing how many talks never quite do that. They leave the audience with nothing they can hold on to. The number one reason for this is that the speaker never had a proper plan for the talk as a whole. It may be constructed from bullet points or even sentence, but there is no throughline.

7. This doesn't mean every talk can only cover one topic, or tell a single story. It just means that all the pieces need to connect. The throughline traces the path

that the journey takes. Ensuring that there are no impossible leaps. **And at the end, the destination, is reached by all.**

8. **Persuasion**. This means convincing an audience that the way they currently see the world isn't quite right. And when this works, it's thrilling for both speaker and audience. It requires taking down the parts that aren't working, and rebuilding something better.

9. **Reason**. Once people have been primed, it's much easier to make your argument with Reason. Reason is capable of delivering a conclusion at a whole different level of certainty than any other mental tool.

10. **And finally:**
    - Inject humour early on
    - Add an anecdote
    - Offer vivid examples
    - Recruit third-party validation
    - Use powerful visuals

MYTH: Idea Heroes are born, not made. You need to be a recognised creative expert to produce something outstanding like a Very! Idea.

REALITY: Both generating ideas and developing them are skills which can be learned. The more you understand about Idea Economics (let's call it the maths of creativity), and the more adept you become at using your Idea Brain, the faster your idea ability will develop. Being a creative contributor to valuable ideas is not a handy extra string to your bow (like DIY or playing the guitar), it will probably play a part in you and your team or company winning. When the going gets tough, the Very! Idea could also be the difference between surviving and going under. Not all Idea Heroes are creative geniuses. Contributing to the development of an idea, and presenting it convincingly, are other routes to recognition.

David Wethey is an author and business adviser living in Gloucestershire and Alderney.

He founded Agency Assessments International (AAI) in 1988 and has undertaken projects in more than 40 countries.

In 2008 he was awarded an Honorary Fellowship by the IPA for services to the Client/Agency Relationship.

David is the bestselling author of Decide, published in 2013 and Mote, published by Urbane in 2016. Mote was shortlisted for the CMI Book of the Year Award in 2016.

QUESTIONNAIRE ON IDEA SKILLS

A. MY IDEA WORLD

1. My work environment encourages ideas and innovation.
2. I can come up with highly creative new ideas.
3. I can readily build on the ideas of others to give them more substance.
4. I can see what is required to turn an idea into action.
5. I can be persuasive in influencing others to adopt my ideas, and the ones I am helping to develop with others.

B. MY IDEA AMBITIONS

1. I believe ideas are the source of all progress, growth and change.
2. I seriously want to be an ideas person.
3. I am also keen to be seen as a creative collaborator.
4. I want to learn new ways of thinking up ideas.
5. I would like to know how to increase the value of ideas.

Please use this rating scale for each question in each of the sections, and add up your scores for each section

3 = Very true   2 = Quite true   1 = Not true at all

Assessing your scores on both sections

5–7:   Plenty of room for improvement. The book should help a lot

8–10: Not bad at all, but you should address particularly any area where you only scored a 1

11–15: You are well on the road, and the Idea Brain and Idea Economist tips in the book should make a real difference

It is highly likely your score on 'My Idea Ambitions' will be higher than on 'My Idea World', and comparing your scores on the two sets of questions should provide something of a route map for improving your idea skills. If you are being held back by work environment, you may need to call on setting an example and persuasion as well as improved performance!

BIBLIOGRAPHY AND SUGGESTIONS FOR FURTHER READING

- De Bono E – *Lateral Thinking* – Penguin (1970)
- De Bono E – *Simplicity* – Penguin (1998)
- De Bono E – *CoRT Thinking* – Penguin (1986)
- Belbin M – *Management Teams* – Butterworth Heinemann (1981)
- Grant A – *Originals* – WH Allen (2016)
- World Economic Forum – *Future of Jobs Report* (2016)
- Altucher J – *Reinvent Yourself* – Create Space Independent Publishing (2017)
- Dennett D – *Consciousness Explained* – Penguin (1991)
- Rothenberg A – *Creativity and Madness* – John Hopkins University Press (1990)
- Christensen T – *The Creativity Challenge* – Simon & Schuster (2015)
- Ogilvy D – *Ogilvy on Advertising* Vintage (1983)
- Bridges C – *In Your Creative Element* – Kogan Page (2016)
- Michalko M – *Cracking Creativity* – Ten Speed Press – (2001)
- Lemley M – *The Myth of the Sole Inventor* (paper) – Michigan Law Review (2011)
- Lehrer J – *Imagine: How Creativity Works* – Houghton Mifflin Company (2012)
- Fox E – *Rainy Brain Sunny Brain* – Heinemann (2012)
- Anchor S – *The Happiness Advantage* – Virgin Books (2010)
- Crabbe A – *Busy* – Little Brown (2014)
- Krznaric R – *Empathy* – Rider (2014)
- Drucker P – *The Age of Discontinuity* – Butterworth Heinemann (1969)
- Drucker P – *Post-Capitalist Society* – Harper Collins (1994)

- Harari YN – *Sapiens* – Vintage Book (2014)
- Earls M – *Welcome to the Creative Age* – Wiley (2003)
- Northcote Parkinson C – *Parkinson's Law* – Buccaneer Books (1957)
- Peter L and Hull R – *The Peter Principle* – Harper Collins (2014)
- McKeown G – *Essentialism* Crown Business (2014)
- Coplin D – *Business Reimagined* – Harriman House (2013)
- Coplin D – *Return of the Humans* – Harriman House (2014)
- Sullivan L – *Hey Whipple Squeeze This* – Wiley (2008)
- Webb Young J – *A Technique for Producing Ideas* – McGraw Hill Classic Edition (2003)
- Griffiths J and Follows T – *98% Pure Potato* – Unbound (2016)
- Kahneman R and Tversky A – *Prospect Theory* – National Emergency Training Center (1979)
- Thaler R and Sunstein C – *Nudge* – Penguin (2009)
- Ed Catmull – *Creativity Inc* – Bantam Press (2014)
- Watson P – *A History of Thought and Invention, from Fire to Freud* – Harper Perennial (2006)
- Sivers D – *Anything you want* – Portfolio (2011)
- Levitin D *The Organized Mind* – Viking (2014)
- Doug Hall – *Jump Start Your Business Brain* – Clerisy Press (2010)
- Johnson S – *Where Good Ideas Come From* – Riverhead Books (2010)
- Puett M – *The Path: What Chinese Philosophers Can Teach Us About the Good Life* – Simon & Schuster (2016)
- Klaff O – *Pitch Anything* – McGraw Hill (2011)
- Allen K – *The Hidden Agenda* – Bibliomotion (2012)
- Anderson C – *TED Talks. The Official Guide to Public Speaking* – Houghton Mifflin (2016)
- Stengel J – *Grow* – Virgin Book (2012)

INDEX

"This is an expert book written by a man whose job it has been to observe successful and unsuccessful meetings." – Chris Satterthwaite, CEO Chime Communications

Analyse the calendar function on the computers, tablets and mobile devices of millions of executives, and what will you find? Wall-to-wall meetings. Even conservative estimates say that we spend more than a quarter of our working lives in meetings, and that over 50% of that meeting time is wasted.

Yet meetings appear central to the way process works in the vast majority of organizations and no-one seems to want to tell the truth about them. Can you embody leadership through meetings? Can you innovate effectively through meetings? Is creativity evolved in meetings?

Mote is that better meeting and a life-changing way forward. When you learn how to mote you open up the pathways to business success. Empower people, inspire innovation, promote productivity, and mote your way to your business goals. Mote is business process re-engineering. Mote can transform YOUR business.

Urbane Publications is dedicated to
developing author voices and publishing business titles that
challenge, educate and inspire.

From trade business titles to innovative
reference books, our goal is to publish what
YOU want to read.

Find out more at
urbanepublications.com